Ayrsh
Street A

CONTENTS

Area of coverage	2 - 3
Ardrossan, Saltcoats, Stevenston & index	4 - 9
Annbank, Mossblown & index	10 - 11
Ayr & Alloway	12 - 17
Auchinleck, Ballantrae, Barr, Barrhill & indices	18 - 19
Beith, Bellsbank & indices	20 - 21
Catrine, Colmonell, Coylton & indices	22 - 23
Crookedholm, Crosshill, Crosshouse, Knockentiber & indices	24 - 25
Cumnock, Dailly, Dalrymple & indices	26 - 29
Dalmellington, Drongan & indices	30 - 31
Dalry, Dunlop & indices	32 - 33
Darvel, Drybridge, Dundonald & indices	34 - 35
Fairlie, Fenwick, Hillhead & indices	36 - 37
Galston, Girvan & indices	38 - 39
Hurlford & index, Irvine (includes Dreghorn & Springside)	40 - 49
Kilbirnie (includes Glengarnock), Kilmaurs, Kirkmichael & indices	50 - 53
Kilmarnock, Kirkoswald & indices	54 - 61
Kilwinning	62 - 63
Largs, Logan, Lugar & indices	64 - 67
Mauchline, Maidens & indices	68 - 69
Maybole, Minishant & indices	70 - 71
Millport & index	72 - 73
Muirkirk & index	74 - 75
New Cumnock & index	76 - 77
Newmilns, Ochiltree, Sorn & indices	78 - 79
Prestwick, Monkton & indices	80 - 83
Patna, Skelmorlie & indices	84 - 85
Stewarton, Symington & indices	86 - 87
Tarbolton, Troon (includes Barassie) & indices	88 - 91
Turnberry & index, West Kilbride & Seamill	92 - 93
Index section:	
West Kilbride & Seamill	94
Ayr (includes Alloway)	94 - 96
Irvine (includes Dreghorn & Springside)	96 - 98
Kilwinning	98 - 99

ISBN 1 86097 239 X

AREA OF COVERAGE

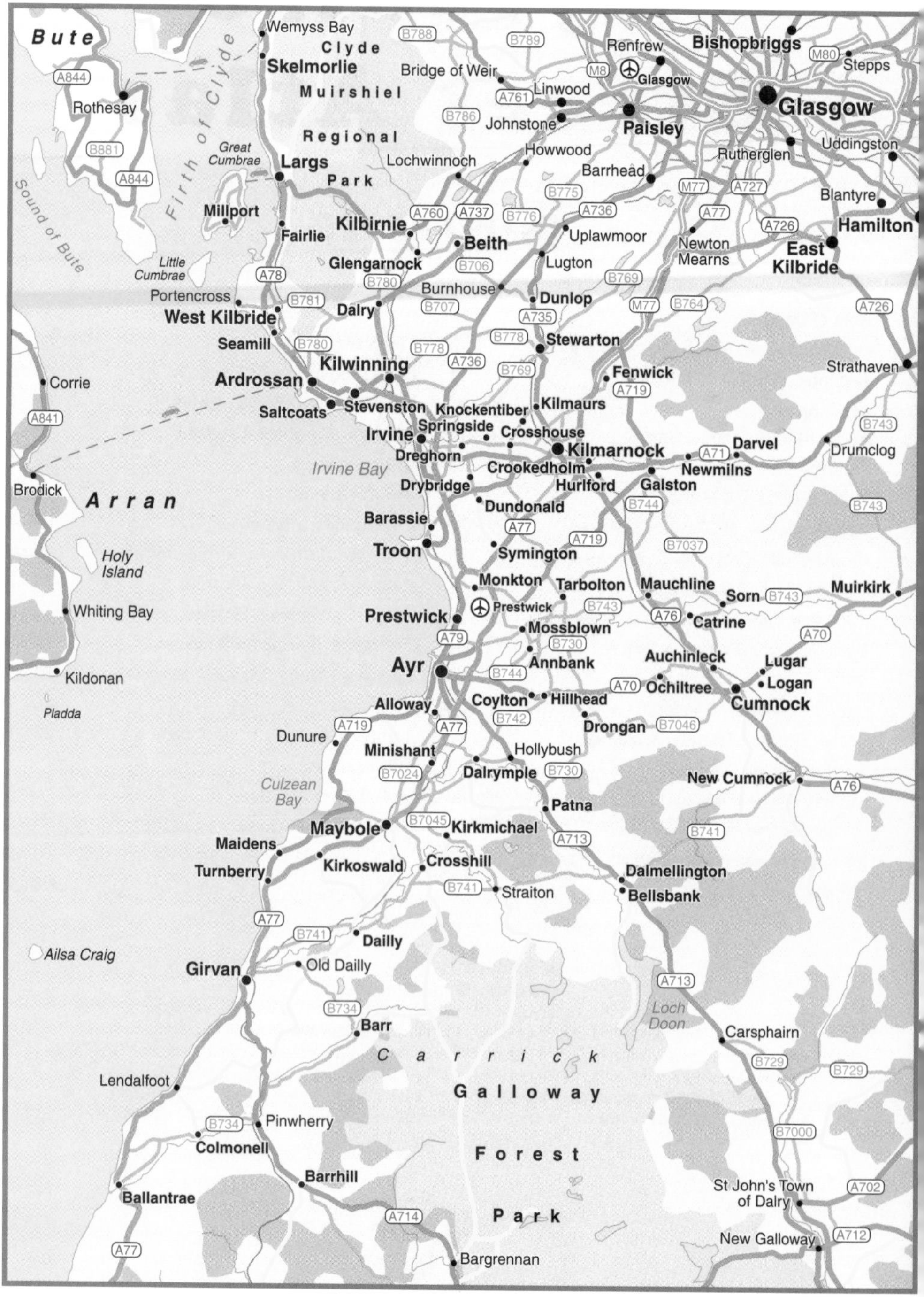

Bute
Wemyss Bay
Clyde
Skelmorlie
Muirshiel
Regional
Park
Renfrew
Bishopbriggs
Stepps
Glasgow
Bridge of Weir
Linwood
Johnstone
Paisley
Glasgow
Rothesay
Firth of Clyde
Great Cumbrae
Largs
Lochwinnoch
Howwood
Barrhead
Rutherglen
Uddingston
Blantyre
Hamilton
Sound of Bute
Millport
Fairlie
Kilbirnie
Beith
Uplawmoor
Newton Mearns
East Kilbride
Glengarnock
Lugton
Little Cumbrae
Portencross
Burnhouse
Dunlop
West Kilbride
Dalry
Seamill
Stewarton
Kilwinning
Fenwick
Strathaven
Corrie
Ardrossan
Saltcoats
Stevenston
Knockentiber
Kilmaurs
Springside
Crosshouse
Irvine
Kilmarnock
Darvel
Dreghorn
Crookedholm
Newmilns
Drumclog
Irvine Bay
Brodick
Drybridge
Hurlford
Galston
Arran
Dundonald
Barassie
Troon
Symington
Holy Island
Monkton
Tarbolton
Mauchline
Sorn
Muirkirk
Prestwick
Prestwick
Catrine
Whiting Bay
Mossblown
Ayr
Annbank
Auchinleck
Lugar
Logan
Kildonan
Alloway
Coylton
Hillhead
Ochiltree
Cumnock
Pladda
Dunure
Drongan
Minishant
Hollybush
Dalrymple
New Cumnock
Culzean Bay
Patna
Maybole
Kirkmichael
Maidens
Turnberry
Kirkoswald
Crosshill
Dalmellington
Bellsbank
Straiton
Dailly
Ailsa Craig
Girvan
Old Dailly
Barr
Loch Doon
Carsphairn
Carrick
Lendalfoot
Galloway
Pinwherry
Colmonell
Forest
Barrhill
St John's Town of Dalry
Ballantrae
Park
New Galloway
Bargrennan

A77 A road dual carriageway
A77 A road single carriageway
B707 B road dual carriageway
Unclassified road
Pedestrianised road
Track
Path
Railway
Disused railway or tunnel
Airport / heliport
Primary school
Secondary school
Special or independent school
Police station
Fire station
Ambulance station
Lifeboat station
Coastguard station
Hospital
Parking
Filling station
Library

Post office
Superstore
Bus station
Railway station
Tourist information centre
Antiquity
Museum
Castle
Historic or visitable house
Battlefield
Garden
Caravan site
Camping
Viewpoint
Other tourist attraction
Church or place of worship
Woodland
Park, recreation, sports or cemetery
Built up area
Rocks
Shingle
Sand

Scale 1:14 000

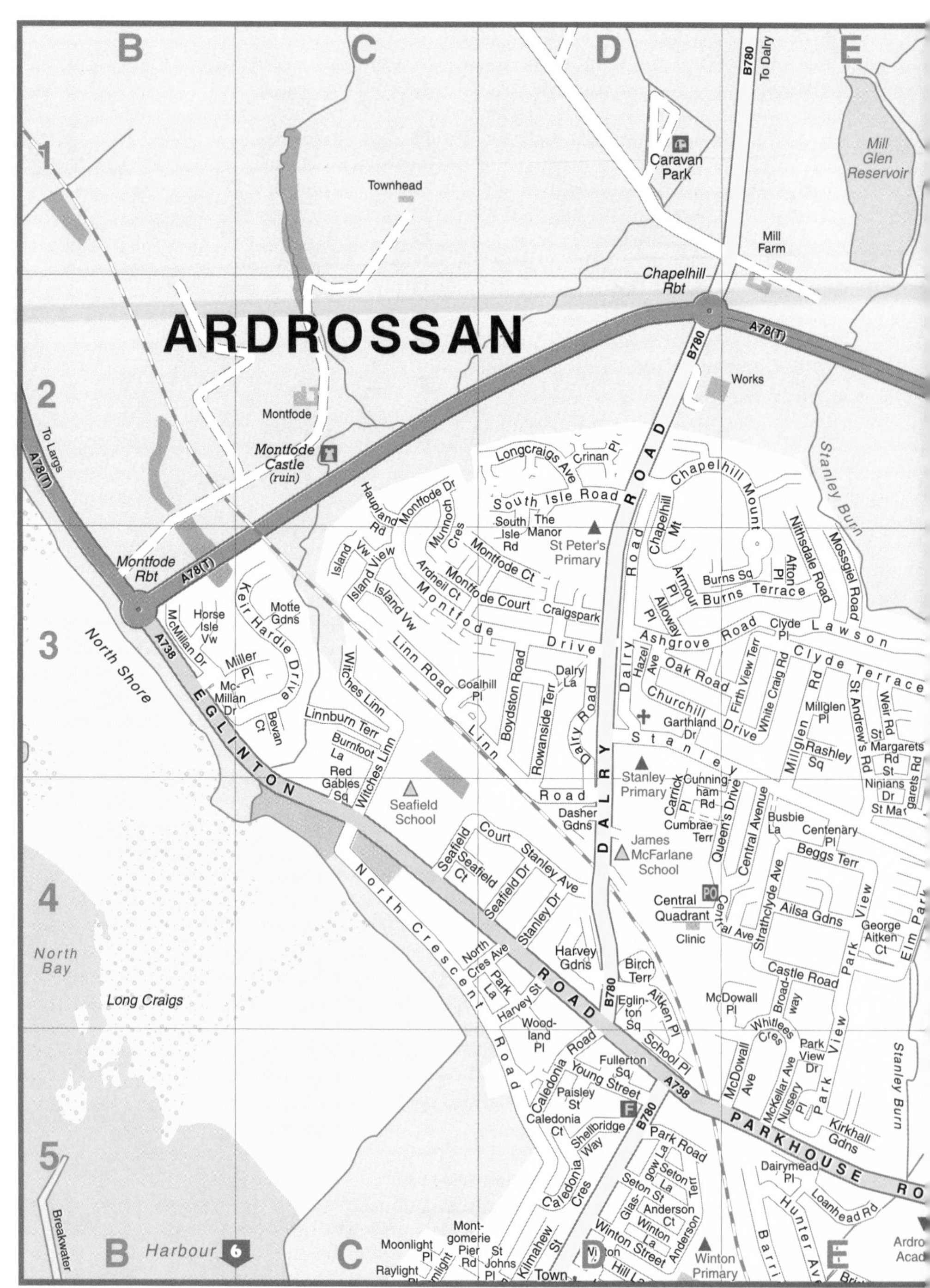
ARDROSSAN
Townhead
Caravan Park
To Dalry
Mill Glen Reservoir
Mill Farm
Chapelhill Rbt
A78(T)
B780
Works
Montfode
Montfode Castle (ruin)
To Largs
Montfode Rbt
Stanley Burn
Longcraigs Ave
Crinan Pl
Chapelhill Mount
South Isle Road
South Isle Rd
The Manor
St Peter's Primary
Dalry Road
Nithsdale Road
Mossgiel Road
Burns Sq
Afton Pl
Burns Terrace
Armour Pl
Alloway Pl
Montfode Dr
Munnoch Cres
Montfode Ct
Montfode Court
Ardneil Ct
Montfode Drive
Craigspark
Haupland Rd
Island Vw
Island View
Linn Road
Horse Isle Vw
Motte Gdns
McMillan Dr
Keir Hardie Drive
Miller Pl
Mc-Millan Dr
Bevan Ct
North Shore
A738
Eglinton Road
Ashgrove Road
Clyde Pl
Lawson
Clyde Terrace
Hazel Ave
Oak Road
Churchill Drive
Firth View Terr
White Craig Rd
Millglen Rd
Millglen Pl
St Andrew's Rd
Weir Rd
St Margarets Rd
Garthland Dr
Stanley Road
Rashley Sq
St Ninians Dr
Coalhill Pl
Boydston Road
Rowanside Terr
Dalry La
Witches Linn
Linnburn Terr
Burnfoot La
Red Gables Sq
Seafield School
Stanley Primary
Carrick Pl
Cunningham Rd
Queen's Drive
Central Avenue
Busbie La
Centenary Pl
Beggs Terr
Dasher Gdns
Cumbrae Terr
James McFarlane School
Seafield Court
Seafield Ct
Stanley Ave
Seafield Dr
Stanley Dr
North Crescent
Central Quadrant
Central Ave
Clinic
Strathclyde Ave
Ailsa Gdns
Park View
George Aitken Ct
Elm Park
Harvey Gdns
North Cres Ave
Park La
Harvey St
Birch Terr
Eglinton Sq
Aitken Pl
Castle Road
Broadway
McDowall Pl
North Bay
Long Craigs
Woodland Pl
School Pl
Whitlees Cres
Park View Dr
Caledonia Road
Fullerton Sq
Young Street
Paisley St
Caledonia Ct
Shellbridge Way
McDowall Ave
McKellar Ave
Nursery Pl
Kirkhall Gdns
Stanley Burn
Parkhouse Road
Park Road
Glasgow La
Seton Terr
Seton La
Seton St
Anderson Ct
Winton La
Anderson
Caledonia Cres
Dairymead Pl
Hunter Ave
Loanhead Rd
Breakwater
Harbour
Moonlight Pl
Mont-gomerie Pier Rd
St Johns Pl
Kilmahew St
Raylight Pl
Winton Street
Winton Primary
Town

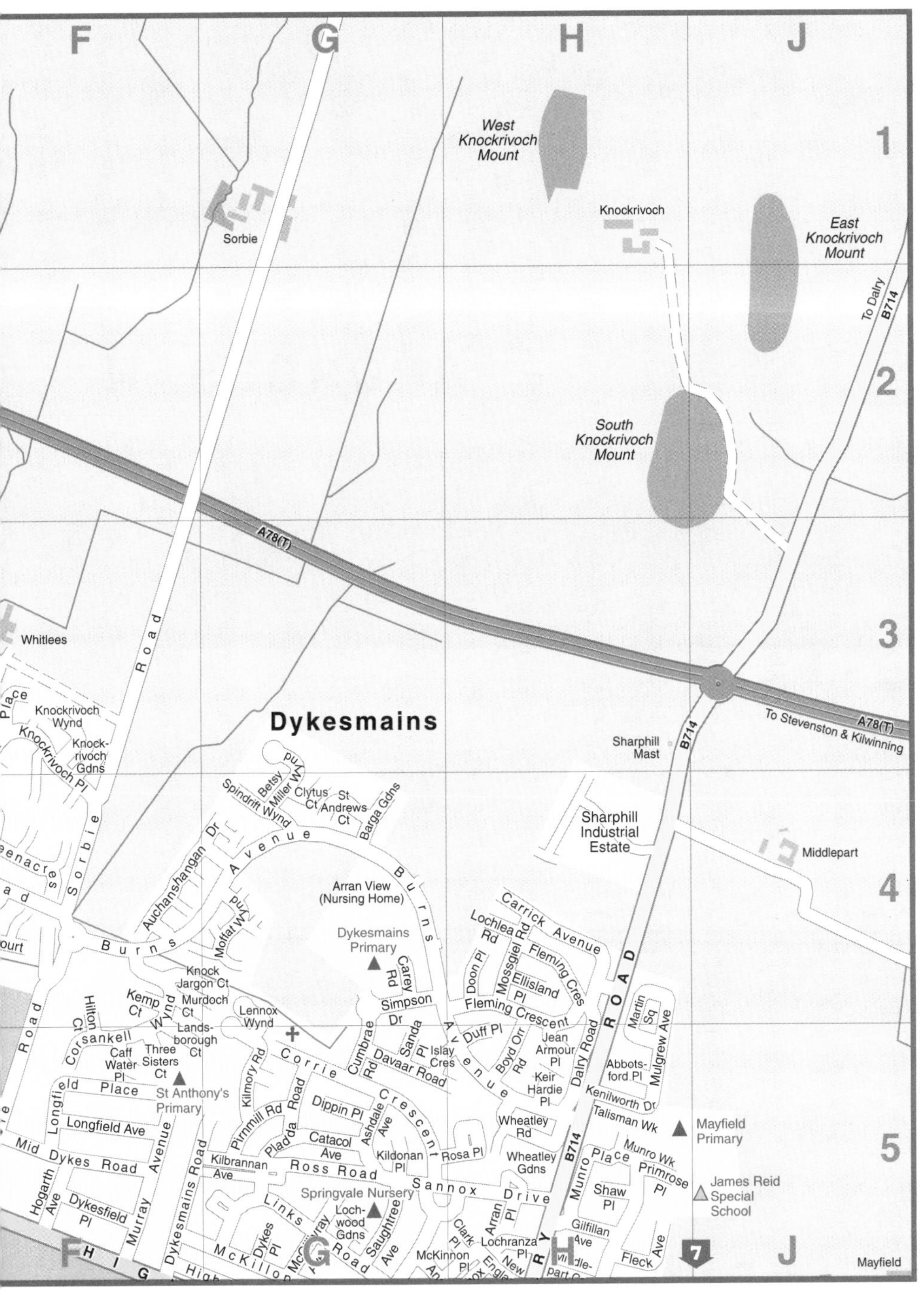
F
G
H
J
1
2
3
4
5
West Knockrivoch Mount
Knockrivoch
East Knockrivoch Mount
Sorbie
To Dalry B714
South Knockrivoch Mount
A78(T)
Whitlees
To Stevenston & Kilwinning
Dykesmains
Sharphill Mast
B714
Sharphill Industrial Estate
Middlepart
Knockrivoch Wynd
Knockrivoch Pl
Knock-rivoch Gdns
Sorbie Road
Betsy Miller Wynd
Clytus Ct
St Andrews Ct
Barga Gdns
Spindrift Wynd
Auchanshangan Dr
Burns Avenue
Arran View (Nursing Home)
Dykesmains Primary
Carrick Avenue
Lochlea Rd
Mossgiel Rd
Fleming Cres
Doon Pl
Ellisland Pl
Moffat Wynd
Knock Jargon Ct
Murdoch Ct
Kemp Ct
Wynd
Hilton Ct
Lennox Wynd
Lands-borough Ct
Corsankell
Caff Water Pl
Three Sisters Ct
St Anthony's Primary
Carey Rd
Simpson Dr
Fleming Crescent
Dalry Road
ROAD
Martin Sq
Mulgrew Ave
Duff Pl
Sanda Pl
Islay Cres
Boyd Orr Rd
Jean Armour Pl
Keir Hardie Pl
Abbots-ford Pl
Kenilworth Dr
Talisman Wk
Mayfield Primary
Corrie Crescent
Cumbrae Rd
Davaar Road
Kilmory Rd
Longfield Place
Longfield Ave
Pirnmill Rd
Road
Dippin Pl
Ashdale Ave
Pladda
Catacol Ave
Kildonan Pl
Rosa Pl
Wheatley Rd
Wheatley Gdns
B714
Munro Place
Munro Wk
Primrose Pl
Mid Dykes Road
Avenue
Kilbrannan Ave
Ross Road
Sannox Drive
Dykesmains Road
Springvale Nursery
Loch-wood Gdns
Saughtree Ave
Arran Pl
Shaw Pl
James Reid Special School
Hogarth Ave
Dykesfield Pl
Murray Avenue
Links Road
Dykes Pl
McKillop
Clark Pl
Lochranza Pl
Gilfillan Ave
Fleck Ave
McKinnon Pl
New England
7
Mayfield

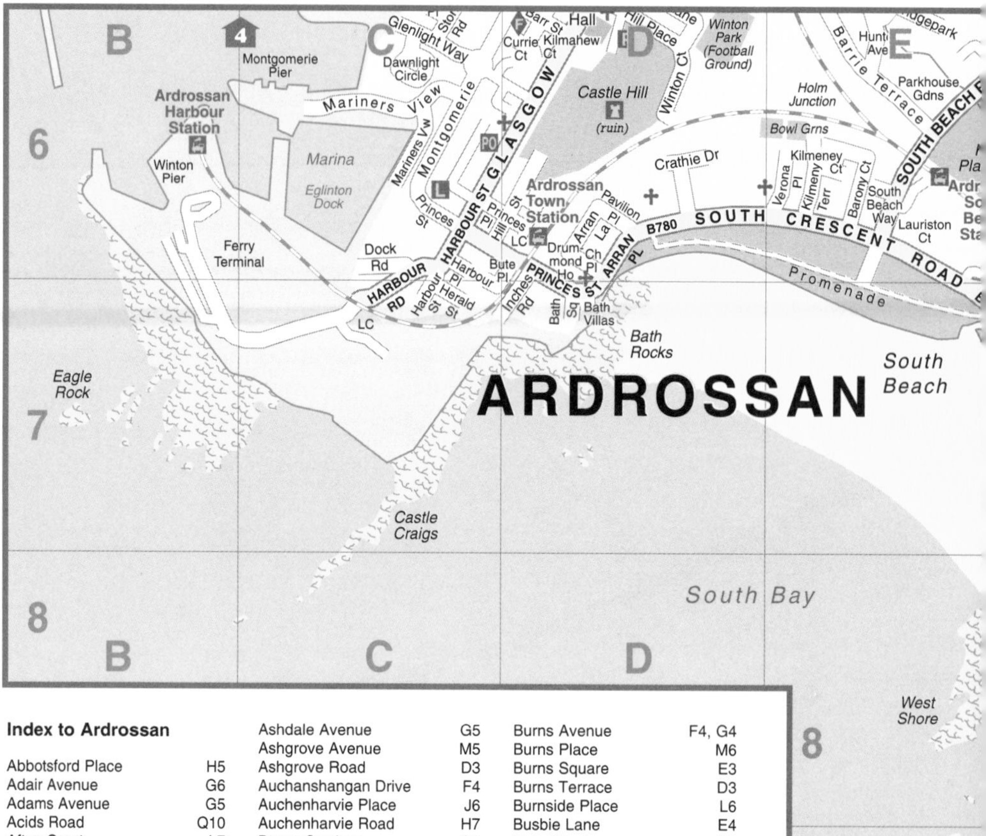

B C D E
6 7 8 9
4
Montgomerie Pier
Ardrossan Harbour Station
Winton Pier
Mariners View
Marina
Eglinton Dock
Ferry Terminal
Glenlight Way
Dawnlight Circle
Mariners Vw
Montgomerie
Princes St
Dock Rd
HARBOUR RD
HARBOUR ST
GLASGOW
Harbour Pl
Harbour St
Herald St
Princes Pl
Hill St
Bute Pl
Inches Rd
PRINCES ST
Bath Sq
Bath Villas
Barr St
Currie Ct
Kilmahew Ct
Hall
Hill Place
Castle Hill (ruin)
Winton Ct
Winton Park (Football Ground)
Ardrossan Town Station
Arran Pl
La
Pavilion
Drummond Ho
Ch Pl
ARRAN PL
B780
SOUTH CRESCENT ROAD
Crathie Dr
Verona Pl
Kilmeney Ct
Kilmeney Terr
Barony Ct
South Beach Way
Lauriston Ct
Bowl Grns
Holm Junction
Hunt Ave
Barrie Terrace
Parkhouse Gdns
SOUTH BEACH
Promenade
LC
PO
L
Bath Rocks
Eagle Rock
Castle Craigs
ARDROSSAN
South Beach
South Bay
West Shore

Index to Ardrossan

Abbotsford Place H5
Adair Avenue G6
Adams Avenue G5
Acids Road Q10
Afton Court L7
Afton Place E3
Afton Road L6
Ailsa Drive K7
Ailsa Gardens E4
Ailsa Road H6
Aitken Place D4
Alexander Avenue M5
Alexander Place L6
Alloway Place D3
Anderson Court D5
Anderson Drive H6
Anderson Terrace D5
Ardchoille Drive M5
Ardchoille Lane M5
Ardeer Lane N9
Ardlui Terrace H7
Ardneil Court C3
Ardoch Court M9
Ardoch Crescent M9
Ardoch Terrace M8
Ardrossan Road F7
Argyle Place F7
Argyle Road G7
Armour Place D3
Arran Court K7
Arran Lane D6
Arran Place (Ard'n) D6
Arran Place (S'coats) H5
Arthur Street (S'coats) H8
Arthur Street (S'ston) L7
Arthurlie Place F7
Ashdale Avenue G5
Ashgrove Avenue M5
Ashgrove Road D3
Auchanshangan Drive F4
Auchenharvie Place J6
Auchenharvie Road H7
Barga Gardens G4
Barnett Court G8
Barnett Crescent G8
Barony Court D6
Barr Street D6
Barra Place N5
Barrie Terrace E6
Bath Square D7
Bath Villas D7
Beattie Court L8
Beggs Terrace E4
Berchem Place G7
Betsy Miller Wynd G4
Bevan Court C3
Birch Terrace D4
Blakely Road J8
Boglemart Street K7
Border Avenue G7
Border Place G7
Boyd Orr Road H5
Boydston Road D3
Bradshaw Street G8
Braehead Place G7
Braes Road F8
Bridgepark E6
Broadway E4
Brown Place G6
Burma Road P10
Burn Road E7
Burnbank Street L7
Burnfoot Lane C3
Burnlea Place M5
Burns Avenue F4, G4
Burns Place M6
Burns Square E3
Burns Terrace D3
Burnside Place L6
Busbie Lane E4
Bute Court K7
Bute Place C7
Bute Terrace F6
Caff Water Place F5
Caledonia Court D5
Caledonia Crescent D5
Caledonia Road (Ard'n) D5
Caledonia Road (S'coats) F6, F7
Caledonian Road M8
Caley Court L8
Cambuskeith Road M4
Campbell Avenue (S'coats) F7
Campbell Avenue (S'ston) L5
Canal Court H8
Canal Crescent L8
Canal Place H8
Canal Street H8
Caponcraig Avenue K6
Carey Road G4
Carment Drive M8
Carmyle Place L8
Carrick Avenue H4
Carrick Place D4
Castle Avenue M4
Castle Road E4
Castlehill Road N5
Catacol Avenue G5
Centenary Place E4
Central Avenue (Ard'n) E4
Central Avenue (S'ston) P10
Central Quadrant D4
Chapelwell Street F
Chaplehill Mount D
Christie Gardens G
Church Place D
Churchill Drive D
Clark Crescent L
Clark Place H
Clements Place M
Clyde Place E
Clyde Terrace E
Clyde View Avenue K
Clytus Court G
Coalhill Place C
Corrie Crescent G
Corsankell Wynd F
Countess Street G

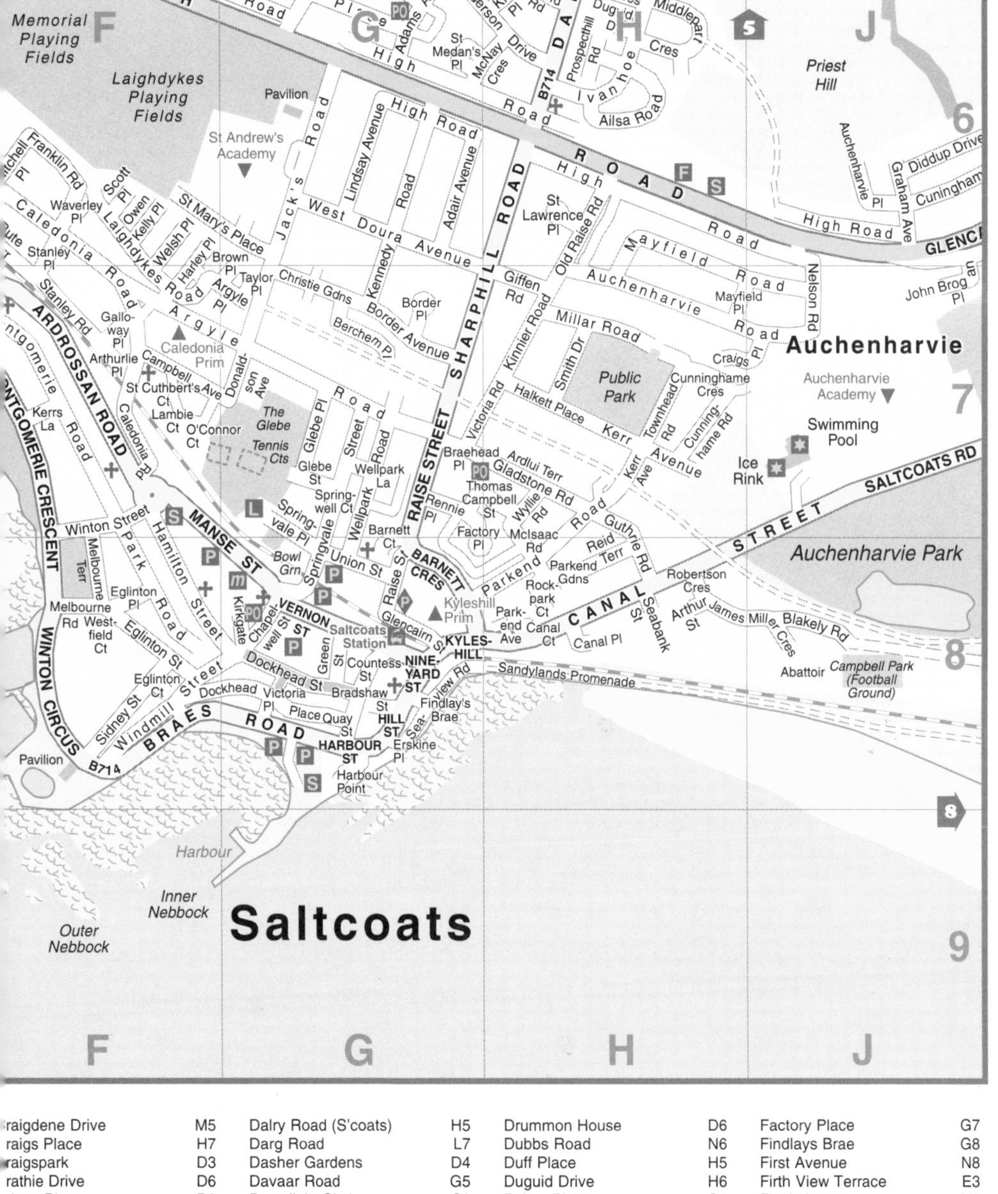

raigdene Drive	M5	Dalry Road (S'coats)	H5	Drummon House	D6	Factory Place	G7
raigs Place	H7	Darg Road	L7	Dubbs Road	N6	Findlays Brae	G8
raigspark	D3	Dasher Gardens	D4	Duff Place	H5	First Avenue	N8
rathie Drive	D6	Davaar Road	G5	Duguid Drive	H6	Firth View Terrace	E3
rinan Place	D2	Dawnlight Circle	C6	Dykes Place	G5	Fleck Avenue	H5
umbrae Road	G5	Deer Park Avenue	M8	Dykesfield Place	F5	Fleming Crescent	H4
umbrae Terrace	D4	Diddup Drive	J6	Dykesmains Road	F5	Forde Crescent	M5
unninghame Crescent	H7	Dippin Place	G5	Eglinton Court	F8	Franklin Road	F6
unninghame Drive	J6	Dock Road	C6	Eglinton Place	F8	Fullerton Place	K7
unninghame Road (Ard'n)	D4	Dockhead Place	G8	Eglinton Road	B3	Fullerton Square	D5
unninghame Road (S'coats)	H7	Dockhead Street	G8	Eglinton Square	D4	Galloway Place	F7
		Donaldson Avenue (S'coats)	G7	Eglinton Street	F8	Garnock Road	L7
urrie Court	D6			Ellisland Place	H4	Garthland Drive	D3
airymead Place	E5	Donaldson Avenue (S'ston)	M5	Elm Park	E4	Garven Road	M8
alry Lane	D3			Elms Place	M5	George Aitken Court	E4
alry Road (Ard'n)	D3	Doon Place	H4	Erskine Place	G8		

continued overleaf....

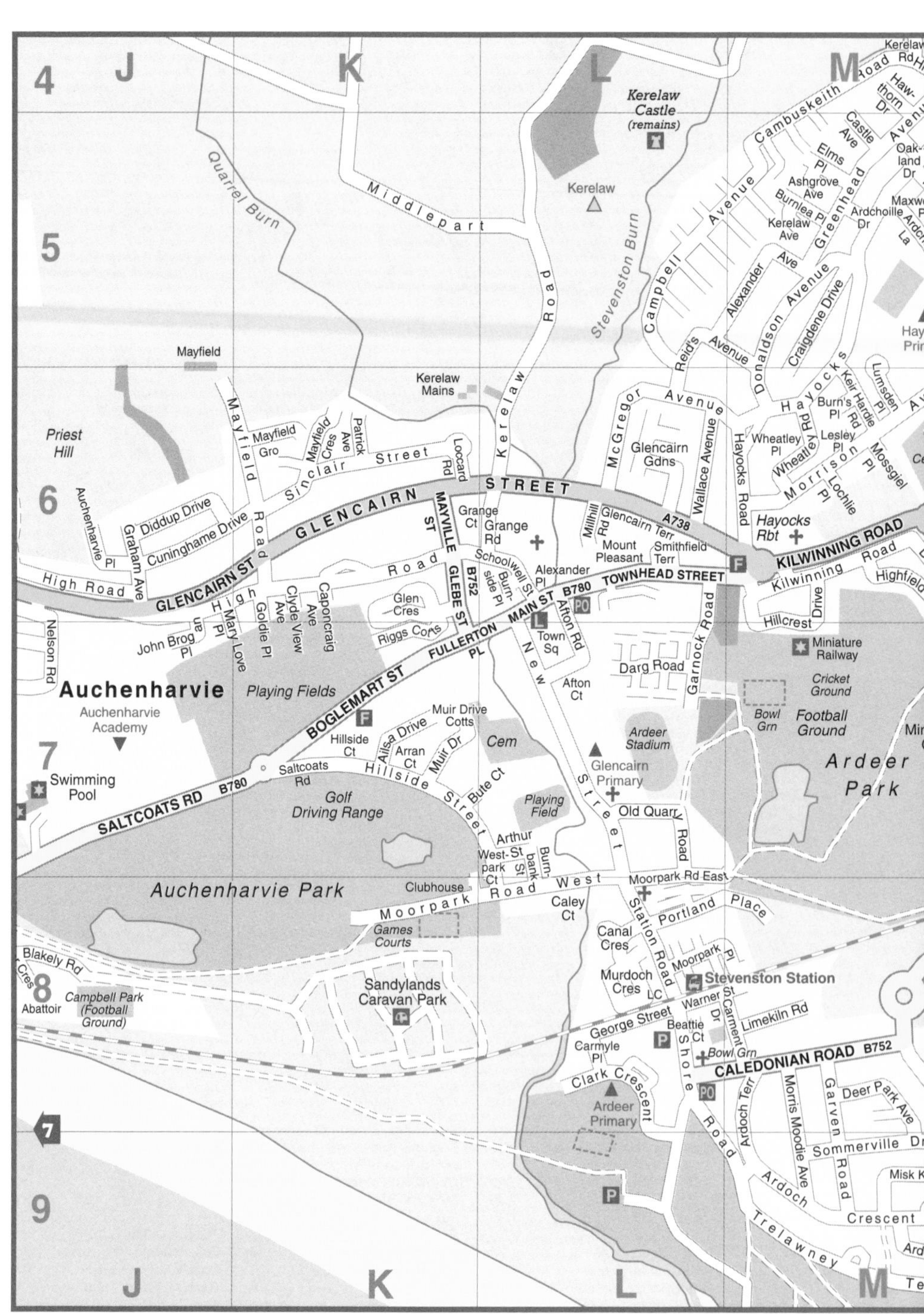
J
K
L
M
4
5
6
7
8
9
Kerelaw Castle (remains)
Kerelaw
Quarrel Burn
Middlepart
Stevenston Burn
Kerelaw Road
Mayfield
Kerelaw Mains
Priest Hill
Mayfield
Mayfield Gro
Mayfield Cres
Patrick Ave
Sinclair Street
Loccard Rd
GLENCAIRN STREET
Auchenharvie Pl
Diddup Drive
Graham Ave
Cuninghame Drive
Road
High Road
GLENCAIRN ST
High Road
MAYVILLE ST
GLEBE ST
B752
Grange Ct
Grange Rd
Schoolwell St
Burnside Pl
Alexander Pl
Glen Cres
Riggs Cotts
Capon craig Ave
Clyde View Ave
Goldie Pl
Mary Love Pl
John Brogan Pl
Nelson Rd
Auchenharvie
Auchenharvie Academy
Playing Fields
BOGLEMART ST
FULLERTON PL
MAIN ST
B780
TOWNHEAD STREET
Town Sq
Afton Rd
New Street
Afton Ct
Darg Road
Garnock Road
Millhill Rd
Glencairn Terr
Mount Pleasant
Smithfield Terr
A738
Hayocks Rbt
KILWINNING ROAD
Kilwinning Road
Highfield
Hillcrest Drive
Hillcrest
Miniature Railway
Cricket Ground
Football Ground
Bowl Grn
Ardeer Park
Ardeer Stadium
Glencairn Primary
Old Quarry Road
Cambuskeith Road
Kerelaw Rd
Hawthorn Dr
Castle Ave
Avenue
Oakland Dr
Elms Pl
Ashgrove Ave
Burnlea Pl
Greenhead
Ardchoille Dr
Kerelaw Ave
Campbell Avenue
Alexander Ave
Donaldson Avenue
Craigdene Drive
Reid's Avenue
McGregor Avenue
Glencairn Gdns
Wallace Avenue
Hayocks Road
Hayocks
Keir Hardie Rd
Burn's Pl
Lumsden Pl
Wheatley Pl
Wheatley Rd
Lesley Pl
Morrison Pl
Lochlie
Mossgiel
Swimming Pool
SALTCOATS RD
B780
Saltcoats Rd
Hillside Ct
Ailsa Drive
Arran Ct
Muir Dr
Muir Drive Cotts
Cem
Hillside Street
Bute Ct
Playing Field
Golf Driving Range
Arthur St
Westpark Ct
West-St
Burnbank
Auchenharvie Park
Clubhouse
Moorpark Road West
Moorpark Rd East
Caley Ct
Games Courts
Station Road
Portland Place
Canal Cres
Murdoch Cres
Moorpark Pl
Stevenston Station
Warner St
LC
Blakely Rd
Abattoir
Campbell Park (Football Ground)
Sandylands Caravan Park
George Street
Beattie Ct
Carment Dr
Limekiln Rd
Carmyle Pl
Shore Road
Bowl Grn
CALEDONIAN ROAD
B752
Clark Crescent
Ardeer Primary
PO
Ardoch Terr
Morris Moodie Ave
Garven Road
Deer Park Ave
Sommerville Dr
Ardoch Crescent
Trelawney
7

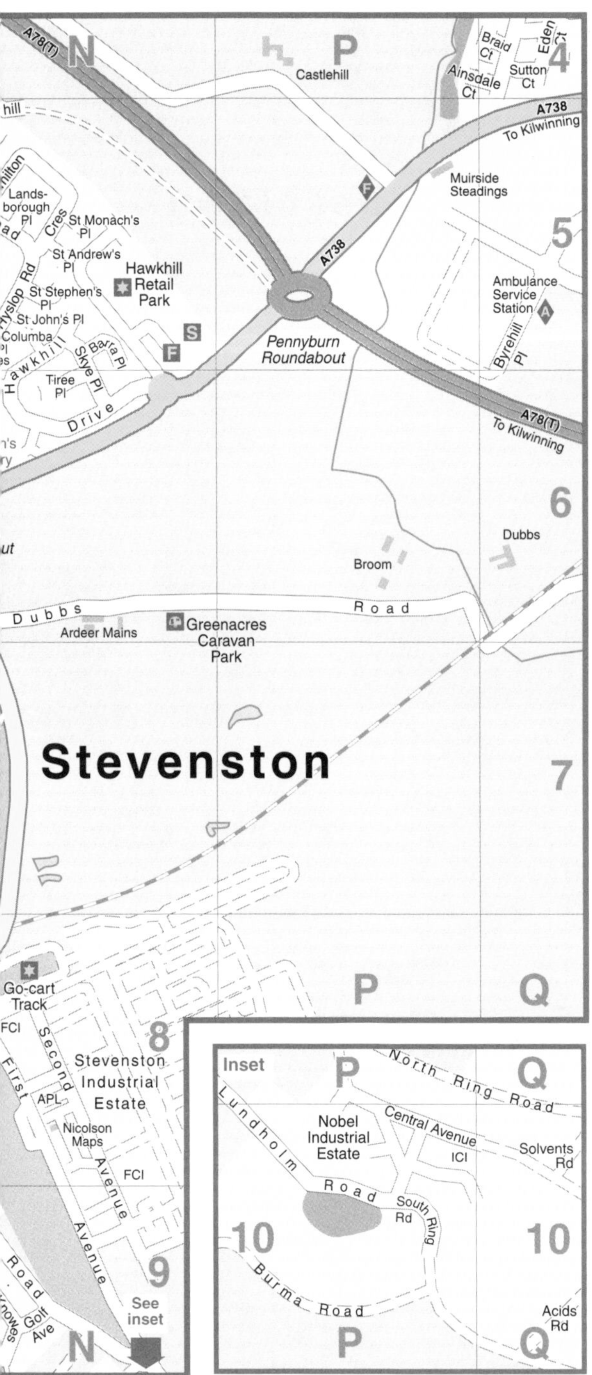

George Street L8
Giffen Road H7
Gilfillan Avenue H5
Gladstone Road H7
Glasgow Lane D5
Glasgow Street D6
Glebe Place G7
Glebe Street (S'coats) G7
Glebe Street (S'ston) K6
Glen Crescent K6
Glencairn Gardens L6
Glencairn Street (S'coats) G8
Glencairn Street (S'ston) K6
Glencairn Terrace L6
Glenlight Way C6
Goldie Place K6
Golf Avenue N9
Graham Avenue J6
Grange Court K6
Grange Road L6
Green Street G8
Greenacres F4
Greenhead Avenue M5
Guthrie Road H7
Halkett Place H7
Hamilton Crescent N5
Hamilton Street F8
Harbour Place C6
Harbour Road C7
Harbour Point G8
Harbour Street (Ard'n) C6
Harbour Street (S'coats) G8
Harley Place F7
Harvey Gardens D4
Harvey Street D4
Haupland Road C2
Hawkhill Drive N6
Hawkhill Place N5
Hawthorn Drive M4
Hayocks Road M5
Hazel Avenue D3
Herald Street C7
High Road G6
Highfield Drive M6
Hill Lane D5
Hill Place D6
Hill Street (Ard'n) D6
Hill Street (S'coats) G8
Hillcrest Drive M6
Hillhead Road M4
Hillside Court K7
Hillside Street K7
Hilton Court F4
Hogarth Avenue F5
Horse Isle View B3
Hunter Avenue E5
Hyslop Road M5
Inches Road C7
Island View C3
Islay Crescent G5
Ivanhoe Drive H5
Jacks Road G6
James Miller Crescent H8
Jean Armour Place H4
John Brogan Place J7
Keir Hardie Drive C3
Keir Hardie Place H5
Keir Hardie Road M6
Kemp Court F4
Kenilworth Drive H5
Kennedy Road G6
Kerelaw Avenue M5
Kerelaw Road L6, M4
Kerr Avenue H7
Kerrs Lane F7
Kilbrannan Avenue G5
Kildonan Place G5
Kilmahew Court D6
Kilmahew Street D5
Kilmeny Court E6
Kilmeny Terrace E6
Kilmory Road G5
Kilwinning Road M6
Kinnier Road H7
Kirkgate G8
Kirkhall Gardens E5
Knock Jargon Court F4
Knockrivoch Gardens F3
Knockrivoch Place F3
Knockrivoch Wynd F3
Knox Place H5
Kyleshill G8
Laighdykes Road F6
Laird Weir E4
Lambie Court F7
Landsborough Court F5
Landsborough Place N5
Lauriston Court E6
Lawson Drive E3
Lennox Wynd G4
Lesley Place M6
Limekiln Road M8
Lindsay Avenue G6
Links Road G5
Linn Road D3
Linnburn Terrace C3
Loanhead Road E5
Loccard Road K6
Lochlea Road H4
Lochlie Place M6
Lochranza Place H5
Lochwood Gardens G5
Longcraigs Avenue D2
Longfield Avenue F5
Longfield Place F5
Lumsden Place M6
Lundholm Road M8
McDowall Avenue E5
McDowall Place D4
McGillivray Avenue G5
McGregor Avenue L6
McIsaac Road H8
McKellar Avenue E5
McKillop Place G5
McKinnon Place H5
McMillan Drive B3
McNay Crescent G6
Main Street L6
Manor, The D2
Manse Street F7
Mariners View C6
Martin Square H4
Mary Love Place J6
Maxwell Place M5
Mayfield Crescent K6

continued overleaf...

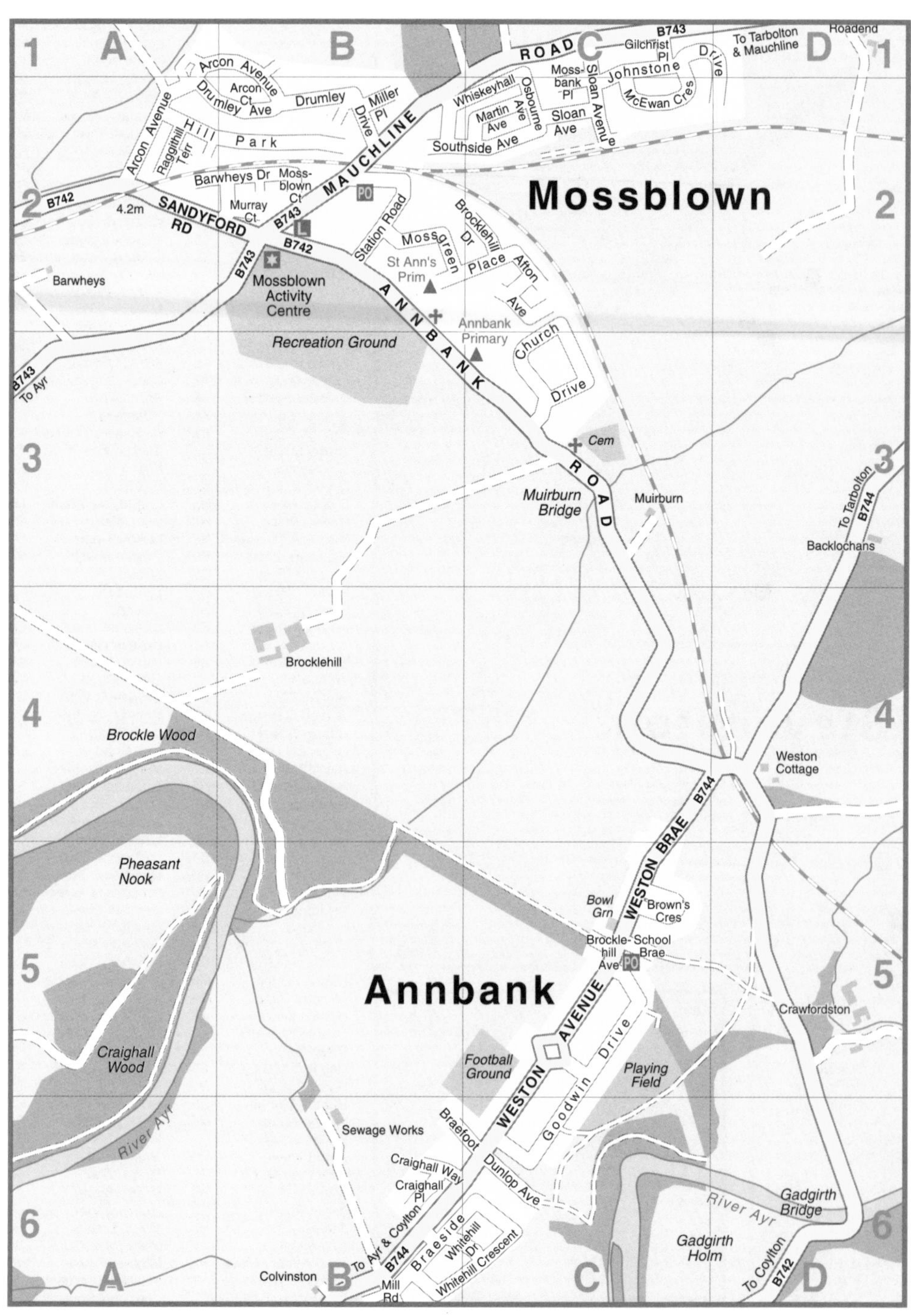
Mossblown
Annbank
MAUCHLINE ROAD
ANNBANK ROAD
SANDYFORD RD
WESTON BRAE
WESTON AVENUE
Arcon Avenue
Arcon Ct
Drumley Ave
Drumley Drive
Miller Pl
Hill Park
Raggithill Terr
Barwheys Dr
Mossblown Ct
Murray Ct
Station Road
Mossgreen
Brocklehill Dr
Place
Afton Ave
St Ann's Prim
Annbank Primary
Church Drive
Cem
Whiskeyhall
Martin Ave
Osbourne Ave
Mossbank Pl
Sloan Avenue
Sloan Ave
Southside Ave
Gilchrist Pl
Johnstone Drive
McEwan Cres
To Tarbolton & Mauchline
Roadend
Barwheys
Mossblown Activity Centre
Recreation Ground
To Ayr
4.2m
Muirburn Bridge
Muirburn
To Tarbolton
Backlochans
Brocklehill
Brockle Wood
Weston Cottage
Pheasant Nook
Bowl Grn
Brown's Cres
Brocklehill Ave
School Brae
Crawfordston
Craighall Wood
Football Ground
Playing Field
Goodwin Drive
River Ayr
Sewage Works
Braefoot
Craighall Way
Craighall Pl
Dunlop Ave
To Ayr & Coylton
Braeside
Whitehill Dr
Whitehill Crescent
Gadgirth Bridge
Gadgirth Holm
To Coylton
Colvinston
Mill Rd
B742
B743
B744

Index to Ardrossan

continued from page 9

Mayfield Grove K6
Mayfield Place H7
Mayfield Road (S'coats) H6
Mayfield Road (S'ston) K6
Mayville Street K6
Melbourne Road F8
Melbourne Terrace F8
Mid Dykes Road F5
Middlepart Crescent H6
Middlepart J5
Millar Road H7
Miller Place B3
Millglen Place E3
Millglen Road E3
Millhill Road L6
Misk Knowes M9
Mitchell Place F6
Moffat Wynd G4
Montfode Court D3
Montfode Drive C3
Montgomerie Crescent F7
Montgomerie Pier Road C5
Montgomerie Road F7
Montgomerie Street C6
Moonlight Place C5
Moorpark Place L8
Moorpark Road East L7
Moorpark Road West K8
Morris Moodie Avenue M8
Morrison Avenue M6
Morrison Court M6
Mossgiel Place M6
Mossgiel Road (Ard'n) E3
Mossgiel Road (S'coats) H4
Motte Gardens C3
Mount Pleasant L6
Muir Drive Cottages K7
Muir Drive K7
Mulgrew Avenue H5
Munnoch Crescent C3
Munro Place H5
Munro Walk H5
Murdoch Court F4
Murdoch Crescent L8
Murray Avenue F5
Nelson Road J7
New England Road H5
New Street L7
Nineyard Street G8
Nithsdale Road E3
North Crescent Avenue D4
North Crescent Road C4
North Ring Road P9
Nursery Place E5
Oak Road D3
Oakland Drive M5
O'Connor Court G7
Old Quarry Road L7
Old Raise Road H6
Owen Kelly Place F6
Paisley Street D5
Park Lane D4
Park Road (Ard'n) D5
Park Road (S'coats) F8
Park View Drive E5
Park View E5
Parkend Avenue H8
Parkend Gardens H8
Parkend Road H8
Parkhouse Gardens E6
Parkhouse Road E5
Patrick Avenue K6
Pavilion Place D6
Pirnmill Road G5
Pladda Road G5
Portland Place L8
Primrose Place H5
Princes Place C6
Princes Street D6
Prospecthill Road H6
Quay Street G8
Queen's Drive D4
Raise Street G6, G7
Rashley Square E3
Raylight Place C6
Red Gables Square C4
Reid Terrace H8
Reid's Avenue L5
Rennie Place G7
Riggs Cottages K7
Roberston Crescent H8
Rockpark Court H8
Rosa Place H5
Ross Road G5
Rowanside Terrace D3
St Andrews Court G4
St Andrew's Place N5
St Andrew's Road E3
St Columba Place N5
St Cuthbert's ourt F7
St James Place N5
St John's Place (Ard'n) D5
St John's Place (S'ston) N5
St Laurence Place H6
St Margaret's Road E3, E4
St Mary's Place F6
St Meddan's Place G6
St Monach's Place N5
St Ninian's Drive E3
St Stephen's Place N5
Saltcoats Road J7
Sanda Place G5
Sandylands Prom H8
Sannox Drive H5
Saughtree Avenue G5
School Place D5
Schoolwell Street L6
Scott Place F6
Seabank Street H8
Seafield Court C4
Seafield Drive D4
Seaview Road G8
Second Avenue N8
Seton Lane D5
Seton Street D5
Sharphill Road G7
Shaw Place H5
Shellbridge Way D5
Shore Road L8
Simpson Drive G4
Sinclair Street K6
Skye Place N5
Smith Drive H7
Smithfield Terrace L6
Solvents Road Q10
Sommerville Drive M9
Sorbie Road E6
Sorbie Road F5
South Beach Road E6
South Beach Way E6
South Crescent Road D6
South Isle Road D2
South Ring Road N10
Spindrift Wynd G4
Springvale Place G7
Springvale Street G7
Springwell Court G7
Stanley Avenue D4
Stanley Drive D4
Stanley Place F7
Stanley Road (Ard'n) D3
Stanley Road (S'coats) F7
Station Road L8
Stormlight Road C6
Strathclyde Avenue E4
Sydney Street F8
Talisman Walk H5
Taylor Place G7
Thistle Terrace M5
Thomas Campbell Street H7
Three Sisters Court F5
Tiree Place N6
Town Square L6
Townhead Road H7
Townhead Street L6
Trelawney Terrace M9
Union Street G8
Vernon Street G8
Verona Place E6
Victoria Place G8
Victoria Road G7
Wallace Avenue L6
Warner Street L8
Waverley Place (1) F6
Weir Road E3
Wellpark Lane G7
Wellpark Road G7
Welsh Place F6
West Doura Avenue G6
West Park Court K7
Westfield Court F8
Wheatley Gardens H5
Wheatley Place M6
Wheatley Road (S'coats) H5
Wheatley Road (S'ston) M6
White Craig Road E3
Whitlees Court F4
Whitlees Crescent E4
Windmill Street F8
Winton Circus F8
Winton Court D6
Winton Lane D5
Winton Place D5
Winton Street (Ard'n) D5
Winton Street (S'coats) F7
Witches Linn C3
Woodland Place D4
Wyllie Road H7
Young Street D5

Index to Annbank

Afton Avenue C2
Annbank Road B2
Arcon Avenue B1
Arcon Court B2
Barwheys Drive A2
Braefoot C6
Braeside B6
Brocklehill Avenue C5
Brocklehill Drive C2
Brown's Crescent C5
Church Drive C3
Craighall Place B6
Craighall Way B6
Drumley Avenue A2
Drumley Drive B2
Dunlop Avenue C6
Gilchrist Place C1
Goodwin Drive C6
Hill Park A2
Johnstone Drive C1
McEwan Crescent C2
Martin Avenue C2
Mauchline Road B2
Mill Road B6
Miller Place B2
Mossbank Place C2
Mossblown Court B2
Mossgreen Place B2
Murray Court B2
Osbourne Avenue C2
Raggethill Terrace A2
Sandyford Road A2
School Brae C5
Sloan Avenue C1, C2
Southside Avenue B2
Station Road B2
Whiskeyhall C2
Weston Avenue C6
Weston Brae C5
Whitehill Drive C6
Whitehill Crescent B6

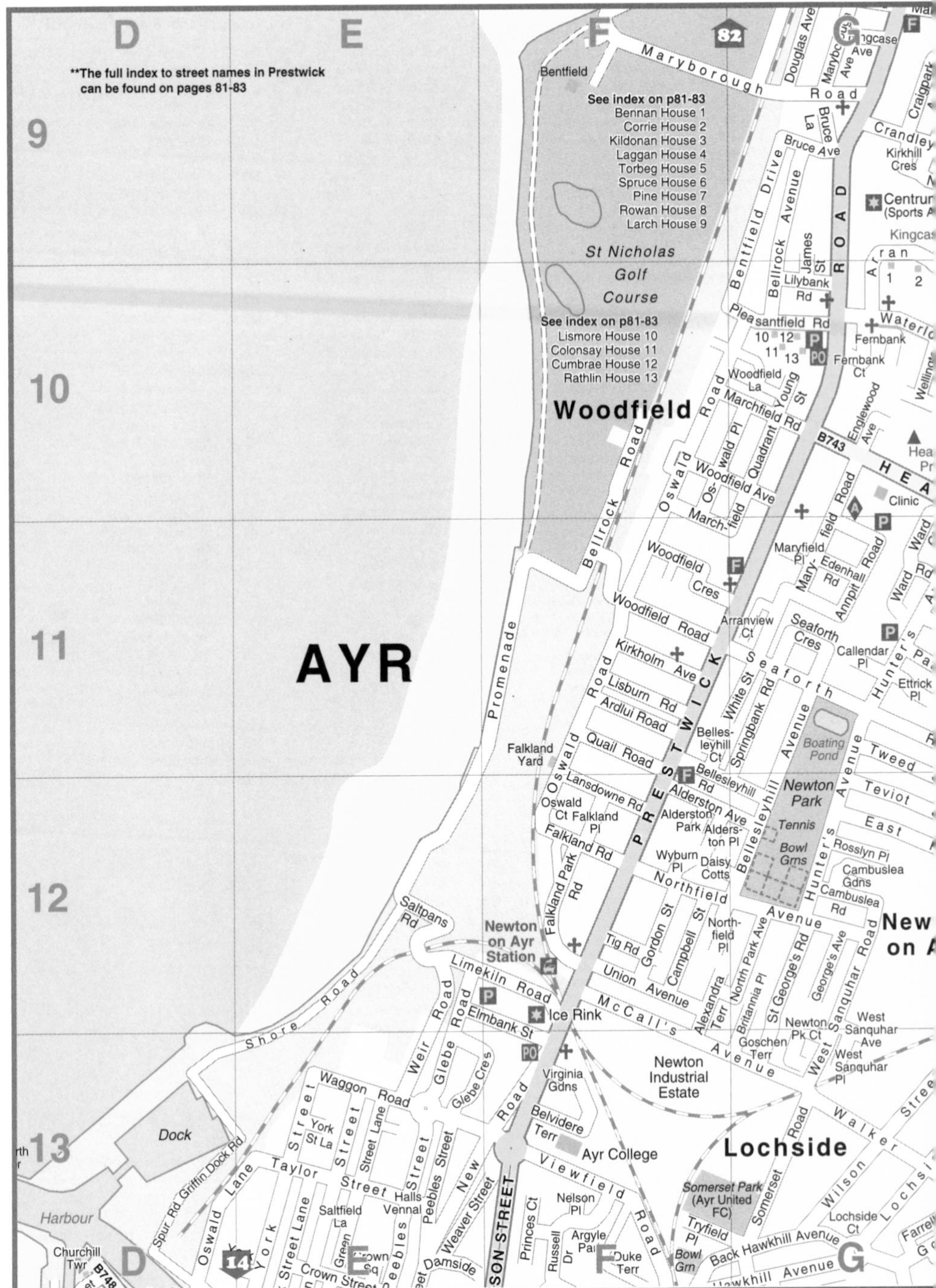
**The full index to street names in Prestwick can be found on pages 81-83
See index on p81-83
Bennan House 1
Corrie House 2
Kildonan House 3
Laggan House 4
Torbeg House 5
Spruce House 6
Pine House 7
Rowan House 8
Larch House 9
St Nicholas Golf Course
See index on p81-83
Lismore House 10
Colonsay House 11
Cumbrae House 12
Rathlin House 13
Woodfield
AYR
Maryborough Road
Bentfield
Newton on Ayr Station
Ice Rink
Newton Industrial Estate
Lochside
Ayr College
Somerset Park (Ayr United FC)
Newton Park
Dock
Harbour
Prestwick Road
Promenade
Shore Road

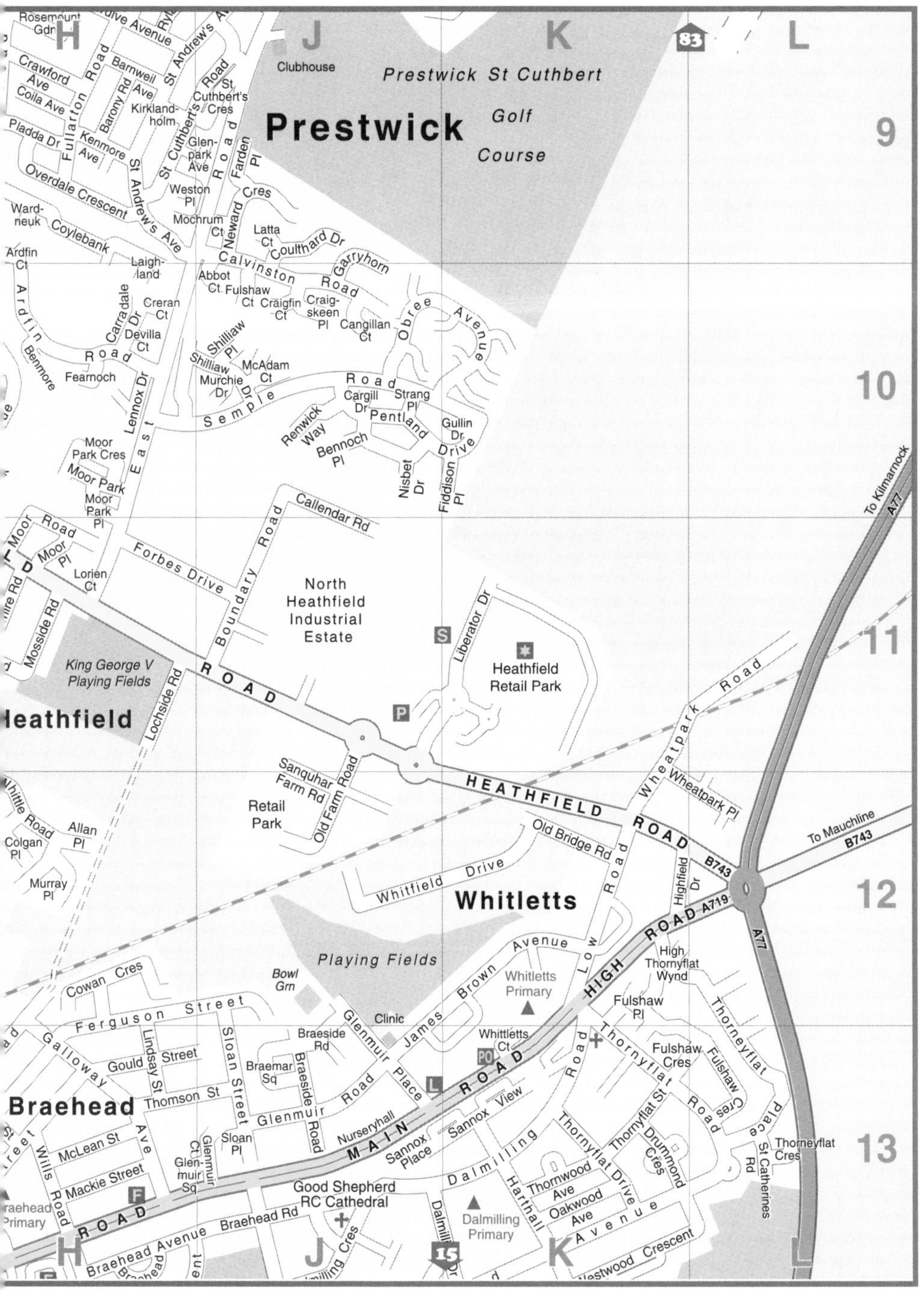

Index to street names can be found starting on page 94

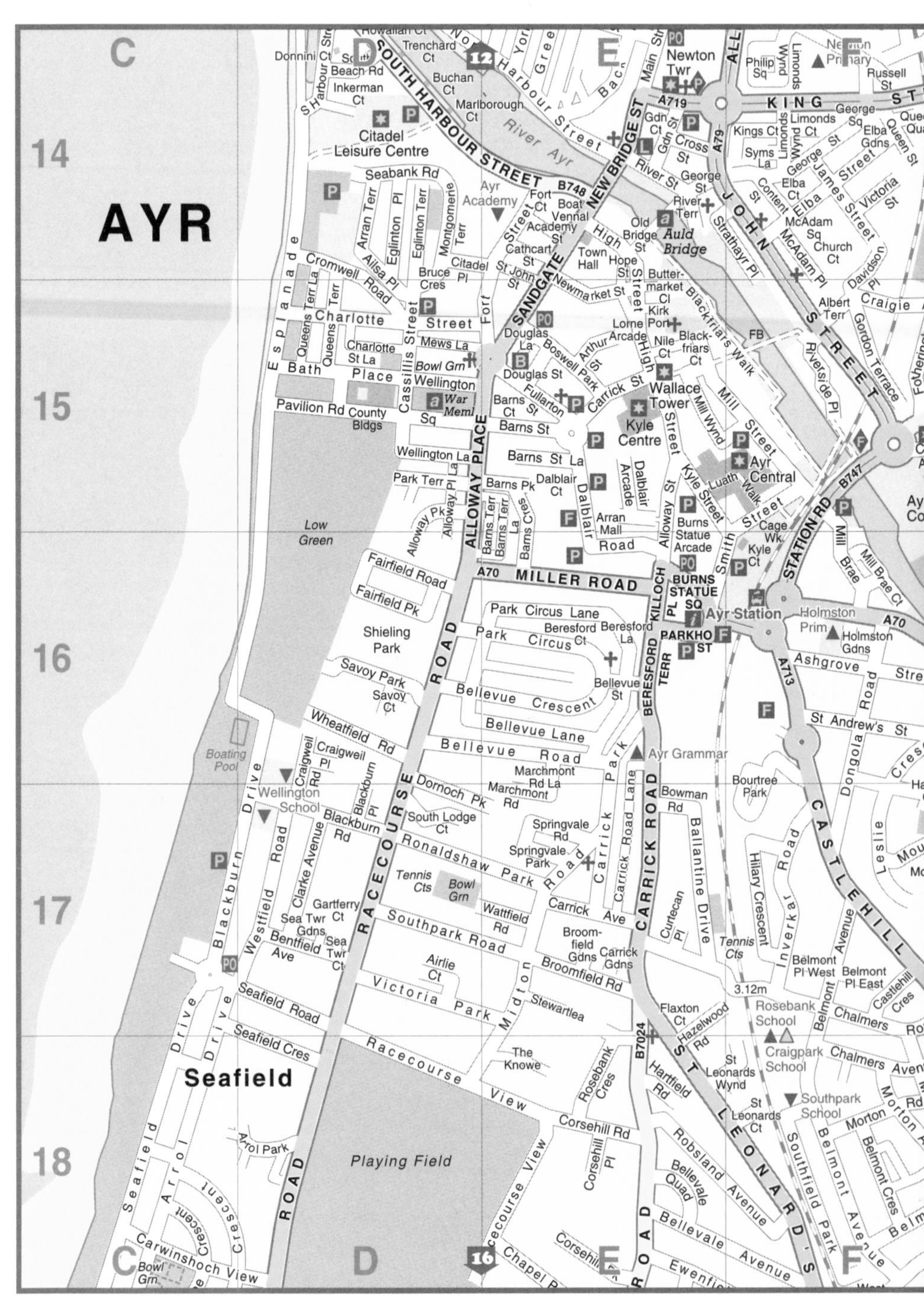

AYR
C
D
E
F
14
15
16
17
18
12
16
Donnini Ct
South Beach Rd
Inkerman Ct
Harbour St
Trenchard Ct
SOUTH HARBOUR STREET
Buchan Ct
Marlborough Ct
North Harbour Street
River Ayr
Citadel Leisure Centre
Seabank Rd
Arran Terr
Eglinton Pl
Eglinton Terr
Montgomerie Terr
Ayr Academy
Fort St
Boat Vennal
Academy St
B748
NEW BRIDGE ST
Main St
Newton Twr
A719
Gdn Ct
Gdn St
Cross St
River St
George St
River Terr
Old Bridge St
Auld Bridge
Town Hall
Hope St
High St
Cathcart St
St John St
SANDGATE
Newmarket St
Butter-market Cl
Kirk Port
Lorne Arcade
Nile Ct
Black-friars Ct
Blackfriars Walk
Esplanade
Cromwell Road
Ailsa Pl
Queens Terr La
Queens Terr
Charlotte Street
Charlotte St La
Cassillis Street
Bruce Cres
Citadel Pl
Mews La
Bowl Grn
Bath Place
Wellington Sq
War Meml
Pavilion Rd
County Bldgs
Douglas La
Douglas St
Boswell Park
Arthur St
Carrick St
Wallace Tower
Kyle Centre
Fullarton St
Barns Ct
Barns St
Barns St La
Wellington La
Park Terr
Alloway Pl La
Alloway Pk
Alloway Pl
ALLOWAY PLACE
Barns Pk
Barns Terr
Barns Terr La
Barns Cres
Dalblair Ct
Dalblair Road
Dalblair Arcade
Arran Mall
Alloway St
Mill Wynd
Mill Street
Ayr Central
Luath Walk
Kyle Street
Burns Statue Arcade
Smith St
Cage Wk
Kyle Ct
Low Green
Fairfield Road
Fairfield Pk
A70
MILLER ROAD
KILLOCH PL
BURNS STATUE SQ
Ayr Station
PARKHOUSE ST
STATION RD
B747
Shieling Park
Park Circus Lane
Park Circus
Beresford Ct
Beresford La
Bellevue St
BERESFORD TERR
Savoy Park
Savoy Ct
Bellevue Crescent
Bellevue Lane
Bellevue Road
Wheatfield Rd
Craigweil Pl
Craigweil Rd
Blackburn Pl
Blackburn Rd
Boating Pool
Wellington School
Marchmont Rd La
Marchmont Rd
Dornoch Pk
South Lodge Ct
Springvale Rd
Springvale Park
Park Road
Ronaldshaw Park
Ayr Grammar
Bowman Rd
Carrick Road Lane
CARRICK ROAD
Ballantine Drive
Curtecan Pl
Blackburn Drive
Westfield Road
Clarke Avenue
Gartferry Ct
Sea Twr Gdns
Sea Twr Ct
Bentfield Ave
Tennis Cts
Bowl Grn
Wattfield Rd
Carrick Ave
Broomfield Gdns
Carrick Gdns
Broomfield Rd
RACECOURSE ROAD
Southpark Road
Airlie Ct
Victoria Park
Midton Road
Stewartlea
Seafield Road
Seafield Cres
Racecourse View
The Knowe
Rosebank Cres
B7024
Flaxton Ct
Hazelwood Rd
Hartfield Rd
ST LEONARD'S ROAD
St Leonards Wynd
St Leonards Ct
Seafield
Seafield Drive
Arrol Drive
Arrol Park
Arrol Crescent
Carwinshoch View
Bowl Grn
Playing Field
Corsehill Rd
Corsehill Pl
Racecourse View
Chapel Park
Robsland Avenue
Bellevale Quad
Bellevale Avenue
Ewenfield Road
Newton Primary
Philip Sq
Wynd St
Limonds Wynd
Russell St
KING STREET
George Sq
Queen St
Limonds Ct
Kings Ct
Syms La
Elba Gdns
Elba Ct
Elba St
Content St
James Street
Victoria St
McAdam Sq
McAdam Pl
Church Ct
Strathayr Pl
JOHN STREET
A79
Davidson Pl
Albert Terr
Craigie Av
Gordon Terrace
Riverside Pl
FB
Holmston Prim
Holmston Gdns
A70
Mill Brae
Mill Brae Ct
A713
Ashgrove Street
Dongola Road
St Andrew's St
Bourtree Park
CASTLEHILL ROAD
Hilary Crescent
Inverkar Road
Leslie
Belmont Pl West
Belmont Pl East
Belmont Avenue
Castlehill Cres
Chalmers Road
Chalmers Avenue
3.12m
Rosebank School
Craigpark School
Southpark School
Southfield Park
Morton Rd
Belmont Cres
Belmont Avenue

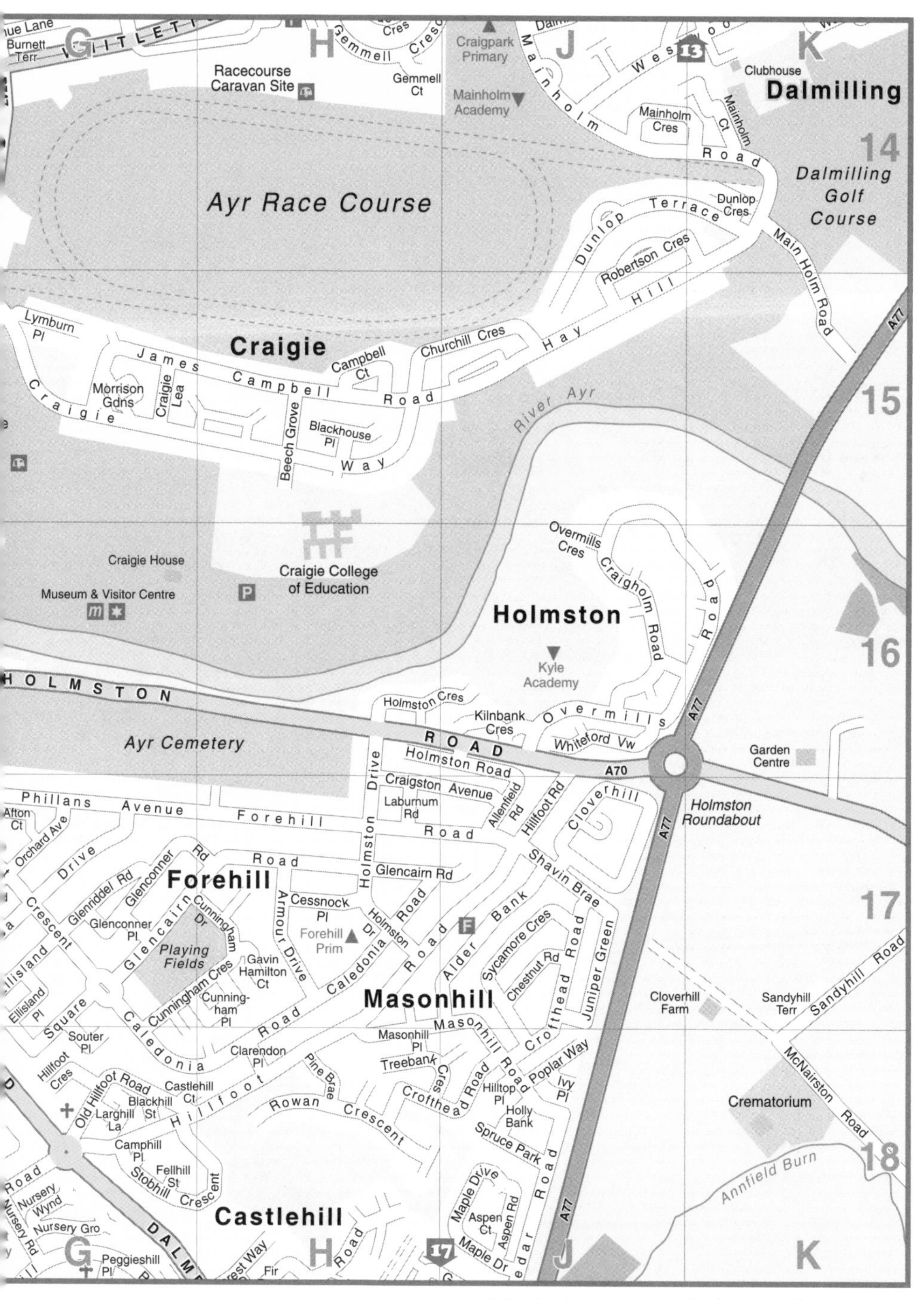

Index to street names can be found starting on page 94

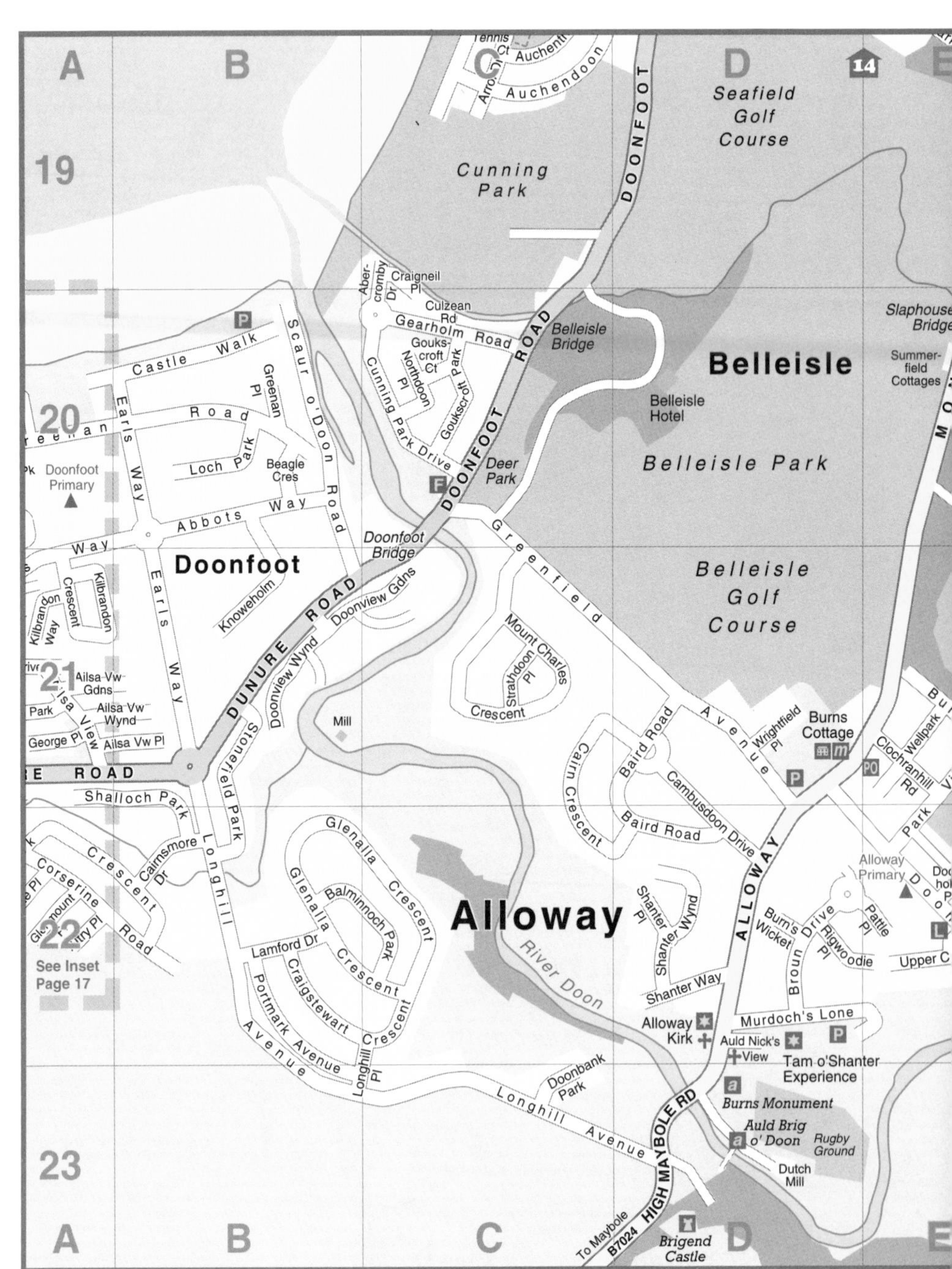
Cunning Park
Seafield Golf Course
Belleisle
Belleisle Hotel
Belleisle Park
Belleisle Golf Course
Belleisle Bridge
Deer Park
Doonfoot
Doonfoot Primary
Doonfoot Bridge
Alloway
River Doon
Alloway Kirk
Auld Nick's View
Tam o'Shanter Experience
Burns Monument
Auld Brig o' Doon
Rugby Ground
Dutch Mill
Brigend Castle
Burns Cottage
Alloway Primary
Mill
Slaphouse Bridge
Summerfield Cottages
DOONFOOT ROAD
DUNURE ROAD
HIGH MAYBOLE RD
B7024 To Maybole
ALLOWAY
Greenfield Avenue
Longhill Avenue
Castle Walk
Earls Way
Abbots Way
Scaur o'Doon Road
Cunning Park Drive
Gearholm Road
Glenalla Crescent
Cambusdoon Drive
Baird Road
Cairn Crescent
Murdoch's Lone
Shanter Way
Shanter Wynd
Portmark Avenue
Craigstewart Crescent
Lamford Dr
Balminnoch Park
Doonbank Park
Stonefield Park
Longhill
Shalloch Park
Doonview Gdns
Doonview Wynd
Knoweholm
Mount Charles Crescent
Strathdoon Pl
See Inset Page 17

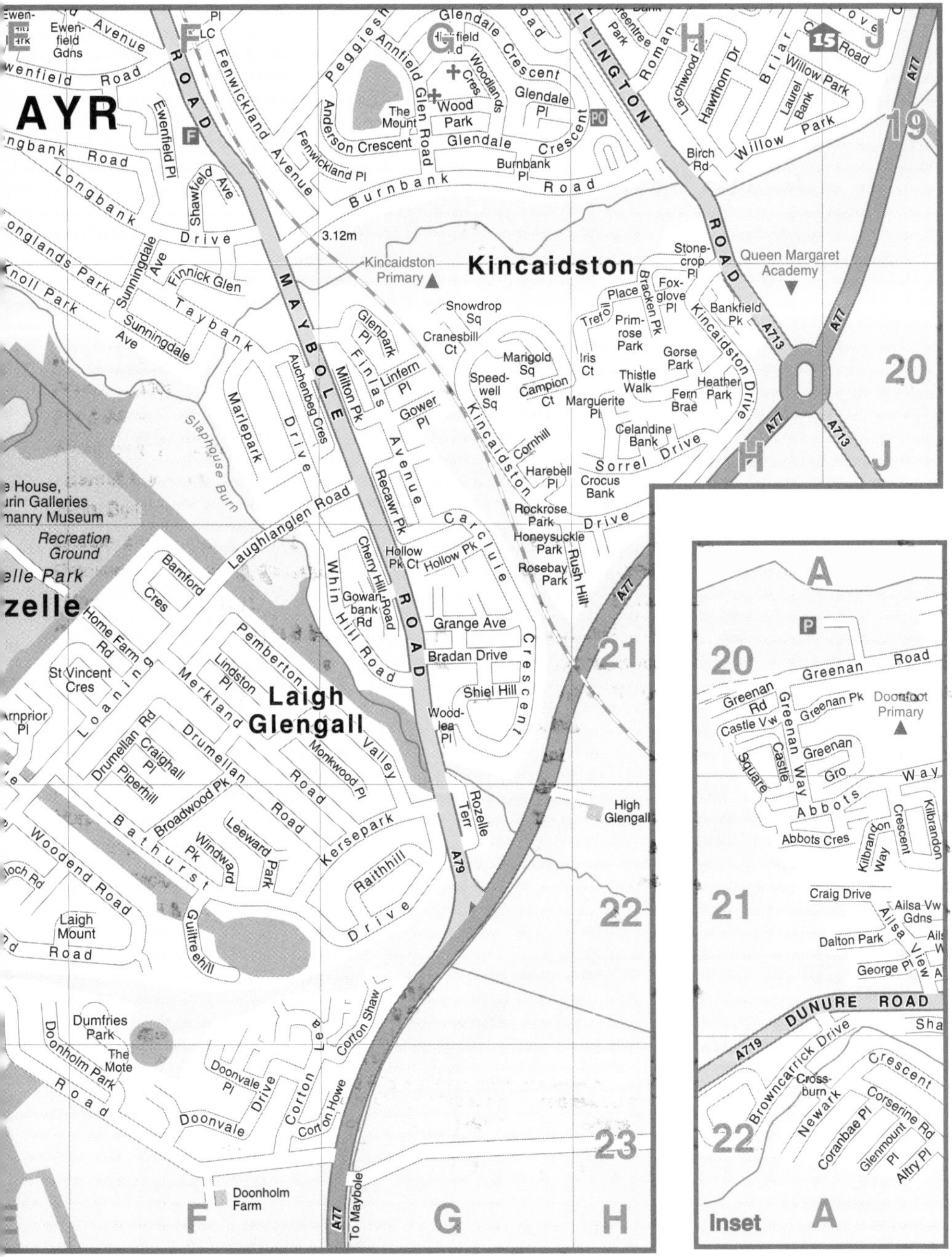

AYR

Kincaidston

Laigh Glengall

Kincaidston Primary

Queen Margaret Academy

Doonfoot Primary

High Glengall

Doonholm Farm

Recreation Ground

MAYBOLE ROAD

DUNURE ROAD

To Maybole

Inset

Auchinleck

Index to Auchinleck

Affleck House C2
Aird Avenue D2
Alma Place D3
Arran Drive C1
Avenue, The B3
Back Rogerton Crescent D2
Ballochmyle Avenue E1
Barbieston Road D2
Barony Road C3
Beechwood Avenue D3
Berry Hill Drive D2
Boswell Drive D3
Cameron Drive D2
Church Hill D3
Church Street D2
Coal Road D3
Dalshalloch Road D2
Darnconner Avenue D2
Darnlaw View B2
Dippol Crescent C2
Easton Place D3
Glennie House C2
Glenshamrock Drive D2
Heathfield Road D2
High House View C3
Hillside Crescent D1
Judge Avenue E2
Knockroon Lane D3
Lambfair Gardens D2
Lord Bute's Walk D4
McTurk Avenue D2
Main Street D3
Market Place C2
Mauchline Road C2
Milne Avenue D2
Old Avenue D2
Park Road D3
Peden Drive E2
Pennylands Road B2
Pentlands View B3
Quarry Knowe D2
Rigg Road F4
Runnels Road B2
Runnels View C3
School Road C2
Searle Terrace C2
Sorn Road C2
Station Road D3
Stoner Crescent D2
Talbot Drive E2
Well Road D2
William McComb Court C2

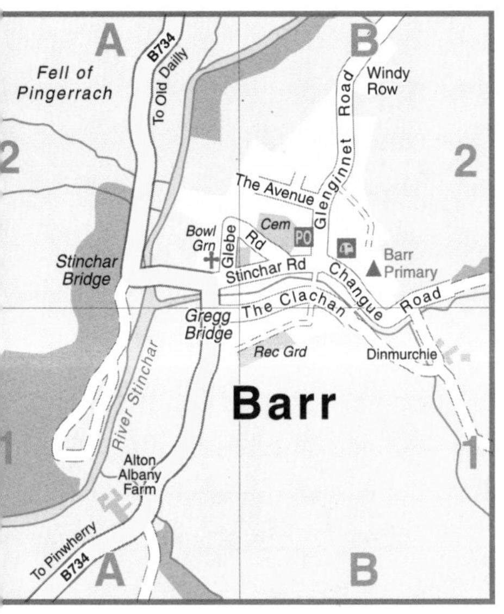

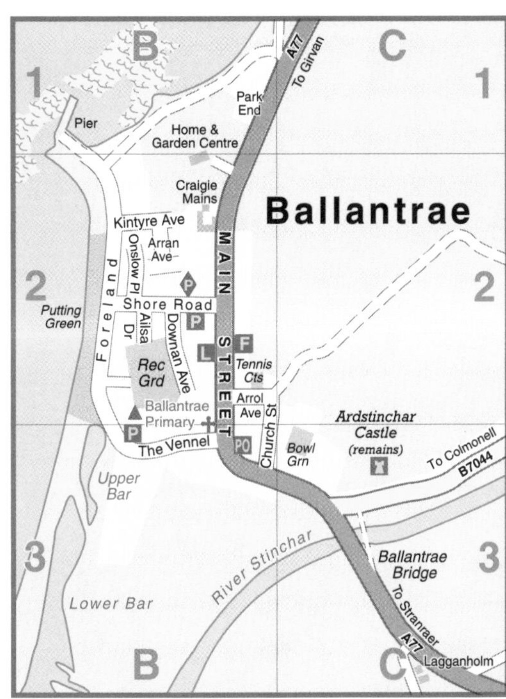

Index to Ballantrae

Ailsa Drive	B2
Arran Avenue	B2
Arrol Avenue	B2
Church Street	B3
Downan Avenue	B2
Foreland	B2
Kintyre Avenue	B2
Main Street	B2
Onslow Place	B2
Park End	B1
Shore Road	B2
Vennel, The	B3

Index to Barr

Avenue, The	B2
Changue Road	B2
Clachan, The	B2
Glebe Road	A2
Glenginnet Road	B2
Stincher Road	A2
Windy Row	B2

Index to Barrhill

Gowlands Terrace	A2
Main Street	A2
Wallace Terrace	B2

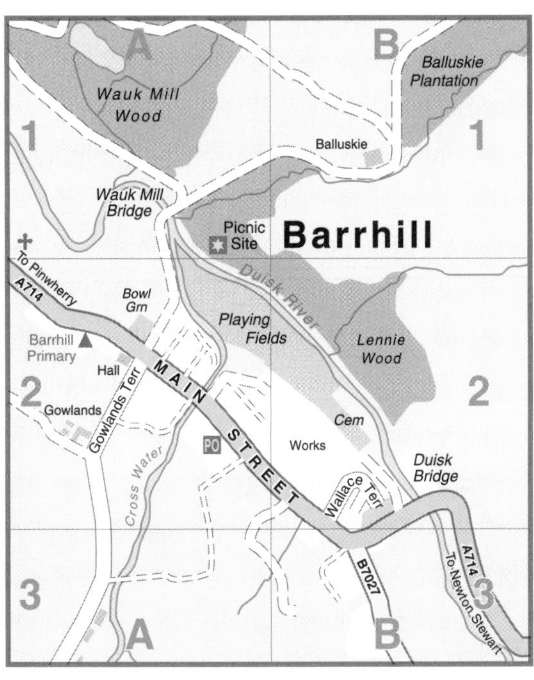

G H J K
2
Muirburn Road
Lodge Wood
Road
Kilbirnie Loch
Ardloch House
Mossneuk
Wotherspoon Dr
Lomond Crescent
Knowehead
A737
3
Thorntree Ave
Cypress Ave
Cherrywood Dr
Belleview
Ash Drive
Sycamore Avenue
Auldlea Road
Beech Avenue
B7049
Cem
Maple Dr
Arran Crescent
ROEBANK RD
Mains House
Sycamore Ct
Kings Road
Janefield Pl
Barrington Ave
BY-PASS ROAD
Threepwood Rd
Bath Burn
Mains Burn
Viewpark
Woodside Rd
Barrington Gdns
TRINITY CRES
BIGHOLM RD
Orr's Public Park
Football
Tennis
Caledonia Rd
Laigh Ct
Laigh Rd
Medine Ave
Somerville Ct
WILSON ST
Crummock Gdns
Trinity Cres
4
Mid Road
Blackthorn Ave
Mains Avenue
Elms Pl
Park Ave
Muirpark Rd
Medine Ct
Crummock St
St Inan's Drive
Mains Road
Kings Ct
Bellmans Cl
Warehouses
Reform Street
MAIN STREET
Main St
Mitchell St
Aitken Drive
Meadowbank Terr
Robert Burns Ct
Bath Lane
Wee Ct
Wee Cl
Kirk Vw
Dickson Ct
Headlands Gro
Meadowside Ct
Keir Hardie Ct
Bellsdale Park (Beith FC)
B777 NEW ST
HEAD ST
Hawthorn Crescent
Cedar Ave
Elder Ave
Barberry Dr
PO
The Cross
Woodburn Rd
Park Ct
Wardrop Terr
B777
WARDROP ST
BEITH
Meadowside Playing Fields
STRAND
Backburn
Academy Brae
Kirk Rd
Rowan Pl
Rowan Ave
Montgomerie Ave
Terrace
Myrtle Bank
Acacia Dr
Meadowside
Guy's La
EGLINTON
Bowl Grn
Boghead
TOWNHEAD ST
William Tricker Cres
5
Square J5
1 Braehead
Laburnum Avenue
Chestnut Avenue
Beith Primary
BARRMILL RD
Larch
Willowyard Road
Oakwood Dr
Glebe Road
Glebe Ct
Balfour Avenue
DALRY ROAD
Morrishill Drive
Cuff Cres
Grahamfield Place
Lancaster Ave
De Morville Pl
Glebe Rd
Glebelands Way
B706
Willowyard Industrial Estate
Old Willowyard Road
Denholm Way
Mac-Donald Ct
Craigvue
6
Beechfield Rd
Willowburn Rd
Spiers Ave
Manuel Ave
Maxwell Ct
McMillan Cres
Lochview Rd
St Andrews Pl
KILBIRNIE ROAD
Jamieson Way
B7049
B777
A737
B777
To Kilbirnie
Spiersland Way
Manrahead Farm
7
To Dalry
A737
Craighouse
B706
To Burnhouse

Index to Beith

Acacia Drive H5
Academy Brae J5
Aitken Drive K4
Arran Crescent K4
Ash Drive J3
Auldlea Road J4
Backburn J5
Balfour Avenue J6
Barberry Drive H5
Barrington Avenue J4
Barrmill Road J5
Bath Lane J4
Beech Avenue J3
Beechfield Place G6
Bellmans Close J4
Bigholm Road K4
Blackthorn Avenue H4
Boghead J5
Braehead (1) J5
By-Pass Road K4
Caledonia Road J4
Cedar Avenue H5
Cherrywood Drive K3
Chestnut Avenue H5
Cross, The J5
Crummock Gardens K4
Crummock Street K4
Cuff Crescent H6
Cypress Avenue K3
Dalry Road H6
De Morville Place J6
Denholm Way H6
Dickson Court K4
Eglinton Street J5
Elder Avenue H5
Elms Place J4
Glebe Court J5
Glebe Road J5, J6
Glebelands Way J6
Grahamfield Place H6
Guy's Lane J5
Hawthorn Crescent H5
Head Street K5
Headlands Grove K4
Jamieson Way H6
Janefield Place J4
Keir Hardie Court J5
Kilbirnie Road G6
Kings Court J4
Kings Road J4
Kirk Road J5
Kirk View J5
Laburnum Avenue H5
Laigh Court J4
Laigh Road J4
Lancaster Avenue J6
Larch Terrace K5
Lochview Road G6
Lomond Crescent K3
MacDonald Court H6
McMillan Crescent H6
Main Street J4
Mains Avenue H4
Mains Road H4
Manuel Avenue H6
Maple Drive J3
Maxwell Court H6
Meadowbank Terrace J4
Meadowside Court H4
Meadowside H5
Medine Avenue J4
Medine Court J4
Mid Road H4
Mitchell Street J4
Montgomerie Avenue K5
Morrishill Drive H6
Muirburn Road H2
Muirpark Road J4
Myrtle Bank H5
New Street J5
Oakwood Drive H5
Old Willowyard Road H6
Park Avenue J4
Park Court K5
Reform Street J4
Robert Burns Court J4
Roebank Road K4
Rowan Avenue K5
Rowan Place K5
St Andrews Place H6
St Inan's Drive K4
Somerville Court J4
Spiers Avenue H6
Spiersland Way J7
Strand J5
Sycamore Avenue J3
Sycamore Court J4
Thorntree Avenue J3
Threepwood Road K4
Townhead Street J5
Trinity Crescent K4
Viewpark J4
Wardrop Street K5
Wardrop Terrace K5
Wee Close J4
Wee Court J4
William Tricker Crescent K5
Willowburn Road G6
Willowyard Road G5
Wilson Street K4
Woodburn Road K5
Woodside Road J4
Wotherspoon Drive J3

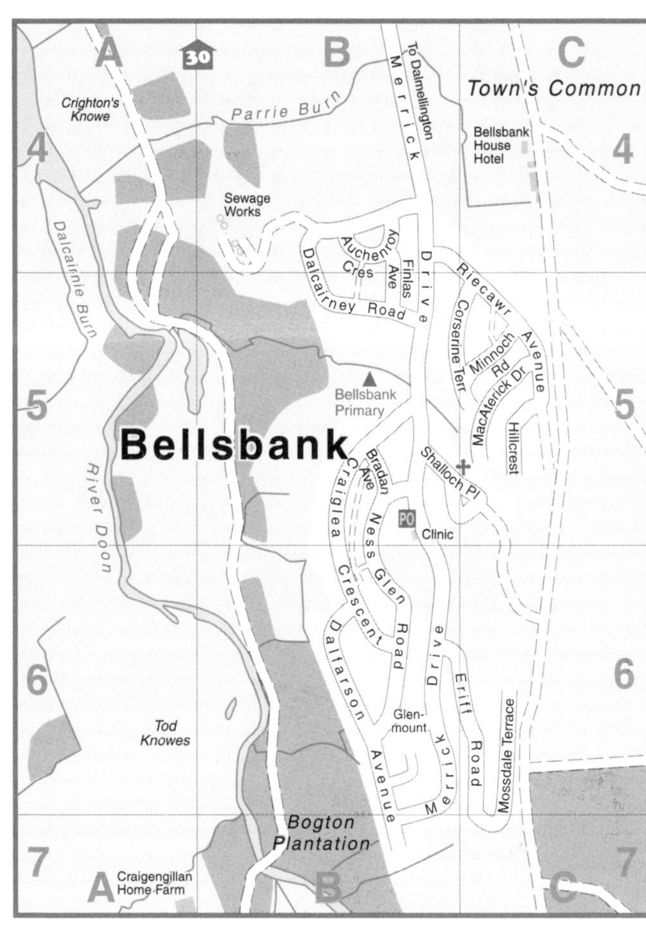

Index to Bellsbank

Auchenroy Crescent B4
Bradan Avenue B5
Corserine Terrace B5
Craiglea Crescent B5
Dalcairney Road B5
Dalfarson Avenue B6
Eriff Road C6
Finlas Avenue B4
Glenmount B6
Hillcrest C5
MacAterick Drive C5
Merrick Drive B4
Minnoch Road C5
Mossdale Terrace C6
Ness Glen Road B6
Riecawr Avenue C5
Shalloch Place B5

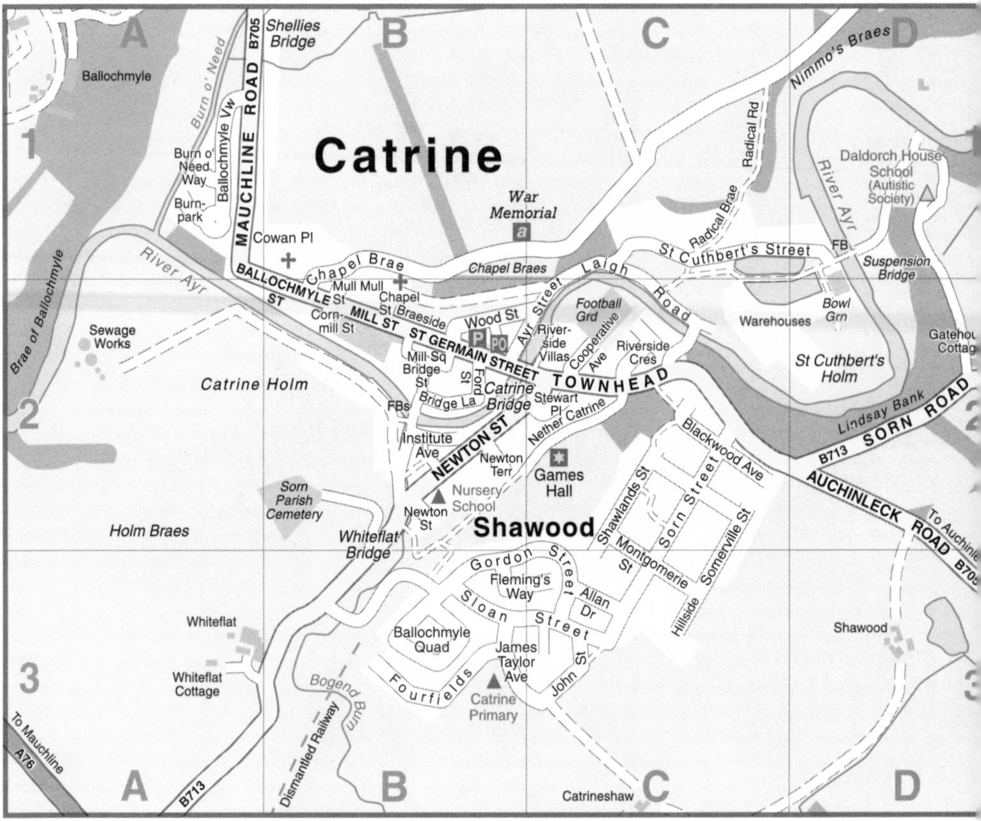

Index to Catrine

Street	Grid
Allan Drive	C3
Auchinleck Road	D2
Ayr Street	B2
Ballochmyle Quadrant	B3
Ballochmyle Street	B2
Ballochmyle View	A1
Blackwood Avenue	C2
Braeside	B2
Bridge Lane	B2
Bridge Street	B2
Burn o' Need Way	A1
Burnpark	A1
Chapel Brae	B1
Chapel Street	B2
Cooperative Avenue	C2
Cornmill Street	B2
Cowan Place	B1
Fleming's Way	B3
Ford Street	B2
Fourfields	B3
Gordon Street	B3
Institute Avenue	B3
James Taylor Avenue	B3
John Street	C3
Laigh Road	C1
Mauchline Road	A1
Mill Square	B2
Mill Street	B2
Montgomerie Street	C3
Mull Mull Street	B2
Nether Catrine	C2
Newton Street	B2
Newton Terrace	B2
Radical Brae	C1
Radical Road	C1
Riverside Crescent	C2
Riverside Villas	C2
St Cuthbert's Street	C1
St Germain Street	B2
Shawlands Street	C2
Sloan Street	B3
Somerville Street	C3
Sorn Road	D2
Sorn Street	C2
Stewart Place	C2
Townhead	C2
Wood Street	B2

Index to Coylton

Street	Grid
Arthurston Terrace	A2
Ashgrove	B2
Ayr Road	A2
Barclaugh Drive	A2
Barngore Drive	B2
Beeches, The	B2
Broadwood	B2
Bryden Place	C3
Burgoyne Drive	B2
Carnell Drive	B2
Carrick View	B1
Chestnut Grove	B2
Coats Place	B3
Dalblair Crescent	B2
Dalrymple View	B3
Douglas Brown Place	B3
Douglas Road	B2
Drumcoyle Drive	B1
Drumsuy Court	B3
Fergus Way	B2
Gadgirth Court	B2
Gallowhill Quadrant	B1
Garvine Road	B2
Glenhead Court	C2
Glenhead Place	C3
Hamilton Place	B3
Highpark Road	B3
Hole Road	B2
John Hodge Court	B2
Kyle Crescent	B1
Laighpark Road	A2
Laighpark View	A2
Lochfergus Crescent	B3
Lochfergus Drive	B3
Lochfergus Place	
Lochfergus Wynd	
Martnaham Drive	
Meadow Park	
Milton Park	
Murray Park	
Park Terrace	
Parklands	
Potterhill Place	
Ramseyston Drive	
St Brides Way	
Shaw Place	
Springs Park	
Sundrum Park	
Thorn Avenue	
Whitehill Way	
Woodhead Road	

Index to Colmonell

Street	Grid
Craigneil Road	
Haddow Place	
Hyslop Crescent	
Kirkhill Crescent	
Main Street	
Manse Road	
Rowantree Street	

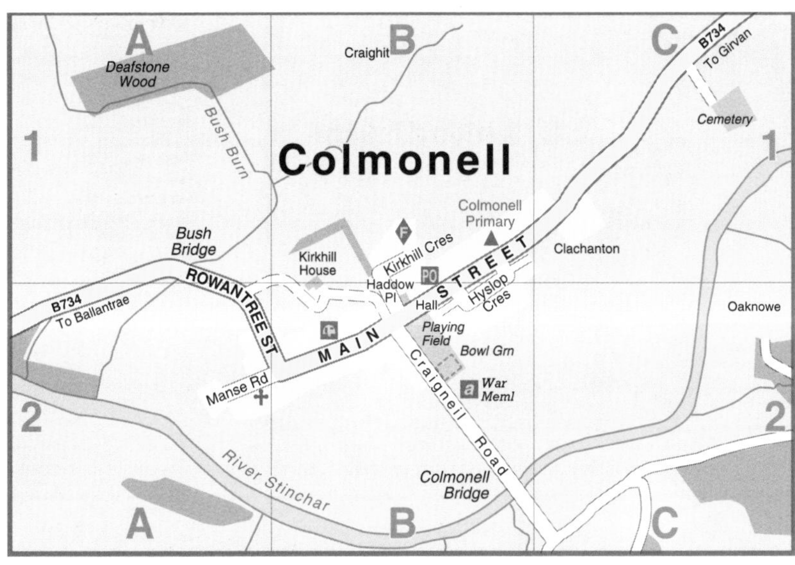
Colmonell
Deafstone Wood
Craighit
Bush Burn
Bush Bridge
B734 To Girvan
Cemetery
Colmonell Primary
Clachanton
Kirkhill House
Kirkhill Cres
Haddow Pl
Hall
ROWANTREE ST
MAIN STREET
Hyslop Cres
B734 To Ballantrae
Oaknowe
Playing Field
Bowl Grn
Manse Rd
War Meml
Craigneil Road
River Stinchar
Colmonell Bridge

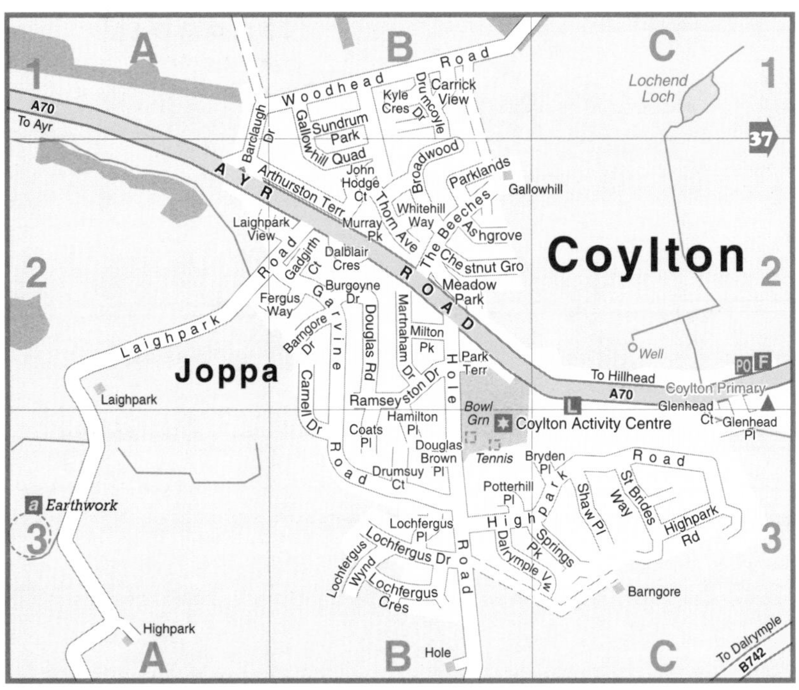
Coylton
Joppa
Woodhead Road
Kyle Cres
Drumcoyle Dr
Carrick View
Lochend Loch
A70 To Ayr
Barclaugh Dr
Gallowhill Quad
Sundrum Park
Broadwood
John Hodge Ct
Arthurston Terr
AYR ROAD
Parklands
Gallowhill
Laighpark View
Murray Pk
Thorn Ave
Whitehill Way
The Beeches
Ashgrove
Gadgirth Ct
Dalblair Cres
The Chestnut Gro
Meadow Park
Burgoyne Dr
Fergus Way
Garvine
Martnaham Dr
Douglas Rd
Milton Pk
Laighpark Road
Barngore Dr
Hole
Park Terr
Well
To Hillhead
A70
Coylton Primary
Laighpark
Carnell Dr
Ramseyston Dr
Bowl Grn
Coylton Activity Centre
Glenhead Ct
Glenhead Pl
Hamilton Pl
Coats Pl
Douglas Brown Pl
Tennis
Bryden Pl
Road
Earthwork
Drumsuy Ct
Potterhill Pl
Shaw Pl
St Brides Way
Highpark Rd
Lochfergus Pl
High park
Springs
Lochfergus Dr
Lochfergus Wynd
Lochfergus Cres
Dalrymple Vw
Pk
Barngore
Highpark
Hole
To Dalrymple B742

CROOKEDHOLM, CROSSHILL, CROSSHOUSE & KNOCKENTIBER

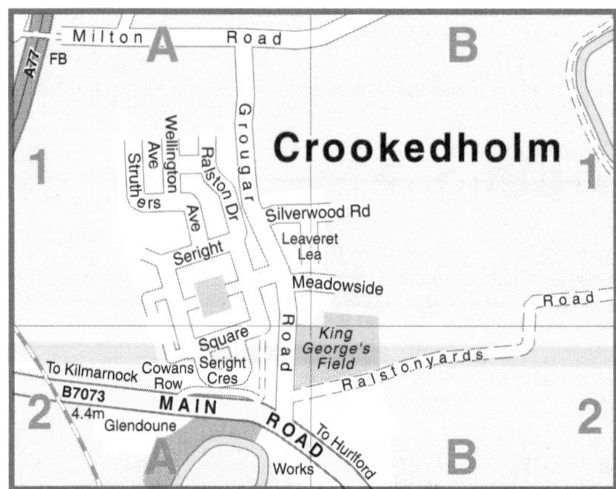

Index to Crookedholm

Street	Grid
Cowans Row	A2
Grougar Road	A1
Leaveret Lea	A1
Main Road	A2
Meadowside	A1
Milton Road	A1
Ralston Drive	A1
Ralstonyards Road	B2
Seright Crescent	A1
Seright Square	A1
Silverwood Road	A1
Struthers Avenue	A1
Wellington Avenue	A1

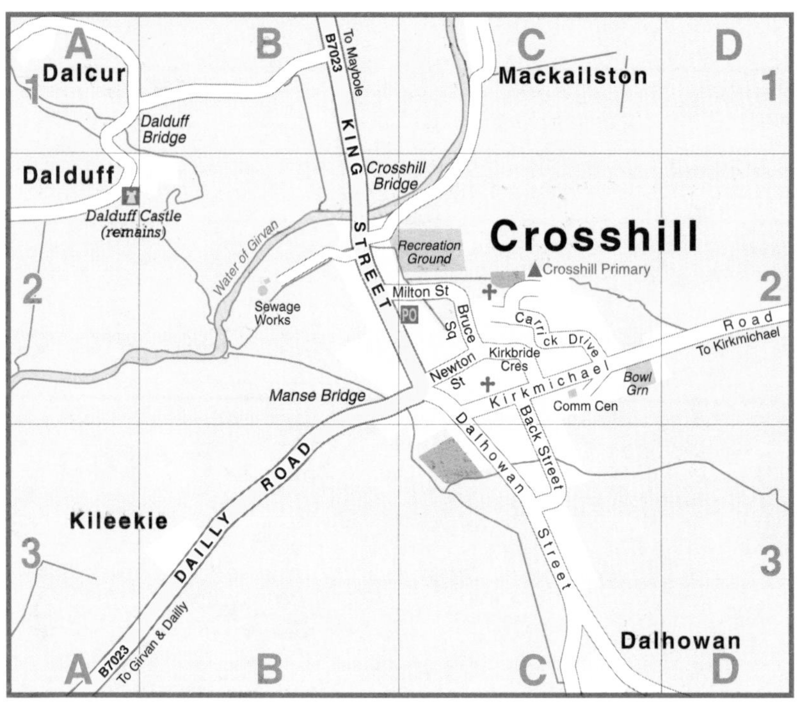

Index to Crosshill

Street	Grid
Back Street	C2
Bruce Square	C2
Carrick Drive	C2
Dailly Road	B3
Dalhowan Street	C2
King Street	B1
Kirkbride Crescent	C2
Kirkmichael Road	C2
Milton Street	C2
Newton Street	C2

Index to Crosshouse & Knockentiber

Annandale Crescent	B3
Annandale Gardens	A3
Annandale Lane	A3
Annandale View	B3
Busbie Gardens	A4
Busbie View	A3
Castle Terrace	B1
Corse Place	B4
Craig Drive	A4
Craigie Place	B4
Craiglea Avenue	A3
Credon Drive	B4
Crossdene Road	A4
Dean Place	B4
Fisher Court	B1
Fardalehill View	B3
Gatehead Road	A3
Greenhill Terrace	B1
Hemphill View	B1
Hunter Road	B3
Irvine Road	A3
Kilmarnock Road	A3
Kilmaurs Road	A2
Laigh Milton Road	A3
Laurieland Avenue	A3
Loudoun Place	B4
Parkhill Avenue	A4
Playingfield Crescent	A3
Playingfield Road	A3
Southhook Road	A1
Springfield Road	B2
Springhill Avenue	A4
Thornton Avenue	A3
Woodbank Road	B3
Woodlea Court	B2
Woodlea Crescent	B2

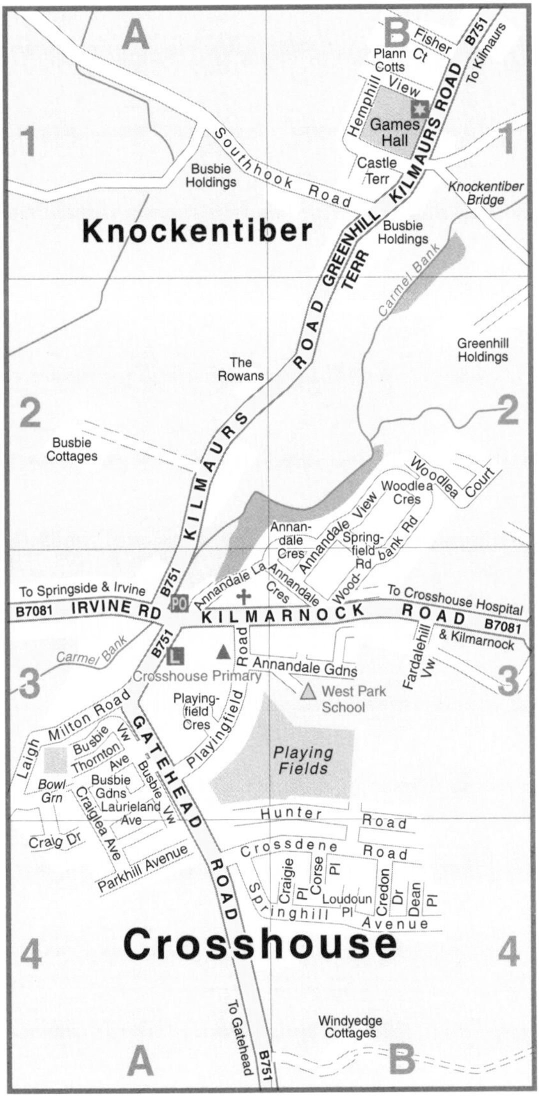

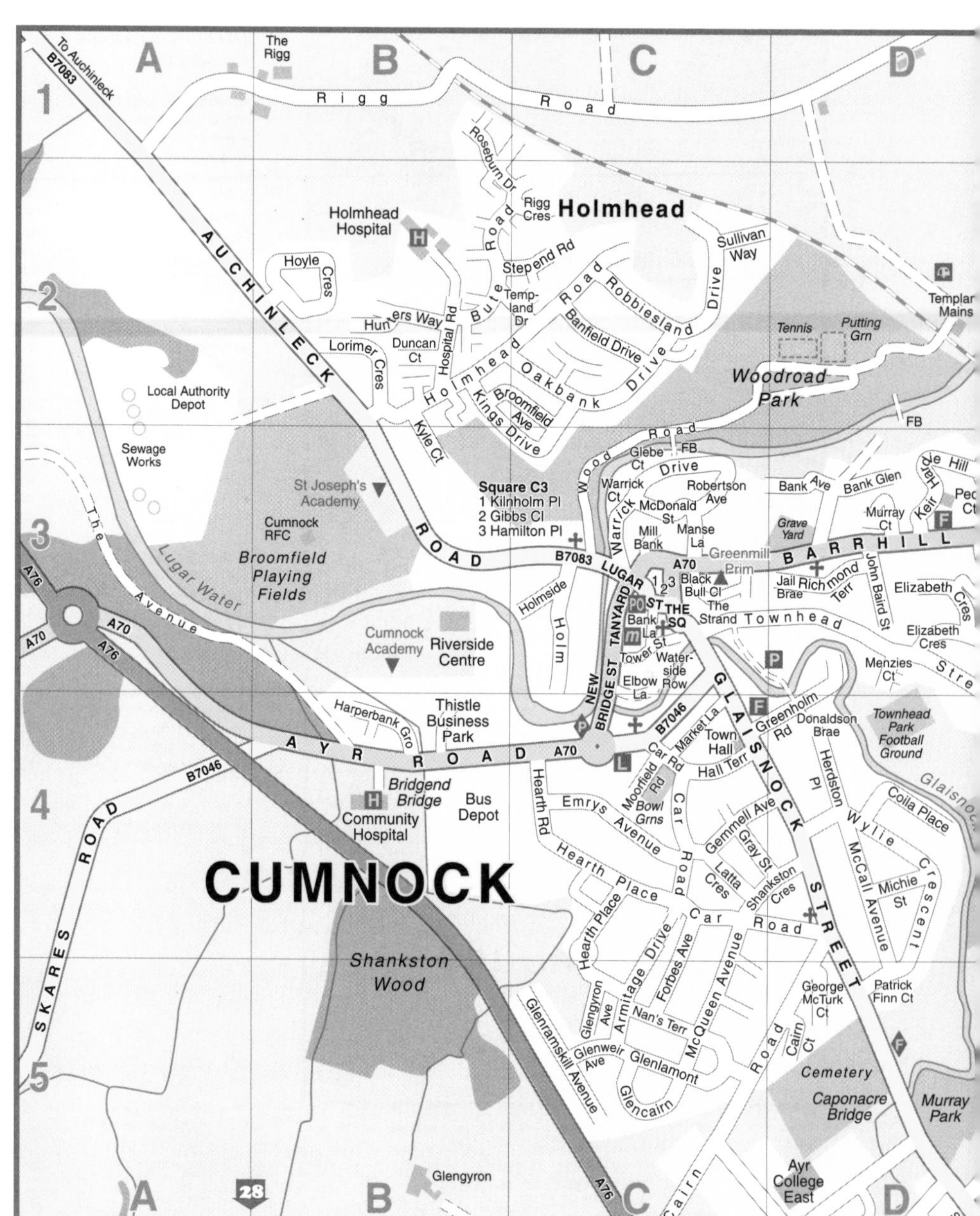

To Auchinleck
B7083
The Rigg
Rigg Road
Holmhead
Holmhead Hospital
Roseburn Dr
Rigg Cres
Road
Stepend Rd
Sullivan Way
Hoyle Cres
Bute
Templand Dr
Robbiesland Drive
Hunters Way
Hospital Rd
Duncan Ct
Lorimer Cres
Banfield Drive
Holmhead
Oakbank Drive
Broomfield Ave
Kings Drive
Kyle Ct
AUCHINLECK ROAD
Tennis
Putting Grn
Templar Mains
Woodroad Park
FB
Local Authority Depot
Sewage Works
St Joseph's Academy
Cumnock RFC
Broomfield Playing Fields
Lugar Water
The Avenue
A76
A70
Square C3
1 Kilnholm Pl
2 Gibbs Cl
3 Hamilton Pl
Wood Road
Glebe Ct
Warrick Ct
Warrick Drive
Robertson Ave
McDonald St
Mill Bank
Manse La
Bank Ave
Bank Glen
Murray Ct
Keir Hill
Grave Yard
Greenmill Prim
B7083 LUGAR ST
BARRHILL
Black Bull Cl
The Strand
Jail Brae
Richmond Terr
John Baird St
Elizabeth Cres
Holmside
Holm
PO
THE SQ
TANYARD
Bank La
Tower St
Waterside Row
Townhead
Elizabeth Cres
Menzies Ct
Street
Cumnock Academy
Riverside Centre
Elbow La
NEW BRIDGE ST
GLAISNOCK STREET
Greenholm Rd
Donaldson Brae
Townhead Park Football Ground
Glaisnock
Harperbank Gro
Thistle Business Park
B7046
Market La
Town Hall
AYR ROAD
A70
Car Rd
Hall Terr
Herdston Pl
Coila Place
B7046
Hearth Rd
Moorfield Rd
Bowl Grns
Bridgend Bridge
Bus Depot
Community Hospital
Emrys Avenue
Car Road
Gemmell Ave
Gray St
Wylie Crescent
McCall Avenue
SKARES ROAD
CUMNOCK
Hearth Place
Latta Cres
Shankston Cres
Michie St
Car Road
Hearth Place
Armitage Drive
Forbes Ave
McQueen Avenue
Shankston Wood
George McTurk Ct
Patrick Finn Ct
Glenramskill Avenue
Glengyron Ave
Nan's Terr
Glenweir Ave
Glenlamont
Road
Cairn Ct
Cemetery
Glencairn
Caponacre Bridge
Murray Park
Glengyron
A76
Cairn
Ayr College East
A
B
C
D
1
2
3
4
5
28

Index to Cumnock

Street	Grid
Armitage Drive	C5
Auchinleck Road	A2
Avenue, The	A3
Avisyard Avenue	F6
Ayr Road	B4
Ballantine Court	E3
Banfield Drive	C2
Bank Avenue	D3
Bank Glen	D3
Bank Lane	C3
Barrhill Road	D3
Barrhill Terrace	E3
Barshare Road	E4
Birchwood Road	E4
Black Bull Close	C3
Blackfaulds Road	E6
Broomfield Avenue	C2
Bute Road	B2
Cairn Court	D5
Cairn Road	C5
Cairnscadden Road	F6
Cameron Crescent	D6
Campbell Court	E4
Car Road	C4
Carsgailloch Avenue	E6
Coila Place	D4
Craigens Place	E6
Craigens Road	E6
Dalgleish Avenue	E3
Davaar Avenue	F5
Donaldson Brae	D4
Drumbrochan Road	D3
Duncan Court	B2
Edgar Avenue	E4
Elbow Lane	C3
Elizabeth Crescent	D3
Emrys Avenue	C4
Forbes Avenue	C5
Gemmell Avenue	C4
George McTurk Court	D5
Gibbs Close (2)	C3
Glaisnock Glen	E7
Glaisnock Road	D5, E7
Glaisnock Street	D4
Glaisnock View	E6
Glebe Court	C3
Glencairn	C5
Glengyron Avenue	C5
Glenlamont	C5
Glenmuir Road	F3
Glenramskill Avenue	C5
Glenweir Avenue	C5
Gray Street	C4
Greenholm Road	D4
Hall Terrace	C4
Hamilton Place (3)	C3
Harperbank Grove	B4
Hearth Place	C4
Hearth Road	C4
Hemmings Way	C4
Herdston Place	D4
Hillview Court	C4
Holland Crescent	E3
Holm	C4
Holmburn Avenue	E5
Holmburn Place	E5
Holmburn Road	E5
Holmhead Road	B2
Holmside	C3
Hospital Road	B2
Hoyle Crescent	B2
Hunter's Way	B2
Jail Brae	D3
James Young Avenue	E6
John Allan Drive	D6
John Baird Street	D3
John Weir Avenue	E4
Jubilee Court	E4
Keir Hardie Hill	D3
Kilbrennan Avenue	F6
Kings Drive	B2
Kings Way	E4
Kilnholm Place (1)	C3
Kyle Court	B3
Lamont Crescent	E6
Latta Crescent	C4
Link Road	D3
Lorimer Crescent	B2
Lugar Street	C3
McCall Avenue	D4
McClymont Court	E4
McDonald Street	C3
McIntyre Crescent	F6
McQueen Avenue	C5
McTurk Road	E6
Manse Lane	C3
Market Lane	C4
Meagher Court	D4
Menzies Avenue	E6
Menzies Court	D3
Michie Street	D4
Mill Bank	C3
Moorfield Road	C4
Muirkirk Road	F3
Murray Court	D3
Nans Terrace	C5
Netherthird Place	E6
Netherthird Road	E6
New Bridge Street	C4
Oakbank Drive	C2
Patrick Finn Court	D5
Phillips Wynd	E7
Peden Court	D3
Richmond Terrace	D3
Rigg Crescent	C2
Rigg Road	B1
River View	E4
Robbiesland Drive	C2
Robertson Avenue	C3
Roseburn Drive	B2
Ryderston Drive	E6
Shankston Crescent	E4
Skares Road	A4

continued overleaf....

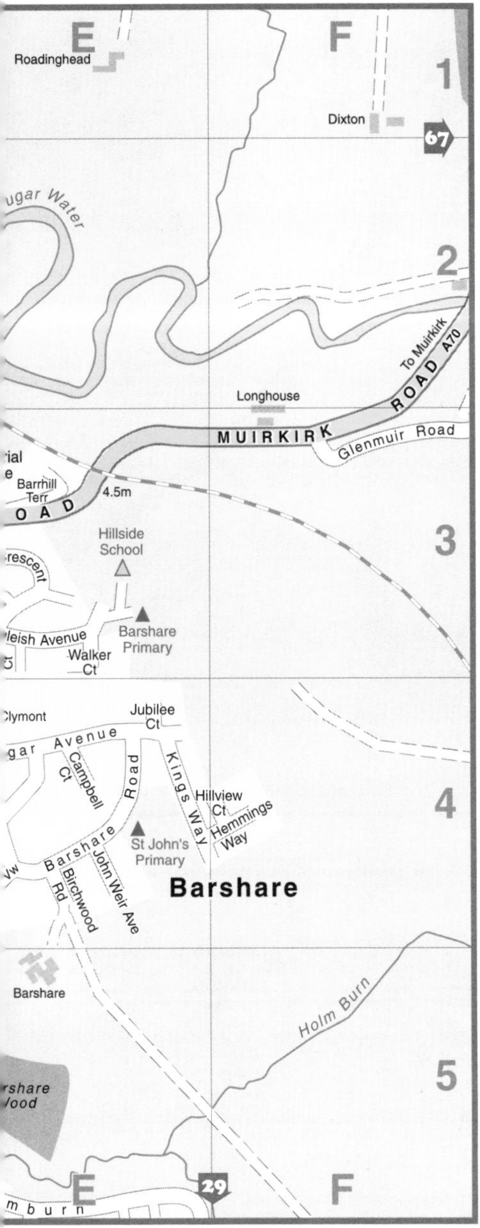

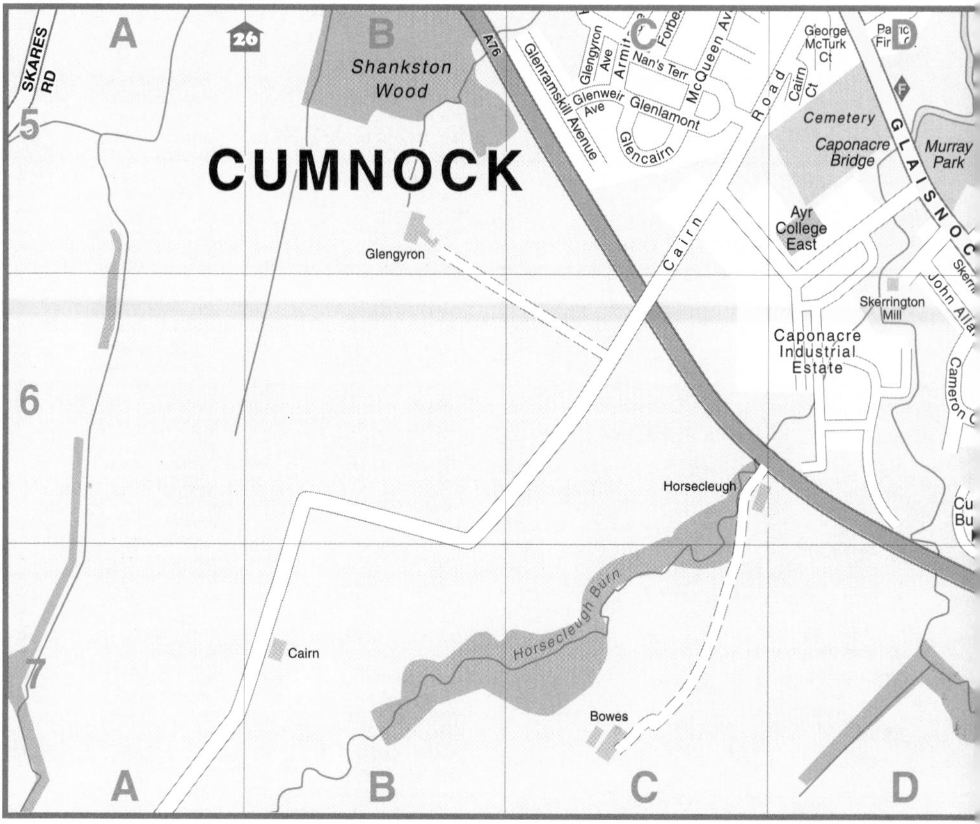

CUMNOCK
A
B
C
D
5
6
7
26
SKARES RD
Shankston Wood
A76
Glenramskill Avenue
Glengyron Ave
Armitage
Forbes
Nan's Terr
McQueen Ave
Glenweir Ave
Glenlamont
Glencairn
Cairn Road
Cairn Ct
George McTurk Ct
Cemetery
Caponacre Bridge
GLAISNOCK
Murray Park
Ayr College East
Glengyron
Skerrington Mill
John Allan
Caponacre Industrial Estate
Cameron
Horsecleugh
Horsecleugh Burn
Cairn
Bowes

Dailly
A
B
C
D
1
2
To Girvan
B741
Mine (dis)
BRIDGE STREET
Brunston Avenue
Brunston Castle Holiday Resort
Water of Girvan
Bowl Grn
Playing Field
LINFERN ROAD
Main St
Green-head St
Road
Dalquharran Castle (remains)
BACK ROAD
To Crosshill
Roan Bridge
Roan
MAIN STREET
Dailly Primary
Victory Cres
Sports Centre
The Loaning
Upper Roan Bridge
Clubhouse
Golf Course Road
Brunston Wynd
Daily Bridge
Smith Cres
Back
West End
Bridge St
Church Cres
Park
Hadyard Terrace
Cemetery
Hazelwood Ave
Brunston Golf Course
Football Ground
Wood St
Woodside
Eldinton Terr
Daily Plantation
Lindsayton Burn
To Girvan
Merkland

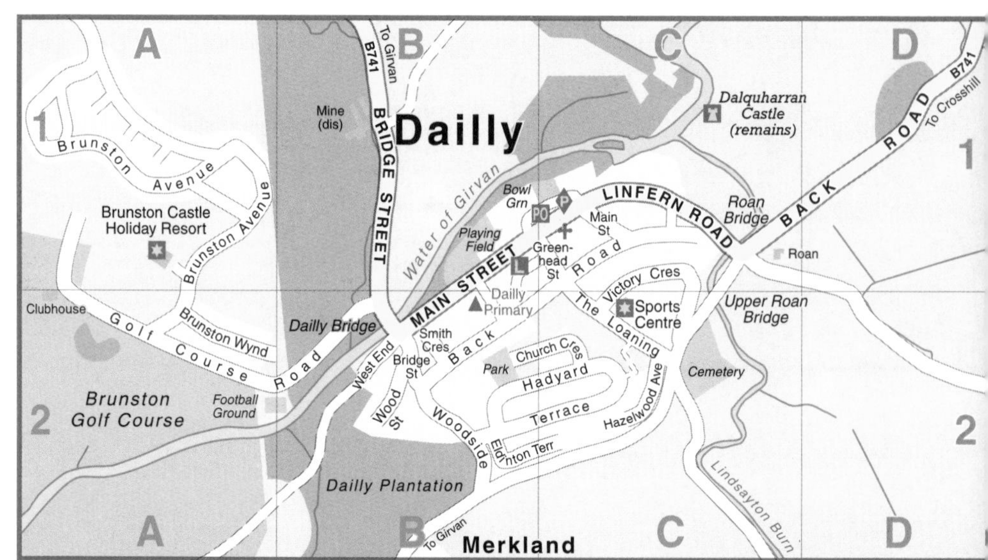

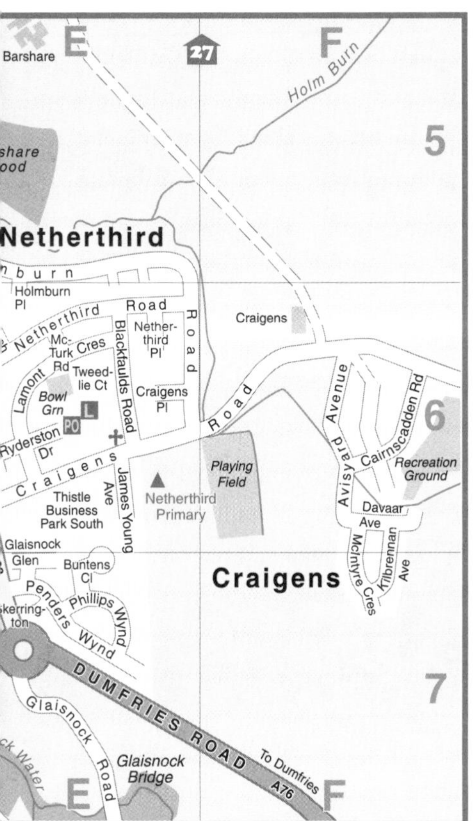

Index to Cumnock

Skerrington	E7
Skerrington Place	D5
Square, The	C3
Stepend Road	C2
Strand, The	C3
Sullivan Way	C2
Tanyard	C3
Templand Drive	C2
Tower Street	C3
Townhead Street	D3
Tweedlie Court	E6
Walker Court	E3
Warrick Court	C3
Warrick Drive	C3
Waterside Row	C3
Wood Road	C3
Wylie Crescent	D4

Index to Dailly

Back Road	B1
Bridge Street	B1
Brunston Avenue	A1
Brunston Wynd	A1
Church Crescent	C1
Eldinton Terrace	B1
Golf Course Road	A1
Greenhead Street	C2
Hadyard Terrace	C1
Hazelwood Avenue	C1
Linfern Road	C2
Loaning, The	C1
Main Street	C2
Main Street	A1
Smith Crescent	C1
Victory Crescent	C2
West End	B1
Wood Street	B1
Woodside	B1

Index to Dalrymple

Barbieston Courtyard	C3
Barbieston Road	B2
Barbieston Terrace	C3
Birch Avenue	C3
Burnside Drive	B2
Burnton Court	B2
Burnton Road	B2
Cedar Terrace	B3
Church Street	A3
Doonvale Avenue	B2
Forglen Road	A2
Fulton Place	B2
Garden Street	A2
Glebe Avenue	A2
Glebe Cottages	A2
Hillview	A2
Holms Farm Road	A3
Kirkton Avenue	B2
Main Street	A3
Maxwell Place	C2
Merkland Drive	C3
Morton Drive	C2
Portland Road	B3
Primpton Avenue	B2
Purclewan Crescent	B2
Riverside Terrace	A3
Robertson Place	C2
Seath Drive	B2
Skeldon Crescent	B3
Skeldon Drive	B3
Viaduct View	C3
Weir Terrace	B2

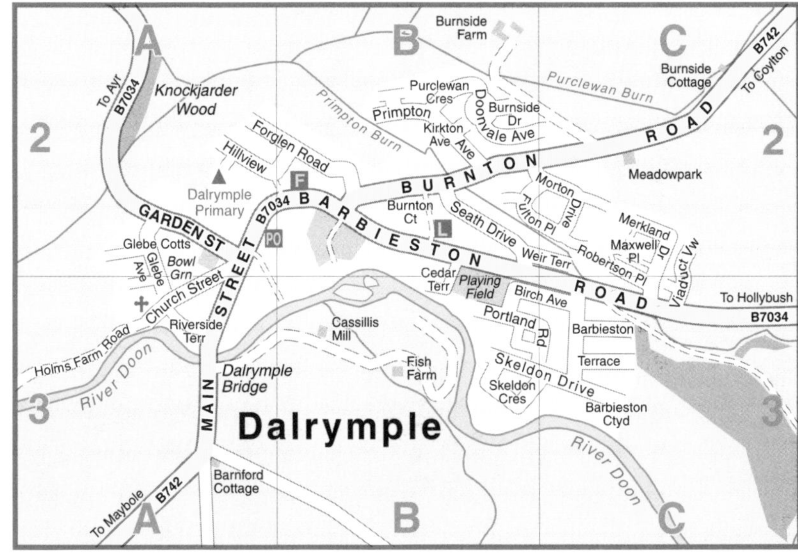

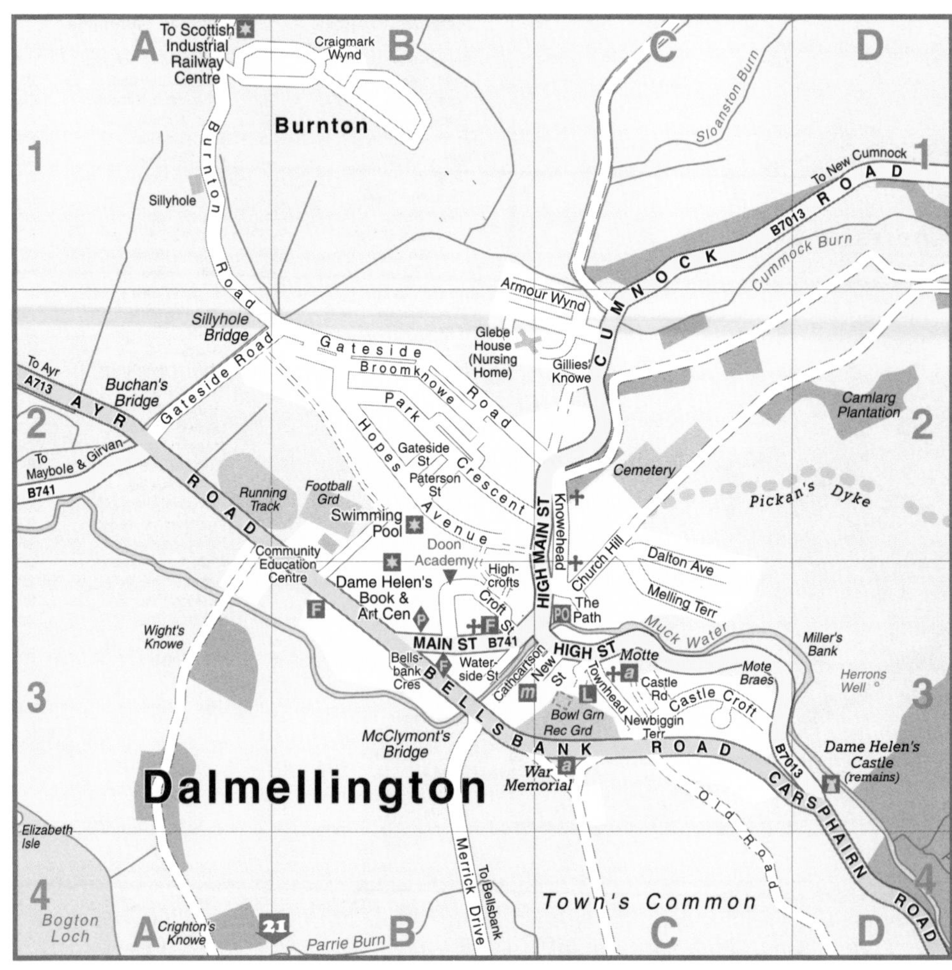

Index to Dalmellington

Armour Wynd	B2	Gillies' Knowe	C2
Ayr Road	A2	High Main Street	C3
Bellsbank Crescent	B3	High Street	C3
Bellsbank Road	B3	Highcrofts	B3
Broomknowe	B2	Hopes Avenue	B2
Burnton Road	A1	Knowehead	C2
Carsphairn Road	D4	Main Street	B3
Castle Croft	C3	Melling Terrace	C3
Castle Road	C3	Merrick Drive	B4
Cathcartson	B3	New Street	C3
Church Hill	C3	Newbiggin Terrace	C3
Craigmark Wynd	B1	Old Road	C3
Croft Street	B3	Park Crescent	B2
Cumnock Road	C1	Paterson Street	C2
Dalton Avenue	C2	Path, The	C3
Gateside Road	B2	Townhead	C3
Gateside Street	B2	Waterside Street	B3

Index to Drongan

Street	Grid
Ailsa Craig View	A3
Arran Court	A3
Barbeith Drive	C3
Barbieston Avenue	C3
Bonnyton Avenue	C3
Byres Road	A3
Cairnston Avenue	B3
Carston Drive	C3
Coronation Road	B3, C3
Corrie Place	A3
Coyle Avenue	B4
Craufurd Drive	B2
Drumwhill Road	B3
Farrell Crescent	B2
Garrowhill Drive	B3
Glencraig Street	B3
Hannahston Avenue	B3
Hodge Crescent	A3
Lane Crescent	B3
Ladies Walk	A3
Littlemill Road	C3
Lochmark Avenue	B3
Lomond Crescent	B1
Lomond View	B1
Mainsford Avenue	C3
Margaret Drain Crescent	B2
Millmannoch Avenue	C3
Mill of Shield Road	B3
Mull Gate	B2
Pettoch Road	A3
Reid Place	C2
Robert Burns Avenue	B2
Rowantree Court	B2
Schaw Avenue	B3
Sinclairston Drive	C3
Stair Drive	C4
Taiglum Place	B2
Torrance Drive	B2
Trabboch Avenue	B3
Truesdale Crescent	A3
Trysting Thorn Wynd	B2
Watson Terrace	B2
Whitegables Court	B2

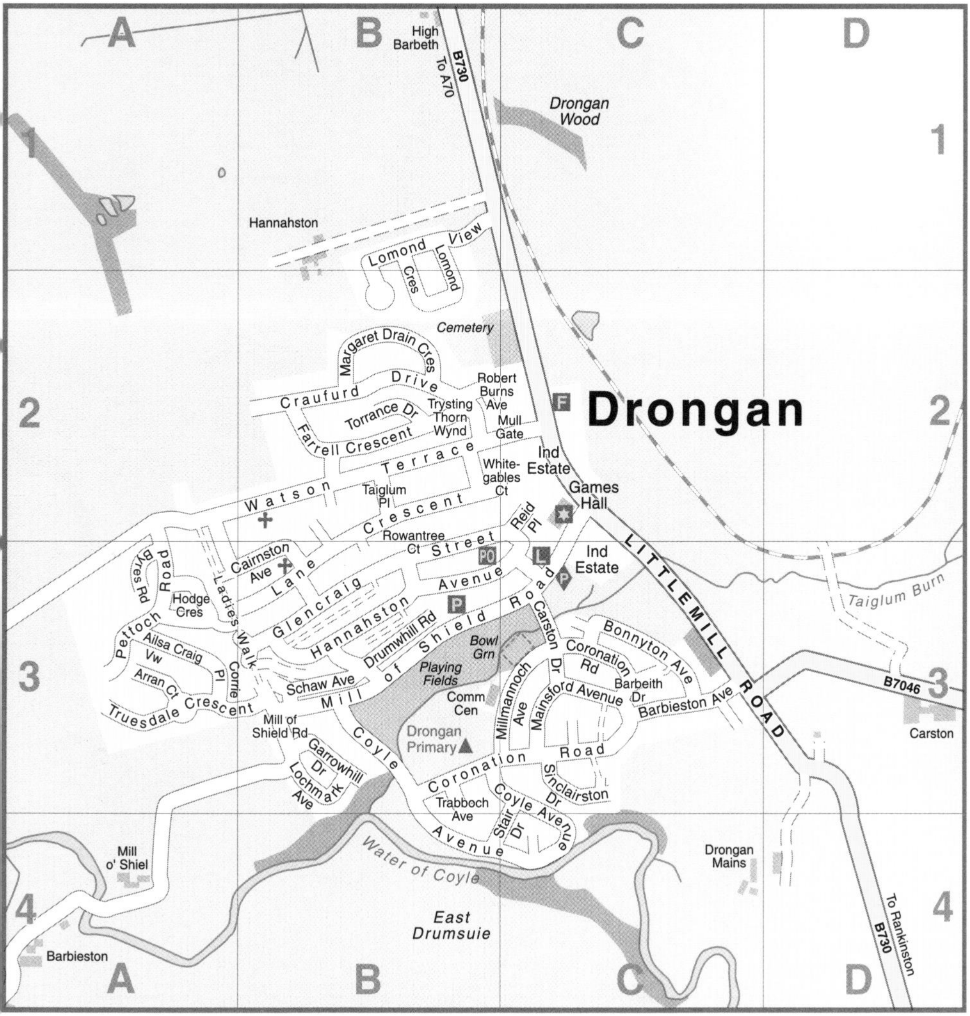

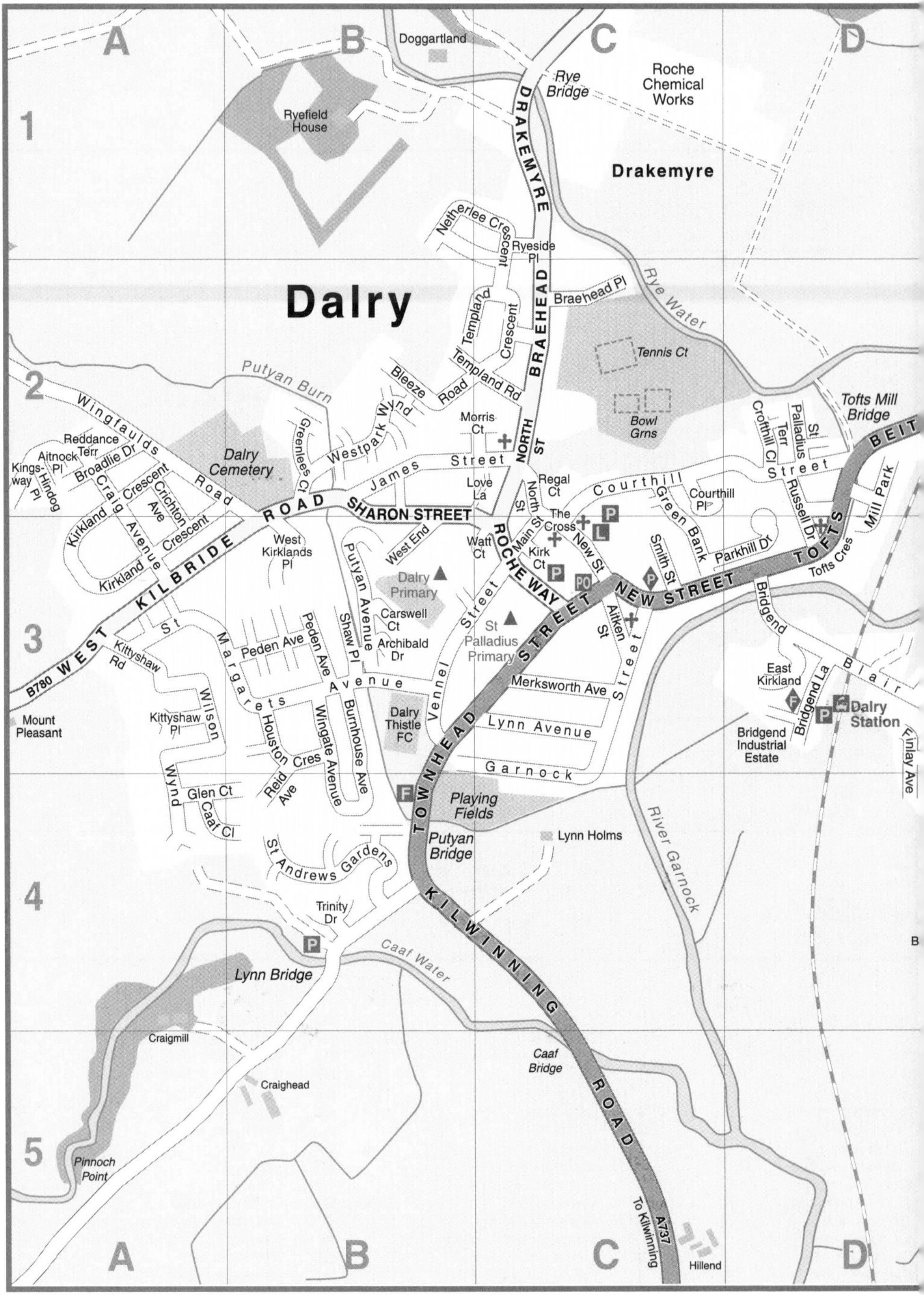

A B C D
1 2 3 4 5

Dalry
Doggartland
Rye Bridge
Roche Chemical Works
Ryefield House
Drakemyre
DRAKEMYRE
Netherlee Crescent
Ryeside Pl
BRAEHEAD
Braehead Pl
Rye Water
Templand Crescent
Templand Road
Templand Rd
Tennis Ct
Bowl Grns
Tofts Mill Bridge
Putyan Burn
Bleeze Road
Westpark Wynd
Morris Ct
NORTH ST
Wingfaulds Road
Reddance Terr
Aitnock Pl
Kings-way
Hindog Pl
Broadlie Dr
Craig Avenue
Crescent
Crichton Ave
Crescent
Kirkland
Kirkland
Dalry Cemetery
Greenlees Ct
James Street
Love La
Regal Ct
North St
Courthill Street
Crofthill Cl
Palladius Terr
St
Russell Dr
BEITH
Mill Park
ROAD
SHARON STREET
West End
The Cross
Main St
Watt Ct
ROCHE WAY
Kirk Ct
New St
Green Bank
Courthill Pl
Parkhill Dr
Smith St
NEW STREET
TOFTS
Tofts Cres
West Kirklands Pl
Putyan Avenue
Dalry Primary
Carswell Ct
Archibald Dr
Shaw Pl
Peden Ave
Peden Ave
Vennel Street
St Palladius Primary
Aitken St
Street
Bridgend
Blair
B780 WEST KILBRIDE
St
Kittyshaw Rd
Margarets Avenue
Merksworth Ave
Lynn Avenue
East Kirkland
Bridgend La
Dalry Station
Finlay Ave
Mount Pleasant
Kittyshaw Pl
Wilson
Houston Cres
Wingate Avenue
Burnhouse Ave
Dalry Thistle FC
TOWNHEAD
Garnock
Bridgend Industrial Estate
Wynd
Glen Ct
Caaf Cl
Reid Ave
Playing Fields
Putyan Bridge
Lynn Holms
River Garnock
St Andrews Gardens
Trinity Dr
KILWINNING
Caaf Water
Lynn Bridge
Craigmill
Caaf Bridge
Craighead
ROAD
Pinnoch Point
A737
To Kilwinning
Hillend
B

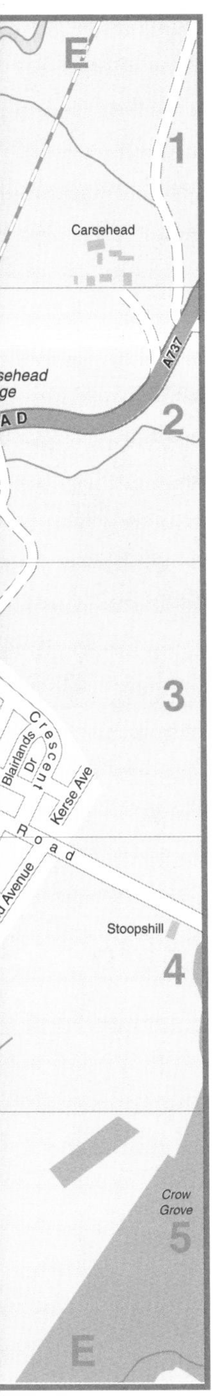

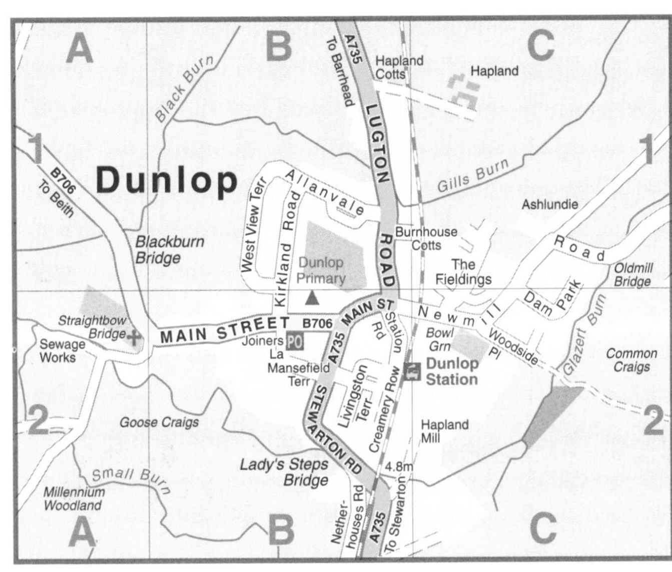

Index to Dalry

Aitken Street	C3
Aitnock Place	A2
Archibald Drive	B3
Beith Road	D2
Blair Road	D3
Blairlands Drive	E3
Bleeze Road	B2
Braehead Place	C2
Braehead	C2
Braidland Avenue	E4
Bridgend Lane	D3
Bridgend	D3
Broadlie Drive	A2
Burnhouse Avenue	B3
Caaf Close	A4
Carswell Court	B3
Cleeves Avenue	D4
Courthill Place	C2
Courthill Street	C2
Craig Avenue	A2
Crichton Avenue	A2
Crofthill Close	D2
Cross, The	C2
Douglas Avenue	D3
Drakemyre	C1
East Kirkland	D3
Finlay Avenue	D3
Garnock Street	C3
Glen Court	A4
Green Bank	C2
Greenlees Court	B2
Hindog Place	A2
Houston Crescent	B3
James Street	B2
Kerse Avenue	E3
Kilwinning Road	B4
Kingsway	A2
Kirk Court	C3
Kirkland Crescent	A3
Kittyshaw Place	A3
Kittyshaw Road	A3
Love Lane	C2
Lynn Avenue	C3
Main Street	C3
Mair Avenue	E3
Merksworth Avenue	C3
Mill Park	D3
Morris Court	B2
Netherlee Crescent	B1
New Street	C3
North Street	C2
Parkhill Drive	C3
Peden Avenue	B3
Putyan Avenue	B3
Reddance Terrace	A2
Regal Court	C2
Reid Avenue	B4
Roche Way	C3
Russell Drive	D2
Ryeside Place	C1
St Andrews Gardens	B4
St Margarets Avenue	A3
St Palladius Terrace	D2
Sharon Street	B2
Shaw Place	B3
Smith Street	C3
Stoopshill Crescent	D3
Templand Crescent	B2
Templand Road	B2
Tofts Crescent	B3
Tofts	B3
Townhead Street	B4
Trinity Drive	B4
Vennel Street	B3
Watt Court	C3
West End	B3
West Kilbride Road	A3
West Kirklands Place	B3
Westpark Wynd	B2
Wilson Wynd	A3
Wingate Avenue	B3
Wingfaulds Avenue	A2

Index to Dunlop

Allanvale	B1
Burnhouse Cottages	B1
Creamery Row	B2
Dam Park	C2
Fieldings, The	C2
Joiners Lane	B2
Kirkland Road	B1
Livingston Terrace	B2
Lugton Road	B1
Main Street	B2
Mansefield Terrace	B2
Netherhouses Road	B2
New Mill Road	C2
Station Road	B2
Stewarton Road	B2
Westview Terrace	B1
Woodside Place	C2

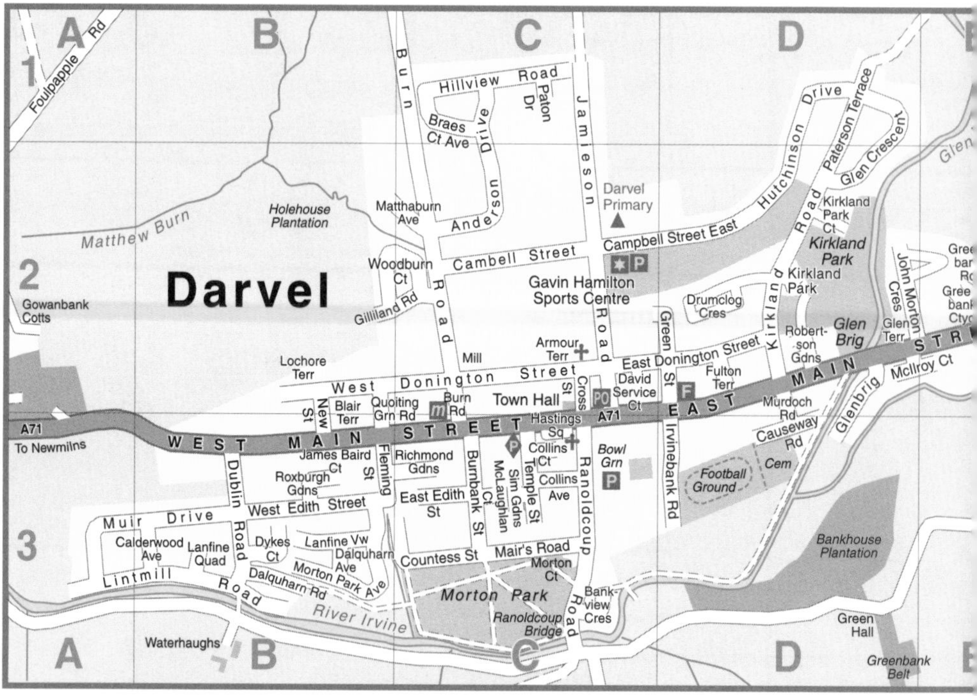

Darvel
Foulpapple Rd
Burn Road
Hillview Road
Paton Dr
Braes Ct Ave
Anderson Drive
Jamieson Road
Darvel Primary
Holehouse Plantation
Matthew Burn
Matthaburn Ave
Campbell Street East
Hutchinson Drive
Paterson Terrace
Glen Crescent
Kirkland Park Ct
Kirkland Park
Woodburn Ct
Cambell Street
Gavin Hamilton Sports Centre
Gowanbank Cotts
Gilliland Rd
Drumclog Cres
Green St
Kirkland Rd
Kirkland Park
Robertson Gdns
Glen Brig
John Morton Cres
Glen Terr
Lochore Terr
Mill
Armour Terr
East Donington Street
Fulton Terr
West Donington Street
David Service Ct
Blair Terr
New St
Quoiting Grn Rd
Burn Rd
Town Hall
Cross St
A71
East Main Street
McIlroy Ct
Murdoch Rd
Glenbrig
To Newmilns
West Main Street
Hastings Sq
Causeway Rd
James Baird Ct
Fleming St
Richmond Gdns
Collins Ct
Bowl Grn
Cem
Roxburgh Gdns
Burnbank St
Sim Gdns
Temple St
McLaughlan Ct
Collins Ave
Irvinebank Rd
Football Ground
Dublin Road
West Edith Street
East Edith St
Ranoldcoup Road
Muir Drive
Calderwood Ave
Lanfine Quad
Dykes Ct
Lanfine Vw
Dalquharn Ave
Countess St
Mair's Road
Morton Ct
Bankhouse Plantation
Lintmill Road
Morton Park Ave
Dalquharn Rd
Morton Park
Bankview Cres
River Irvine
Ranoldcoup Bridge
Green Hall
Waterhaughs
Greenbank Belt 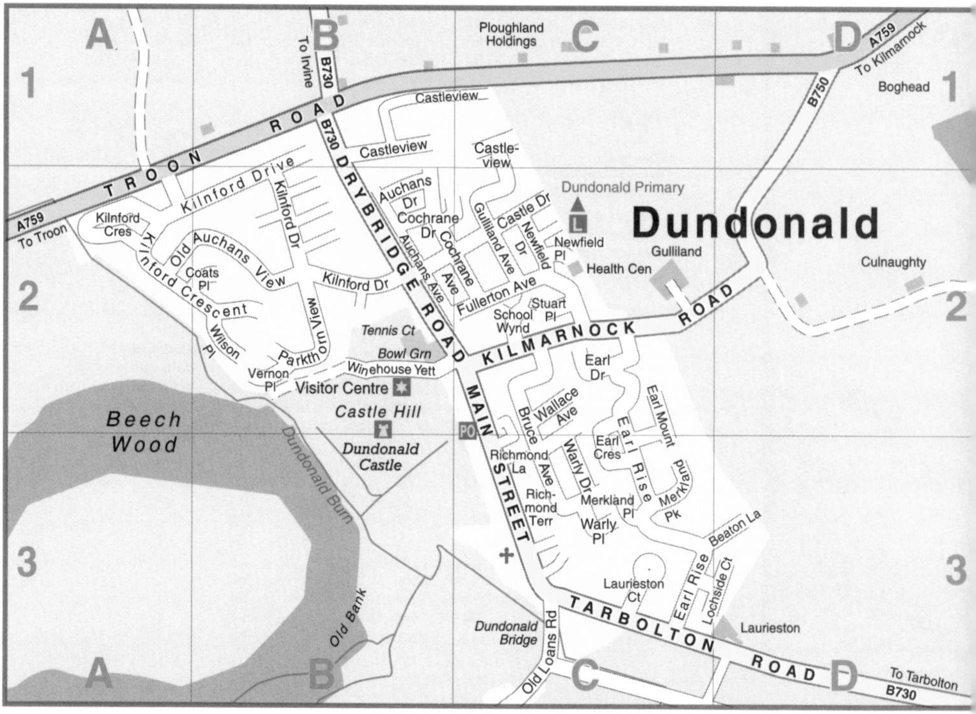
Glen

Dundonald
Ploughland Holdings
To Irvine
B730
A759
To Kilmarnock
B750
Boghead
Troon Road
Castleview
Castleview
Castle-view
Dundonald Primary
A759 To Troon
Kilnford Drive
Kilnford Dr
Auchans Dr
Cochrane Dr
Drybridge Road
Castle Dr
Newfield Dr
Newfield Pl
Gulliland
Kilnford Cres
Old Auchans View
Gulliland Ave
Health Cen
Culnaughty
Kilnford Crescent
Coats Pl
Kilnford Dr
Auchans Ave
Cochrane Ave
Fullerton Ave
Stuart Pl
School Wynd
Kilmarnock Road
Wilson Pl
Orn View
Tennis Ct
Bowl Grn
Parkthorn View
Vernon Pl
Winehouse Yett
Visitor Centre
Earl Dr
Earl Mount
Beech Wood
Castle Hill
Dundonald Castle
Wallace Ave
Main Street
Bruce Ave
Earl Cres
Earl Rise
Merkland Pk
Dundonald Burn
Richmond La
Warly Dr
Richmond Terr
Merkland Pl
Warly Pl
Beaton La
Laurieston Ct
Earl Rise
Lochside Ct
Old Bank
Dundonald Bridge
Old Loans Rd
Tarbolton Road
Laurieston
To Tarbolton
B730

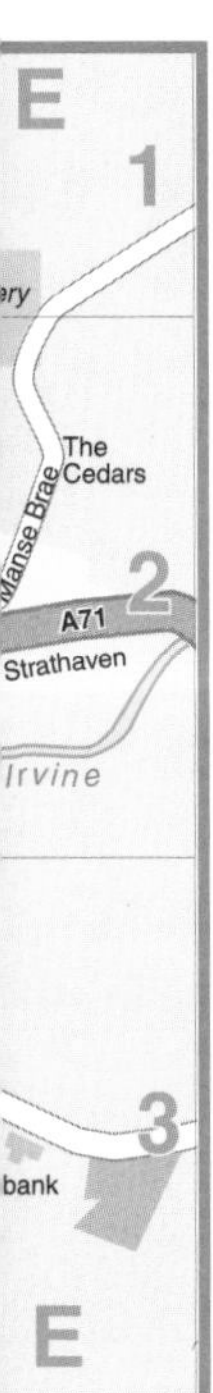

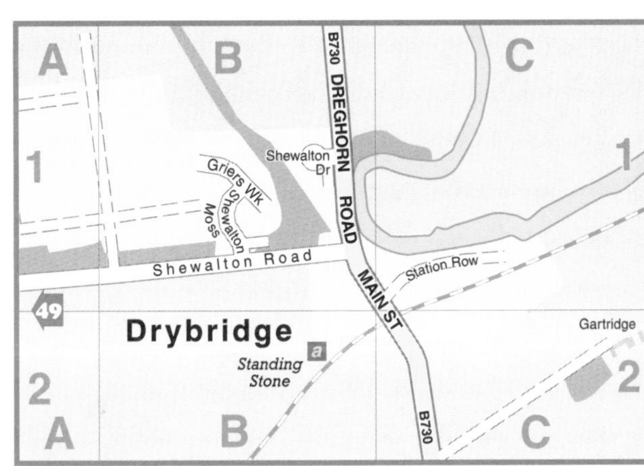

Index to Darvel

Anderson Drive C2
Armour Terrace C2
Bankview Crescent C3
Blair Terrace B2
Braes Court Avenue C1
Burn Road C1
Burn Road C2
Burnbank Street C3
Calderwood Avenue B3
Campbell Street East C2
Campbell Street C2
Causeway Road D3
Collins Avenue C3
Collins Court C3
Countess Street C3
Cross Street C2
Dalquharn Avenue B3
Dalquharn Road B3
David Service Court C2
Drumclog Crescent D2
Dublin Road B3
Dykes Court B3
East Donington Street D2
East Edith Street C3
East Main Street D2
Fleming Street B3
Foulpapple Road A2
Fulton Terrace D2
George Young Drive E2
Gilliland Road B2
Glen Crescent D2
Glen Terrace D2
Glenbrig D2
Gowanbank Cottages A2
Green Street D2
Greenbank Courtyard E2
Greenbank Road E2
Hastings Square C3
Hillview Road C1
Hutchison Drive D2
Irvinebank Road D3
James Baird Court B3
Jamieson Road C1
John Murton Crescent D2
Kirkland Park D2
Kirkland Park Court D2
Kirkland Road D2
Lanfine View B3
Lanfine Quadrant B3
Lintmill Road A3
Lochore Terrace B2
McIlroy Court D2
Mclauchlan Court C3
Mairs Road C3
Matthaburn Avenue B2
Morton Court C3
Morton Park Avenue B3
Muir Drive A3
Murdoch Road D2
New Street B2
Paterson Terrace D2
Paton Drive C1
Quoiting Green Road B2
Ranoldcoup Road C3
Richmond Gardens C3
Robertson Gardens D2
Roxburgh Gardens B3
Sim Gardens C3
Temple Street C3
Townhead E2
West Donington Street C2
West Edith Street B3
West Main Street B3
Woodburn Court B2

Index to Darvel

Dreghorn Road B1
Griers Walk B1
Main Street B1
Shewalton Drive B1
Shewalton Moss B1
Shewalton Road B1
Station Row C1

Index to Dundonald

Auchans Avenue B2
Auchans Drive B2
Beaton Lane D3
Bruce Avenue C2
Castle Drive C2
Castleview B1, C1
Coats Place B2
Cochrane Avenue B2
Cochrane Drive B2
Drybridge Road B2
Earl Crescent C3
Earl Drive C2
Earl Mount C2
Earl Rise C2, C3
Fullerton Avenue C2
Gulliland Avenue C2
Kilmarnock Road C2
Kilnford Crescent A2
Kilnford Drive B2
Laurieston Court C3
Lochside Court C3
Main Street C2
Merkland Park C3
Merkland Place C3
Newfield Drive C2
Newfield Place C2
Old Auchans View B2
Old Loans Road C3
Parkthorn View B2
Richmond Lane C3
Richmond Terrace C3
School Wynd C2
Stuart Place C2
Tarbolton Road C3
Troon Road A2
Vernon Place B2
Wallace Avenue C2
Warly Drive C3
Warly Place C3
Wilson Place B2
Winehouse Yett B2

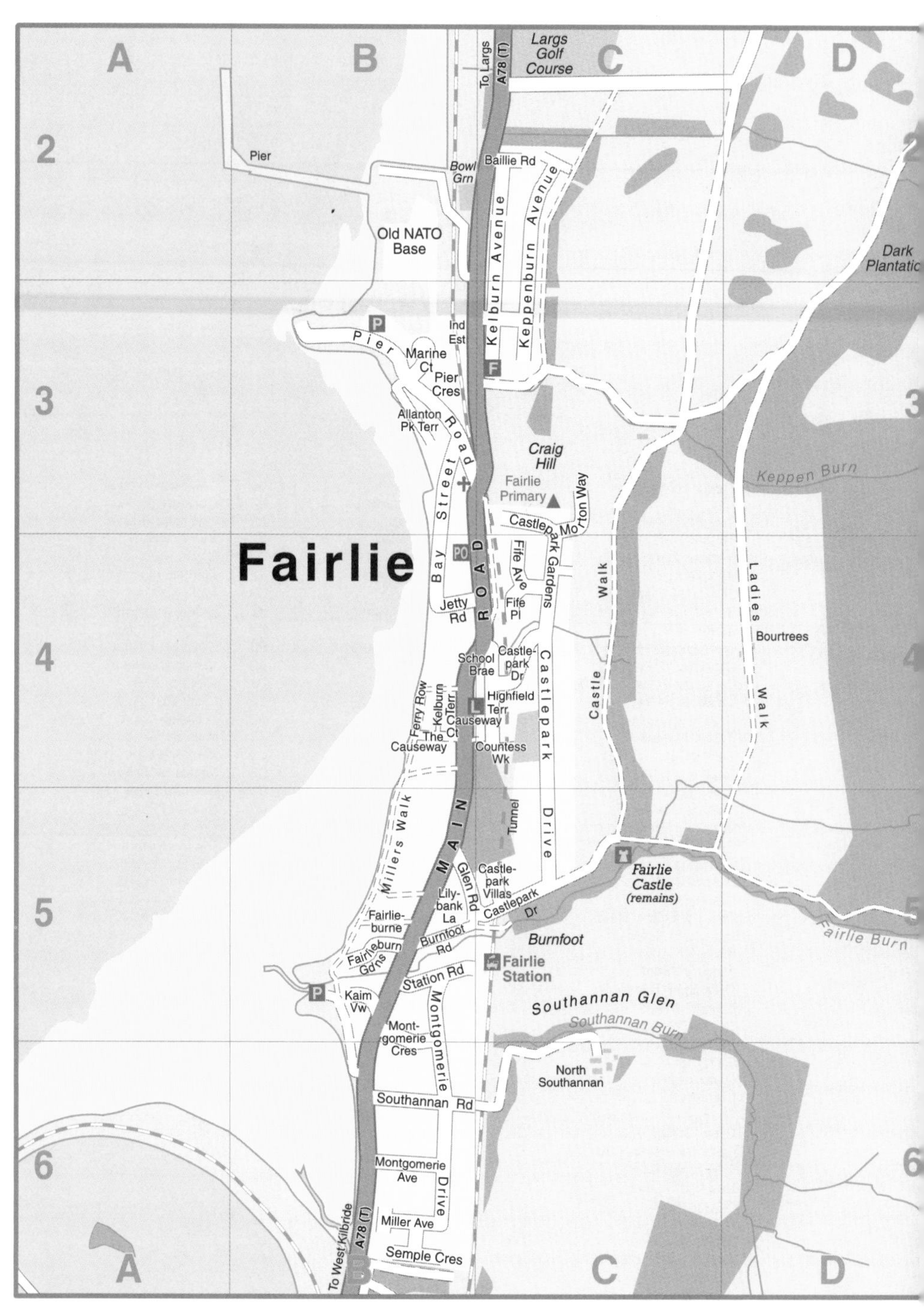
A
B
C
D
2
3
4
5
6
Largs
Golf
Course
To Largs
A78 (T)
Pier
Bowl
Grn
Baillie Rd
Kelburn Avenue
Keppenburn Avenue
Old NATO
Base
Dark
Plantatic
Ind
Est
Pier
Marine
Ct
Pier
Cres
Allanton
Pk Terr
Road
Craig
Hill
Keppen Burn
Fairlie
Primary
Morton Way
Castlepark Gardens
Bay Street
Fairlie
ROAD
Fife Ave
Walk
Ladies Walk
Jetty
Rd
Fife
Pl
Bourtrees
School
Brae
Castle-
park
Dr
Castlepark Drive
Castle
Ferry Row
Kelburn
Terr
Ct
Highfield
Terr
Causeway
The
Causeway
Countess
Wk
Tunnel
Millers Walk
MAIN
Glen Rd
Castle-
park
Villas
Fairlie
Castle
(remains)
Lily-
bank
La
Castlepark
Dr
Fairlie-
burne
Burnfoot
Rd
Burnfoot
Fairlie Burn
Fairlieburn
Gdns
Fairlie
Station
Station Rd
Kaim
Vw
Southannan Glen
Southannan Burn
Mont-
gomerie
Cres
Montgomerie
Drive
North
Southannan
Southannan Rd
Montgomerie
Ave
Drive
Miller Ave
Semple Cres
To West Kilbride
A78 (T)

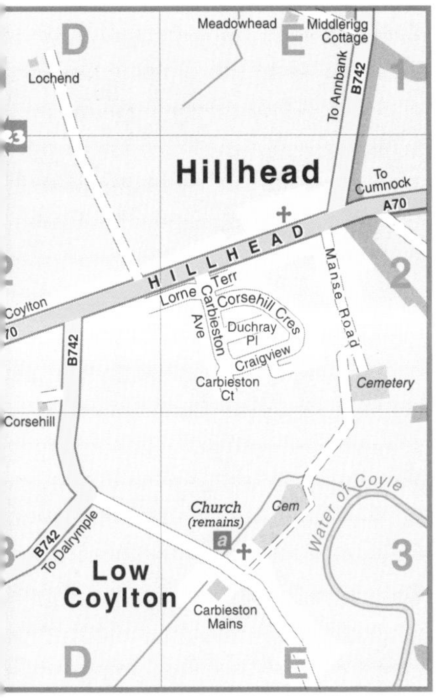

Gardrum
Glaister
To Stewarton
B778
STEWARTON
To Glasgow
A77
M77
Rysland Drive
B751
Blackfaulds Dr
Black-faulds Gdns
Skernieland
Road
Fenwick Cemetery
The Rowans
Rowallan Piggery
Glaister Bridge
ROAD
B778
Fenwick Hill
Gardrum Mill Burn
Fenwick Primary
Hall
PO
Kirkton
Creelshaugh Rd
Fairlie Park
Glebe Terrace
Fenwick
Kirkton Pl
Road
Kirkton Bridge
Poles Road
Dunselma Cotts
Dunlop St
Murchland Ave
Brae-head Rd
Raith
Glencraig Terr
Auchans Pl
Holm Cres
Road
Maunsheugh Road
MAIN ROAD
Langside
Little Fenwick
Bowl Grn
Holm Cres
Laigh Fenwick
Fenwick Water
Waterslap
Fenwick Bridge
KILMAURS RD
B751
To Kilmarnock
M77
A77
B751
A
B
C
1
2
3
4

ex to Fairlie

nton Park Terrace B3
lie Road C2
Street B4
nfoot Road B5
tle Walk B4
tlepark Drive C4
tlepark Gardens C4
tlepark Villas C5
seway Court B4
seway, The B4
ntess Walk C4
lieburne Gardens B5
lieburne B5
y Row B4
Avenue C4
Place C4
n Road B5
nfield Terrace C4
y Road B4
m View B5
ourn Avenue C3
ourn Terrace B4
penburn Avenue C3
ies Walk C4
bank Lane B5
n Road B5
ine Court B3
er Avenue B6
ers Walk B5
ntgomerie Avenue B6
ntgomerie Crescent B5
ntgomerie Drive B5
Crescent B3
Pier Road B3
School Brae C4
Semple Crescent B6
Southannan Road B6
Station Road B5

Index to Fenwick

Auchans Place C3
Blackfaulds Drive B2
Blackfaulds Gardens B2
Braehead Road B3
Creelshaugh Road C2
Dunlop Street B3
Dunselma Cottages B3
Glebe Terrace B2
Glencraig Terrace C3
Holm Crescent C4
Kilmaurs Road A4
Kirkton Place B3
Kirkton Road C2
Main Road B3
Maunsheugh Road B3
Murchland Avenue B3
Poles Road B3
Raith Road C3
Rysland Drive B1
Skernieland Road B2
Stewarton Road B2
Waterslap B4

Index to Hillhead

Carbieston Avenue E2
Carbieston Court E2
Corsehill Crescent E2
Craigview E2
Duchray Place E2
Hillhead D2
Lorne Terrace E2
Manse Road E2

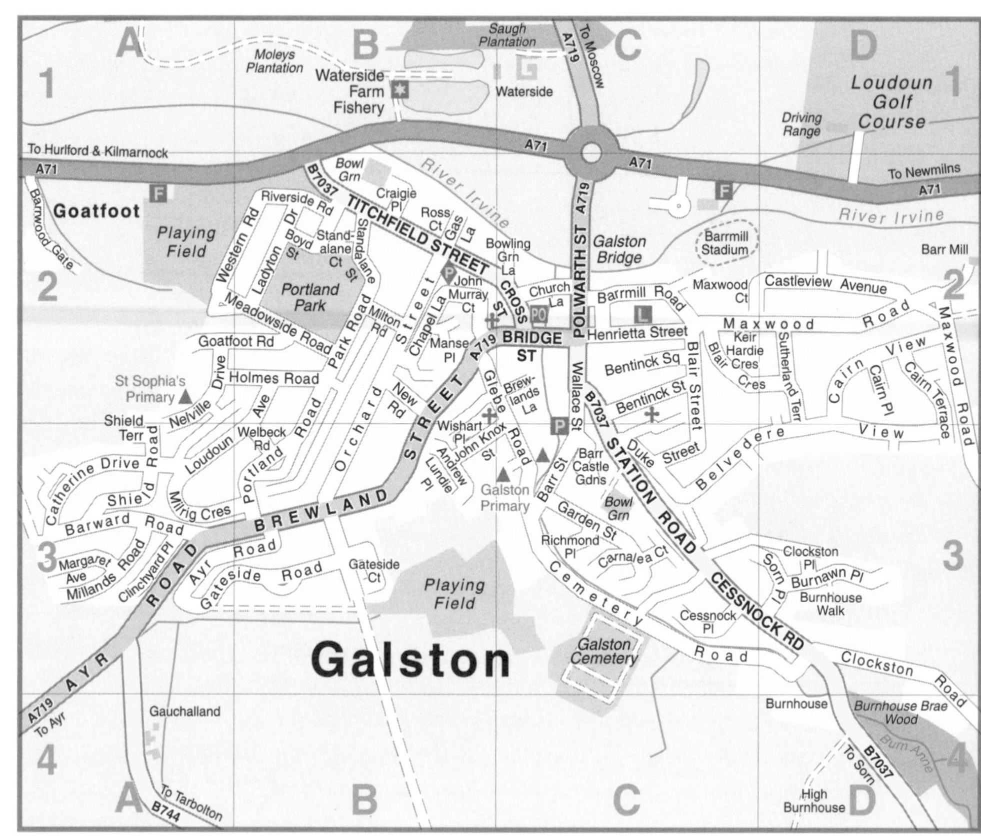

Index to Galston

Street	Grid
Andrew Lundie Place	B3
Ayr Road	A3
Barr Castle Gardens	C3
Barr Street	C3
Barrmill Road	C2
Barward Road	A3
Barwood Gate	A2
Belvedere View	C3
Bentinck Square	C2
Bentinck Street	C2
Blair Crescent	C2
Blair Street	C2
Bowling Green Lane	C2
Boyd Street	B2
Brewlands Lane	C2
Brewland Street	B3
Bridge Street	C2
Burnawn Place	D3
Burnhouse Walk	D3
Cairn Place	D2
Cairn Terrace	D2
Cairn View	D2
Carnalea Court	C3
Castleview Avenue	D2
Catherine Drive	A3
Cemetery Road	C3
Cessnock Place	C3
Cessnock Road	C3
Chapel Lane	B2
Church Lane	C2
Clinchyard Place	A3
Clockston Place	D3
Clockston Road	D3
Craigie Place	B2
Cross Street	C2
Duke Street	C3
Garden Street	C3
Gas Lane	B2
Gatehouse Court	B3
Gateside Road	A3
Glebe Road	B2
Goatfoot Road	A2
Henrietta Street	C2
Holmes Road	B2
John Knox Street	B3
John Murray Court	B2
Keir Hardie Crescent	C2
Ladyton Drive	B2
Loudoun Avenue	B3
Manse Place	B2
Margaret Avenue	A3
Maxwood Court	C2
Maxwood Road	D2
Meadowside Road	B2
Millands Road	A3
Milrig Crescent	A3
Milton Road	B2
Nelville Drive	A2
New Road	B2
Orchard Street	B3
Park Road	B2
Polwarth Street	C2
Portland Road	B3
Richmond Place	C3
Riverside Road	B2
Ross Court	B2
Shield Road	A3
Shield Terrace	A3
Sorn Place	D3
Standalane Court	B2
Standalane Street	B2
Station Road	C3
Sutherland Terrace	D2
Titchfield Street	B2
Wallace Street	C2
Welbeck Road	B3
Western Road	A2
Wishart Place	B3

Index to Girvan

Street	Grid
Ailsa Place	B3
Ailsa Street East	B3
Ailsa Street West	A3
Ainslie Road	A5
Ardmillan Road	C2
Arran Court	B4
Arran View	A2
Avenue, The	C3
Assel Place	C4
Ballochtoul	C4
Ballybroke Street	A4
Bay Terrace	A5
Beech Way	B5
Bennane Road	A5
Birch Terrace	B5
Bourtreehall	B2
Boyle Court	B2
Bridge Street	B2
Byne Court	C4
Carrick Street	B2
Cauldshore	A5
Chalmers Arcade	B3
Chalmers Court (1)	B3
Cherry Drive	B5
Chestnut Drive	B4
Church Square	B2
Clyde View	C3
Coalpots Road	C4
Connor Court	C3
Craig Court	B3
Cuddieston	C4
Dalrymple Street	B4
Deacons Place	B3
Doune Street	A4
Douneburn Crescent	A5
Downhill Road	B4

continued on page 40...

GIRVAN
Square B3
1 Chalmers Ct
Clubhouse
Water of Girvan
Golf Course
Watermouth Park
Golf Course Road
Strathavon Caravan Park
Girvan Station
Hamilton Park (Football Ground)
Houdston Hill
To Turnberry
B734
To Old Dailly
McCreath Park
Swim Pool
Harbour
Promenade
Stair Park
Doune Cem
Girvan Primary
Victory Park
Girvan Academy
Fauldribbon
Coalpots Bridge
Glendoune Farm
Well
Spring
Picnic Site
Viewing Tower
To Stranraer
Shallochpark Roundabout
Wood Hill
Davidson Cottage Hospital
Mill Burn
Henrietta Street
Kirkpatrick St
Glendoune Street
Bennane Road
Dalrymple St
A77
A714

Index to Girvan

continued from page 39...

Duff Street A4
Duncan Street A3
Eastburn Drive C4
Edmiston Drive A4
Elder Avenue B5
Elm Court B5
Fauldribbon Road B4
Firth Terrace A4
George Street A4
Glendoune Street A4
Golf Course Road A2
Greenside A3
Gregg Place C4
Hamilton Street B2
Harbour Lane A3
Harbour Street A3
Hawthorn Drive B5
Henrietta Street A3
Hervey Road B4
High Street B2
Inglis Way C4
Kerr Court B4
Killochan Street B2
Kings Gait B2
Kirkpatrick Street A4
Kirkwood Place A5
Knockcushion Street A2
Knockcusion Gardens A2
Laggenwhilly B2
Lendal Quadrant C2
Linden Avenue B4
Lousia Drive A3
Maple Drive B5
Maxwell Street B2
Mcconnel Square B2
Mcculloch Road C4
Mcmaster Terrace B4
Mcmillan Court B2
Miller Avenue A5
Montgomerie Place B2
Montgomerie Street B2
Motehill Crescent B4
Motehill Road B4
Newton Kennedy A2
Newton Place A2
North Drive C3
North Park Avenue B3
Nursery Court B2
Old Street B2
Orange Arch A3
Orchard Avenue B3
Park Circus A4
Park Road B4
Penkill Road C2
Piedmount Road B4
Piedmount Square B4
Pine Quadrant B5
Promenade A3
Queens Drive C3
Rajput Drive A5
Richard Edminston Way B3
Rodney Drive C3
Roodlands Road B3
Rowan Court A3
Rowan Road B5
Roxburgh Road B4
St Andrews Court B2
Saughhill Road B4
Shalloch Square B4
Smith Crescent B4
Snow Street B4
South Park Avenue B4
Stair Park Terrace A4
Sycamore Drive B5
Threadneedle Crescent B2
Todd Street B4
Torcy Drive C4
Torcy Way C4
Troweir Road B2
Urnfield C4
Vicarton Street B2
Victory Park Road B3
Wesley Place B3
Wesley Road B3
Wheatfield Road C3
Whiteford C4
Willow Drive B5
Wilson Place A3
Wilson Street A3
Woodlands Square B3
Wreck Road B4
Young Street A5

Index to Hurlford

Academy Court B3
Academy Street B3
Ashton Drive C4
Barleith Court C4
Barnweil Drive B4
Bellfield Avenue A3
Bellfield Court A3
Blair Avenue B3
Blair Crescent B3
Blair Road B3
Cadgers Row C3
Cessnock Avenue C4
Cessnock Drive C4
Cessnock Gardens C3
Cessnock Road C3
Craigie Road C4
Cross,The C3
Drumleyhill Drive C4
Dykehead Drive C4
Furnace Court B3
Galston Road C3
Graham Court B3
Holyoake Court C2
Kaimshill Cottages A3
Kerrmuir Avenue C4
Kersland Crescent B3
Knowehead Road C4
Leven Court C3
Leven Drive C3
Lifnock Avenue C3
Lomond Avenue C3
Marchmont Court C2
Mauchline Road C3
Maxwell Gardens B3
Mayfield Avenue D4
Morris Crescent B3
Moss Court C4
Portland Court B3
Portland Brae B2
Reid Court B2
Riccarton Road A3
Riccarton Mill Cottages A3
Richardson Avenue D4
Roxburgh Road B2
Salisbury Avenue C2
Sherwood Road C3
Station Drive A3
Union Street B3
Walden Road B3
Walker Court C3
Wallace Court A3

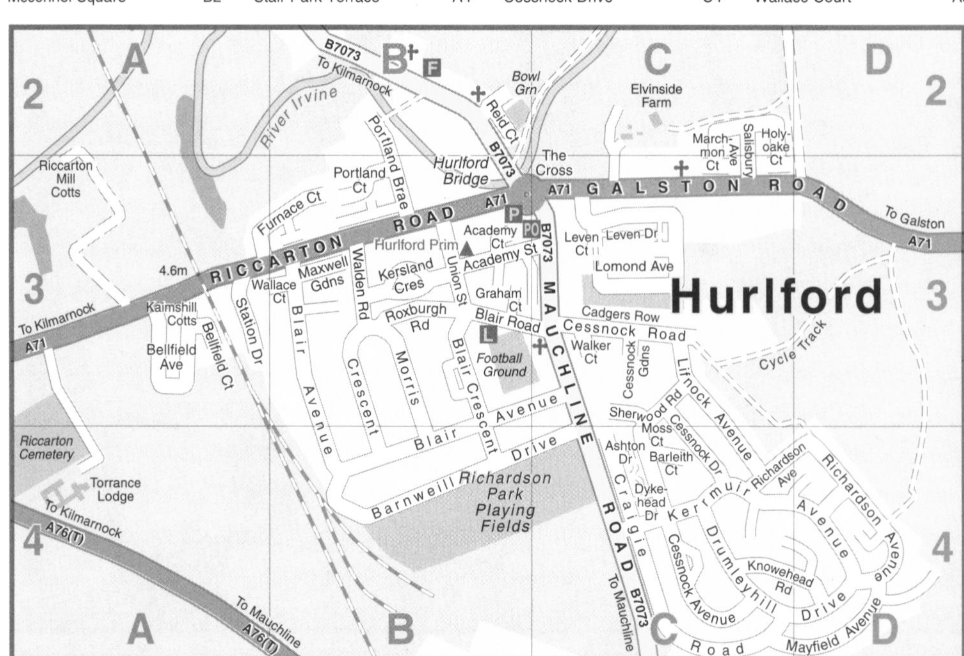

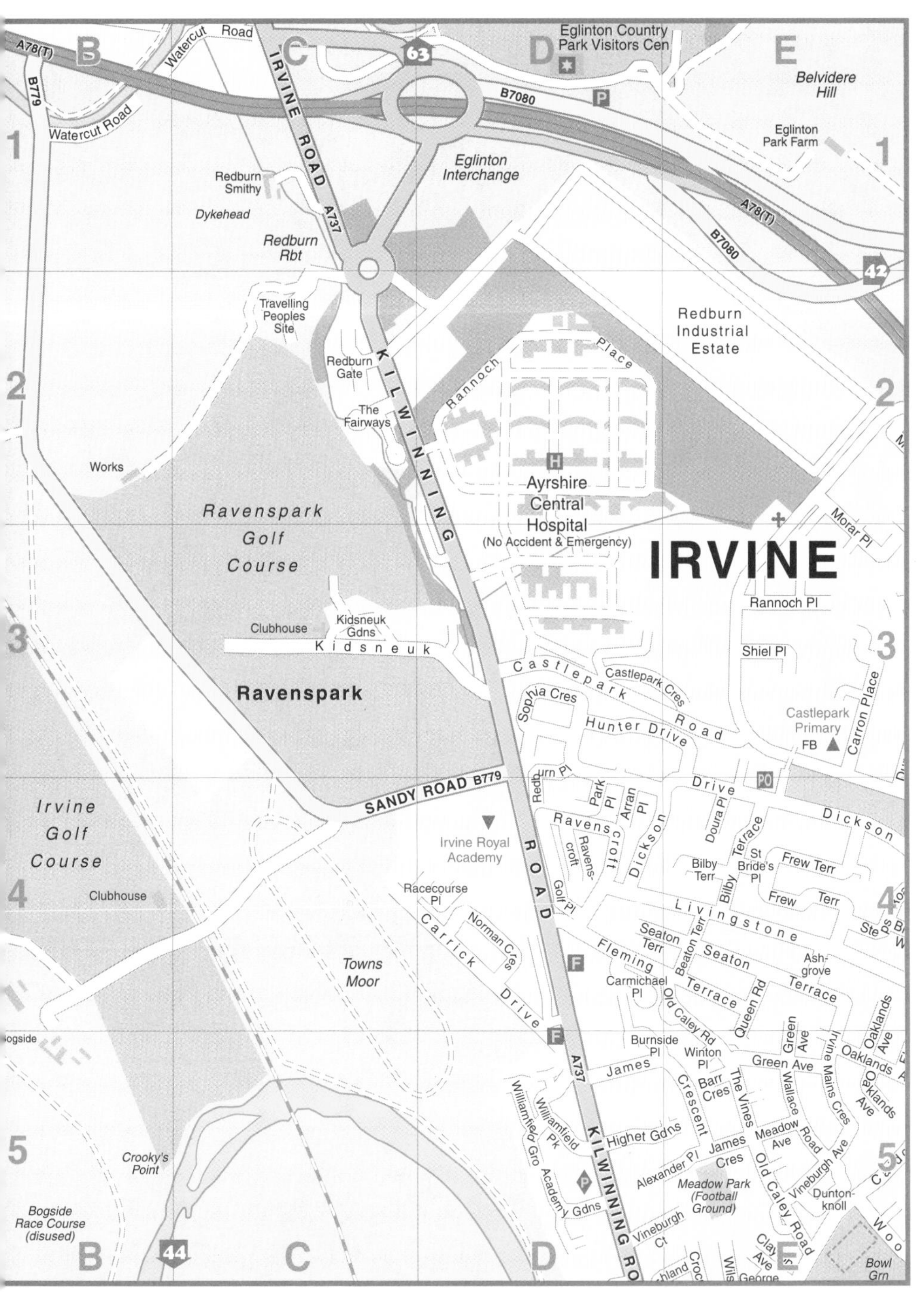
IRVINE
Eglinton Country Park Visitors Cen
Belvidere Hill
Eglinton Park Farm
Eglinton Interchange
Redburn Smithy
Dykehead
Redburn Rbt
Travelling Peoples Site
Redburn Gate
The Fairways
Redburn Industrial Estate
Ayrshire Central Hospital
(No Accident & Emergency)
Works
Ravenspark Golf Course
Clubhouse
Kidsneuk Gdns
Ravenspark
Castlepark Primary
Irvine Golf Course
Irvine Royal Academy
Towns Moor
Crooky's Point
Bogside Race Course (disused)
Meadow Park (Football Ground)
Bowl Grn

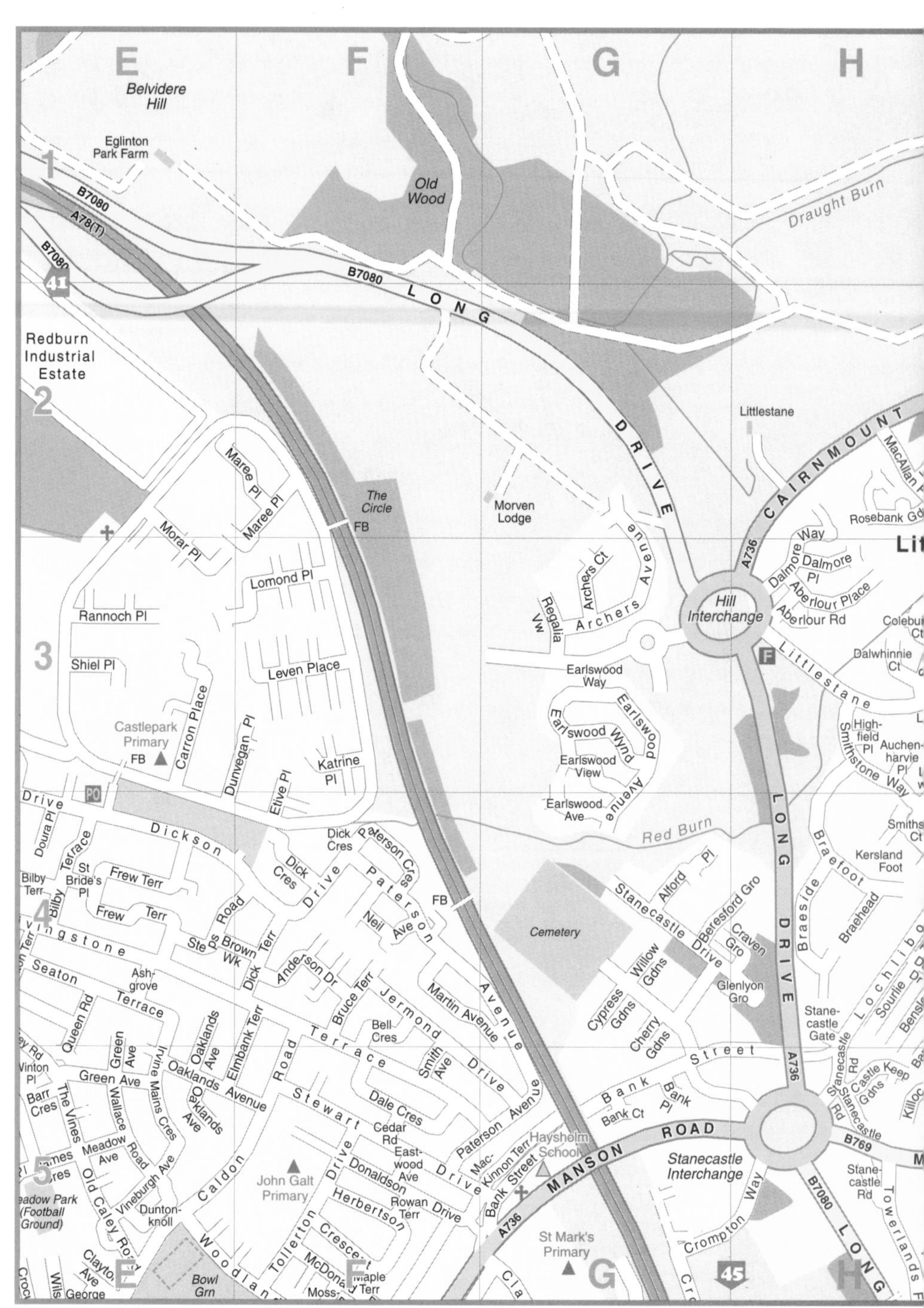
E
F
G
H
Belvidere Hill
Eglinton Park Farm
Old Wood
Draught Burn
B7080
A78(T)
B7080 LONG
Redburn Industrial Estate
DRIVE
Littlestane
CAIRNMOUNT
MacAllan Pl
Rosebank Gdns
The Circle
FB
Morven Lodge
Maree Pl
Maree Pl
Morar Pl
Lomond Pl
Rannoch Pl
Shiel Pl
Leven Place
Carron Place
Dunvegan Pl
Etive Pl
Katrine Pl
Castlepark Primary
PO
Archers Ct
Archers Avenue
Regalia Vw
Hill Interchange
A736
Dalmore Way
Dalmore Pl
Aberlour Place
Aberlour Rd
Littlestane
Dalwhinnie Ct
Earlswood Way
Earlswood Wynd
Earlswood Avenue
Earlswood View
Earlswood Ave
High-field Pl
Auchen-harvie Pl
Smithstone Way
Red Burn
LONG DRIVE
Braefoot
Braeside
Braehead
Kersland Foot
Drive
Dickson
Doura Pl
Terrace
Dick Cres
Paterson Cres
Dick Drive
Paterson
St Bride's Pl
Frew Terr
Frew Terr
Bilby Terr
Bilby
Road
Steps
Brown Wk
Dick Terr
Neil Ave
FB
Cemetery
Stanecastle Drive
Alford Pl
Beresford Gro
Craven Gro
Willow Gdns
Glenlyon Gro
Seaton
Ash-grove
Terrace
Anderson Dr
Bruce Terr
Jermond
Martin Avenue
Avenue
Queen Rd
Green Ave
Oaklands Ave
Elmbank Terr
Bell Cres
Smith Ave
Drive
Cypress Gdns
Cherry Gdns
Stane-castle Gate
Stanecastle Rd
Castle Keep
Sourlie
Lochlibo
Green Ave
Irvine Mains Cres
Oaklands Avenue
Terrace
Road
Street
Bank Pl
Bank Ct
Barr Cres
The Vines
Wallace Road
Oaklands Ave
Stewart
Dale Cres
Paterson Avenue
Stanecastle Gdns
Stanecastle Rd
Killoch
Meadow Ave
Cedar Rd
East-wood Ave
Mac-Kinnon Terr
Haysholm School
ROAD
B769
Stanecastle Interchange
Caldon
John Galt Primary
Drive
Donaldson
MANSON
Bank Street
Stane-castle Rd
Old Caley Road
Vineburgh Ave
Dunton-knoll
Herbertson
Rowan Terr
Drive
A736
Way
B7080
Towerlands
Meadow Park (Football Ground)
Woodlands
Tollerton
Crescent
St Mark's Primary
Crompton
LONG
Clayton Ave
Bowl Grn
McDonald
Maple Terr
Moss-
George
45
41
1
2
3
4
5

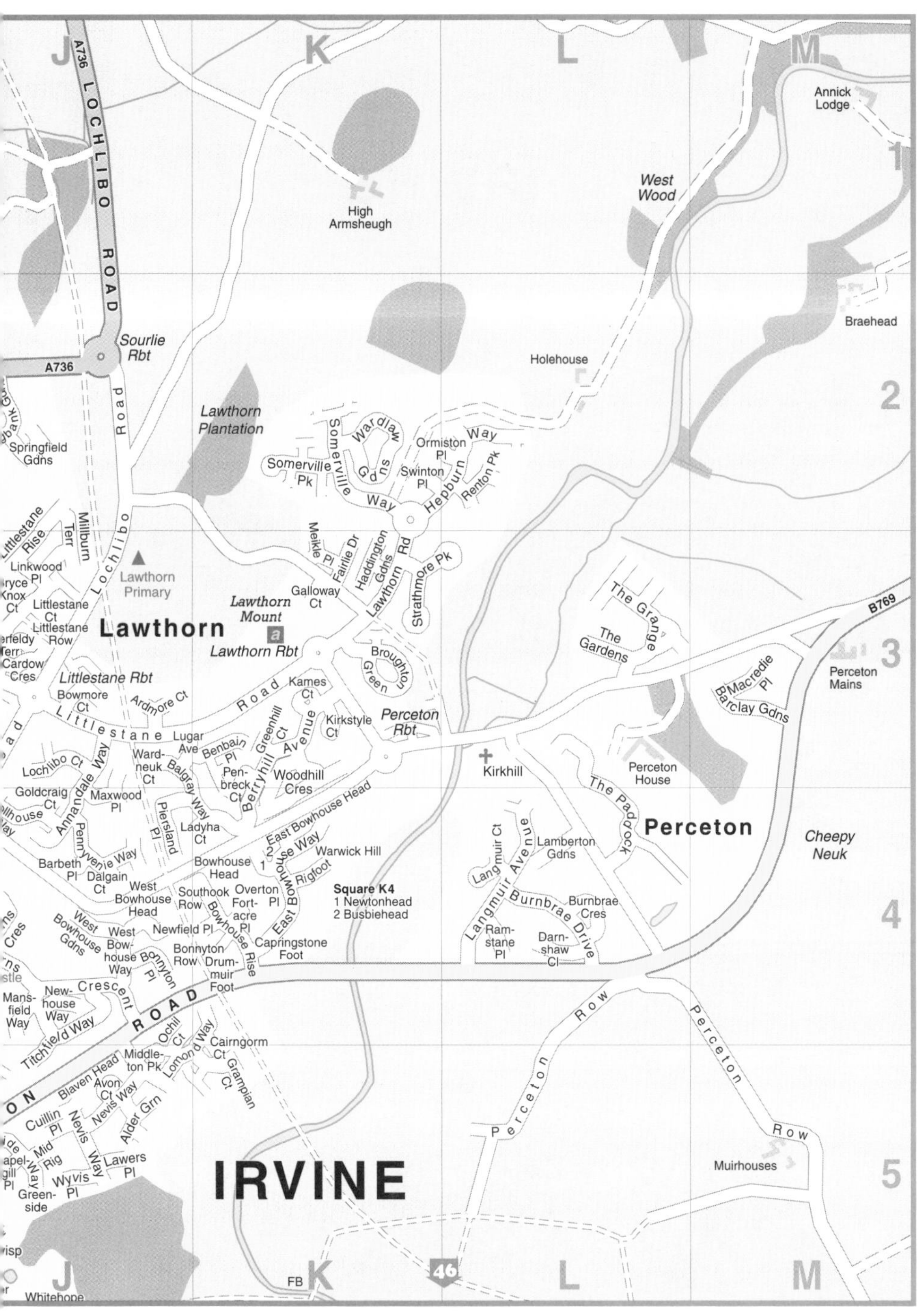

Index to street names can be found starting on page 96

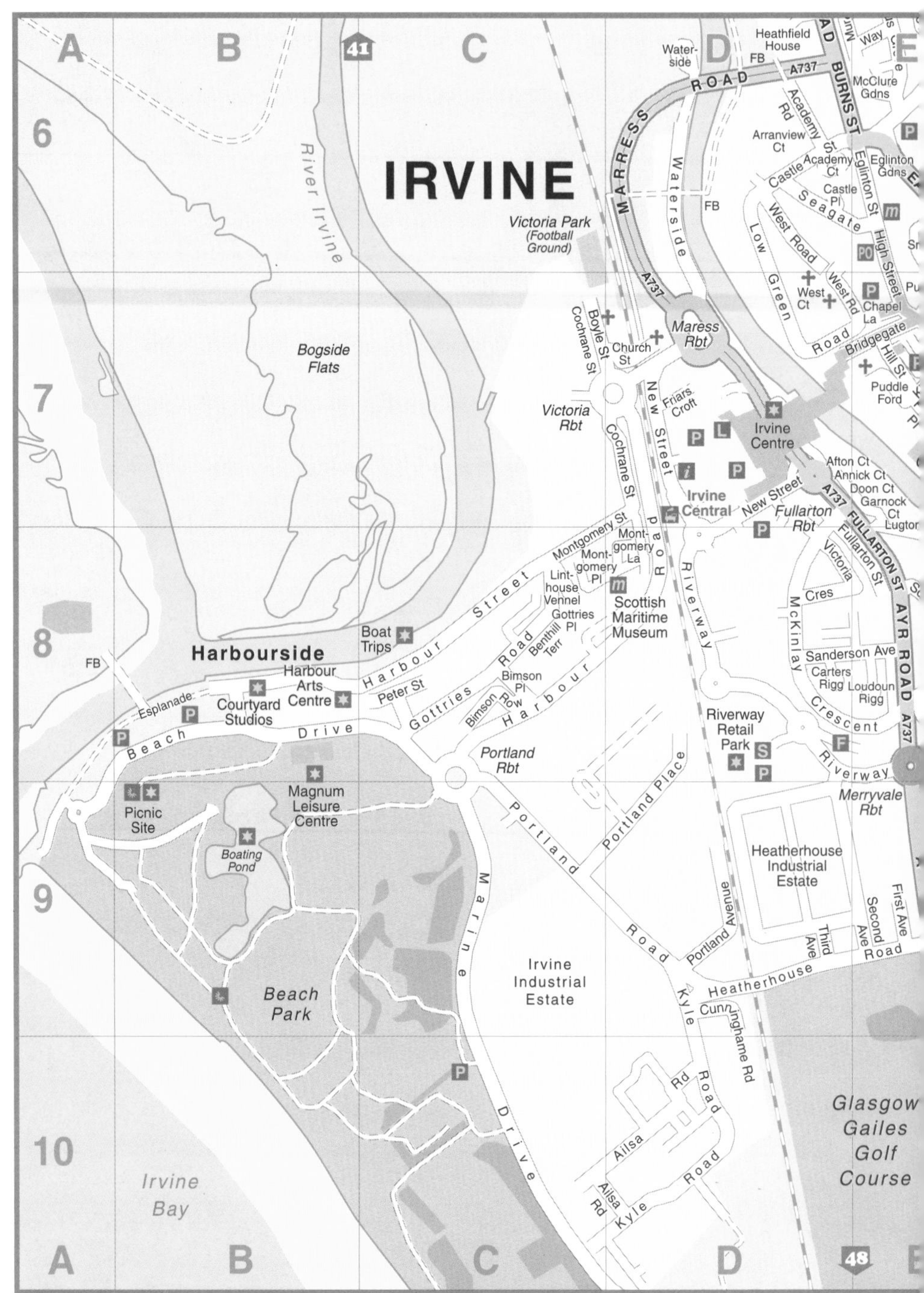
IRVINE
A
B
C
D
E
6
7
8
9
10
41
48
River Irvine
Bogside Flats
Victoria Park (Football Ground)
Harbourside
Boat Trips
Harbour Arts Centre
Courtyard Studios
Esplanade
FB
Beach Drive
Picnic Site
Magnum Leisure Centre
Boating Pond
Beach Park
Irvine Bay
Marine Drive
Harbour Street
Peter St
Gottries Road
Bimson Pl
Bimson Row
Harbour Road
Benthill Terr
Gottries Pl
Linthouse Vennel
Montgomery Pl
Montgomery La
Montgomery St
Scottish Maritime Museum
Portland Rbt
Portland Road
Portland Place
Portland Avenue
Irvine Industrial Estate
Kyle Road
Cunninghame Rd
Ailsa Rd
Ailsa Road
Kyle Road
Heatherhouse Road
Heatherhouse Industrial Estate
Third Ave
Second Ave
First Ave
Glasgow Gailes Golf Course
Victoria Rbt
Cochrane St
Boyle St
Church St
New Street
New Road
Riverway
Irvine Central
Irvine Centre
Friars Croft
Maress Rbt
MARESS ROAD
A737
Waterside
Waterside
FB
Heathfield House
Academy Rd
BURNS ST
McClure Gdns
Arranview Ct
Academy St
Academy Ct
Castle St
Castle Pl
Seagate
Eglinton St
Eglinton Gdns
West Road
Low Green Road
West Ct
West Rd
High Street
Chapel La
Bridgegate
Hill St
Puddle Ford
Afton Ct
Annick Ct
Doon Ct
Garnock Ct
Lugton
New Street
Fullarton Rbt
FULLARTON ST
Fullarton St
Victoria Cres
McKinlay Crescent
Sanderson Ave
Carters Rigg
Loudoun Rigg
AYR ROAD
Riverway Retail Park
Riverway
Merryvale Rbt

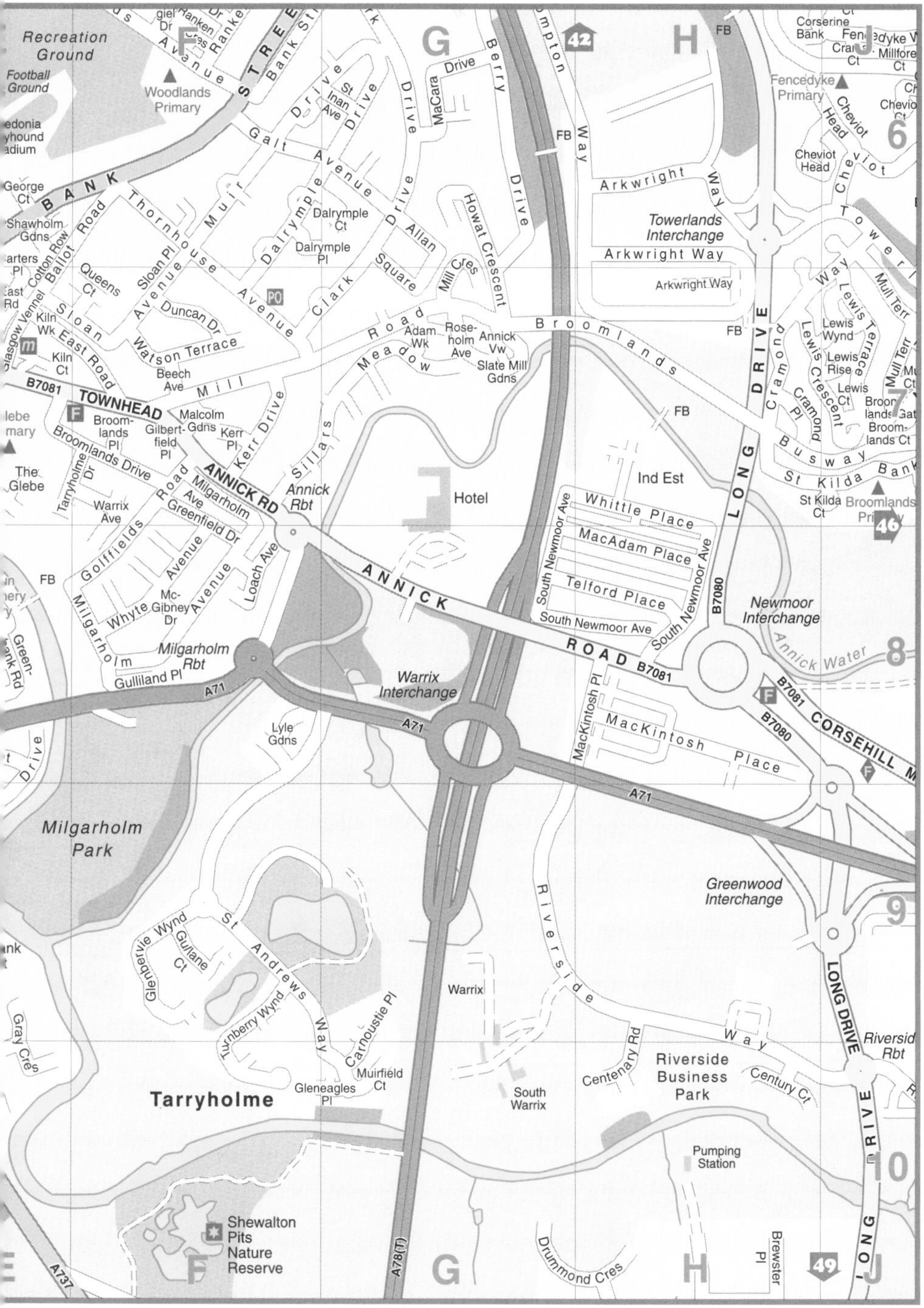

F G H J

6 7 8 9 10

Recreation Ground
Football Ground
Woodlands Primary
Caledonia Greyhound Stadium
George Ct
Shawholm Gdns
Carters Pl
East Rd
Glasgow Vennel
Cotton Row
Ballot Road
Kiln Wk
Kiln Ct
Sloan East Road
Queens Ct
Sloan Pl
Thornhouse Avenue
Muir
Duncan Dr
Watson Terrace
Beech Ave
Mill
Malcolm Gdns
Kerr Pl
Kerr Drive
Gilbertfield Pl
Broomlands Pl
Broomlands Drive
Glebe Primary
The Glebe
Tarryholme Dr
Warrix Ave
Golffields Road
Milgarholm Ave
Greenfield Dr
Avenue
McGibney Dr
Avenue
Whyte
Loach Ave
Milgarholm
Gulliland Pl
Milgarholm Rbt
Annick Rbt
B7081 TOWNHEAD
ANNICK RD
ANNICK ROAD B7081
A71
A71
A71
Lyle Gdns
Gilmour Ranken Dr
Ranken Cres
Avenue
Bank Street
BANK STREET
Galt Avenue
Drive
St Inan Ave
Drive
Dalrymple Ct
Dalrymple Pl
Dalrymple
Clark
Square
Allan Drive
PO
Avenue
Road
Meadow
Sillars
Adam Wk
Roseholm Ave
Annick Vw
Slate Mill Gdns
Mill Cres
Howat Crescent
Drive
MaCara Drive
Berry Drive
Drive
Hotel
Warrix Interchange
Milgarholm Park
St Andrews Way
Glenbervie Wynd
Gullane Ct
Turnberry Wynd
Carnoustie Pl
Muirfield Ct
Gleneagles Pl
Tarryholme
Shewalton Pits Nature Reserve
Gray Cres
Green Bank Rd
Drive
A737
A78(T)
Warrix
South Warrix
Drummond Cres
Riverside Way
Centenary Rd
Riverside Business Park
Century Ct
Pumping Station
Brewster Pl
49
42
Crompton Way
FB
Arkwright Way
Towerlands Interchange
Arkwright Way
Arkwright Way
Broomlands
FB
FB
Ind Est
Whittle Place
MacAdam Place
Telford Place
South Newmoor Ave
South Newmoor Ave
South Newmoor Ave
MacKintosh Pl
MacKintosh Place
B7080
Newmoor Interchange
Annick Water
LONG DRIVE
Cramond Pl
Cramond
Lewis Crescent
Lewis Wynd
Lewis Rise
Lewis Ct
Lewis Terrace
Mull Terr
Mull Terr
Mull Ct
Broomlands Gate
Broomlands Ct
Busway
St Kilda Bank
St Kilda Ct
Broomlands Primary
46
Towerlands Way
Fencedyke Primary
Corserine Bank
Fencedyke Way
Corserine Ct
Millfore Ct
Cheviot Head
Cheviot Ct
Cheviot Head
Cheviot
B7081 CORSEHILL MOUNT
B7080
Greenwood Interchange
LONG DRIVE
Riverside Rbt
LONG DRIVE

Index to street names can be found starting on page 96

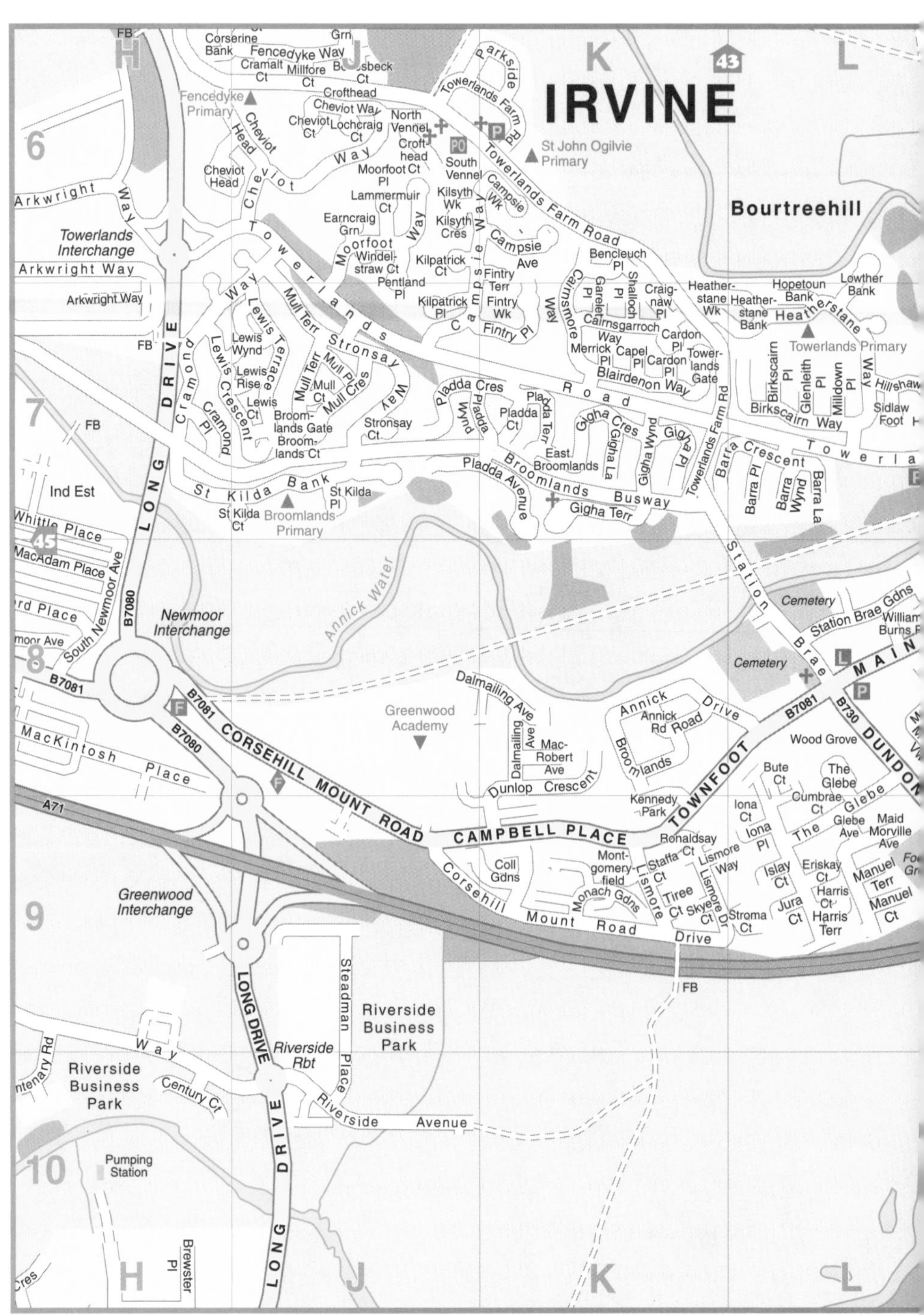
IRVINE
Bourtreehill
H
J
K
L
6
7
8
9
10
43
45
Corserine Bank
Fencedyke Way
Cramalt Ct
Millfore Ct
Crofthead
Cheviot Way
Cheviot Ct
Lochcraig Ct
North Vennel
Crofthead Ct
South Vennel
PO
Fencedyke Primary
Cheviot Head
Moorfoot Ct
Moorfoot Pl
Lammermuir Ct
Earncraig Grn
Windelstraw Ct
Pentland Pl
Kilsyth Wk
Kilsyth Cres
Kilpatrick Ct
Kilpatrick Pl
Campsie Way
Campsie Wk
Campsie Ave
Fintry Terr
Fintry Wk
Fintry Pl
Parkside
Towerlands Farm Rd
Towerlands Farm Road
St John Ogilvie Primary
Arkwright Way
Towerlands Interchange
Towerlands Road
Lewis Terrace
Lewis Wynd
Lewis Rise
Lewis Ct
Lewis Crescent
Mull Terr
Mull Pl
Mull Ct
Mull Cres
Stronsay Way
Stronsay Ct
Broomlands Gate
Broomlands Ct
Cramond Way
Cramond Pl
Long Drive
FB
Benclеuch Pl
Cairnsmore Way
Garelet Pl
Shalloch Pl
Craignaw Pl
Cairnsgarroch Way
Merrick Pl
Capel Pl
Cardon Pl
Towerlands Gate
Blairdenon Way
Heatherstane Wk
Heatherstane Bank
Heatherstane Way
Hopetoun Bank
Lowther Bank
Towerlands Primary
Birkscairn Pl
Glenleith Pl
Milldown Pl
Birkscairn Way
Hillshaw
Sidlaw Foot
Pladda Cres
Pladda Wynd
Pladda Ct
Pladda Terr
Pladda Avenue
East Broomlands
Gigha Cres
Gigha La
Gigha Wynd
Gigha Pl
Gigha Terr
Broomlands Busway
Barra Crescent
Barra Pl
Barra Wynd
Barra La
Ind Est
St Kilda Bank
St Kilda Pl
St Kilda Ct
Broomlands Primary
Whittle Place
MacAdam Place
South Newmoor Ave
B7080
Newmoor Interchange
Annick Water
Station Brae
Cemetery
Station Brae Gdns
William Burns
Main
B7081
MacKintosh Place
Corsehill Mount Road
A71
Dalmailing Ave
Greenwood Academy
MacRobert Ave
Dunlop Crescent
Annick Drive
Annick Rd
Broomlands
Kennedy Park
Townfoot
Campbell Place
B730
Dundonald
Wood Grove
Bute Ct
The Glebe
Cumbrae Ct
Iona Ct
Iona Pl
Glebe Ave
Maid Morville Ave
Ronaldsay Ct
Staffa Ct
Lismore Way
Lismore Ct
Lismore Dr
Coll Gdns
Montgomeryfield
Monach Gdns
Tiree Ct
Skye Ct
Islay Ct
Eriskay Ct
Harris Ct
Harris Terr
Manuel Terr
Manuel Ct
Stroma Ct
Jura Ct
Corsehill Mount Road Drive
Greenwood Interchange
Steadman Place
Riverside Business Park
Riverside Rbt
Riverside Avenue
Centenary Rd
Century Ct
Pumping Station
Brewster Pl

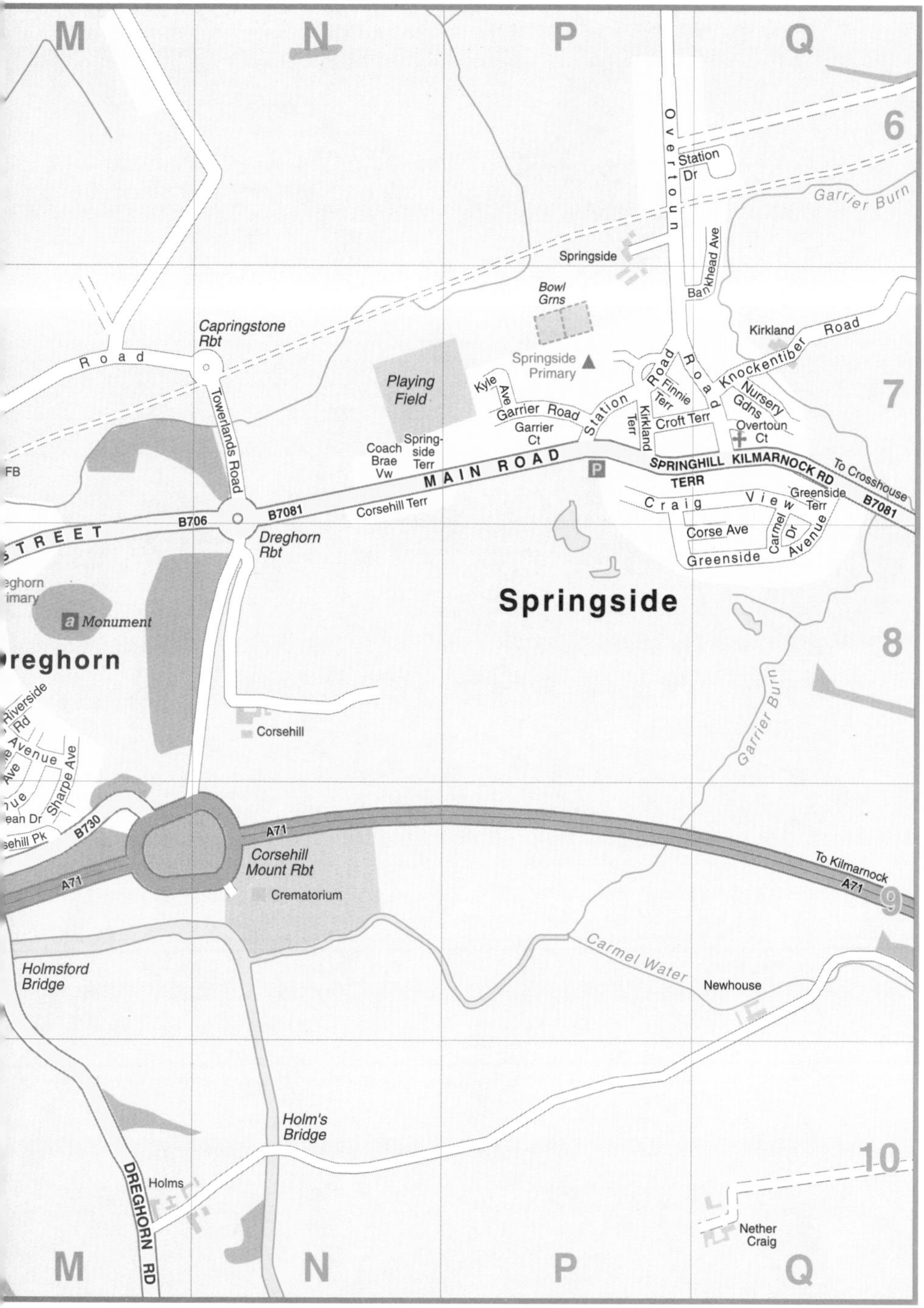

M N P Q

6 7 8 9 10

Capringstone Rbt
Road
Towerlands Road
Dreghorn Rbt
B706
B7081
STREET
MAIN ROAD
Corsehill Terr
Playing Field
Coach Brae Vw
Spring-side Terr
Kyle Ave
Garrier Road
Garrier Ct
Station Road
Kirkland Terr
Finnie Terr
Croft Terr
Bowl Grns
Springside Primary
Springside
Overtoun Road
Station Dr
Bankhead Ave
Kirkland
Knockentiber Road
Nursery Gdns
Overtoun Ct
SPRINGHILL TERR
KILMARNOCK RD
To Crosshouse
B7081
Greenside Terr
Craig View
Corse Ave
Carmel Dr
Avenue
Greenside
Garrier Burn
Springside
Monument
Dreghorn
Riverside Rd
Avenue
Ave
Sharpe Ave
B730
Corsehill
A71
Corsehill Mount Rbt
Crematorium
To Kilmarnock
Carmel Water
Newhouse
Holmsford Bridge
Holm's Bridge
Holms
DREGHORN RD
Nether Craig
FB

Index to street names can be found starting on page 96

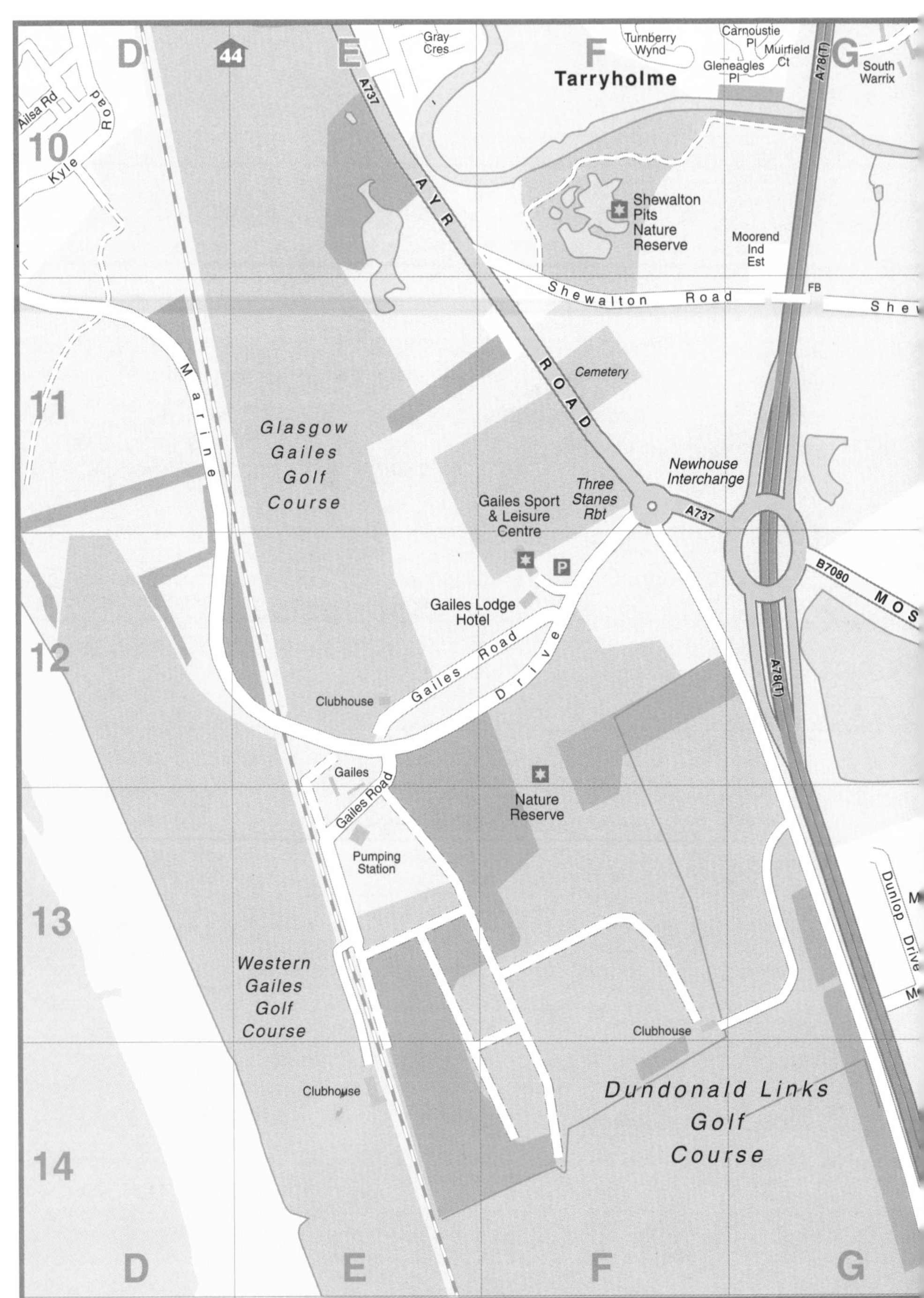

D
E
F
G
44
10
11
12
13
14
Ailsa Rd
Road
Kyle
Gray Cres
Turnberry Wynd
Carnoustie Pl
Muirfield Ct
Gleneagles Pl
Tarryholme
South Warrix
A737
A78(T)
AYR ROAD
Shewalton Pits Nature Reserve
Moorend Ind Est
Shewalton Road
FB
Shew
Cemetery
Marine
Glasgow Gailes Golf Course
Newhouse Interchange
Three Stanes Rbt
Gailes Sport & Leisure Centre
A737
B7080
MOS
P
Gailes Lodge Hotel
Gailes Road
Drive
Clubhouse
Gailes
Gailes Road
Nature Reserve
Pumping Station
Dunlop Drive
Western Gailes Golf Course
Clubhouse
Clubhouse
Dundonald Links Golf Course
D
E
F
G

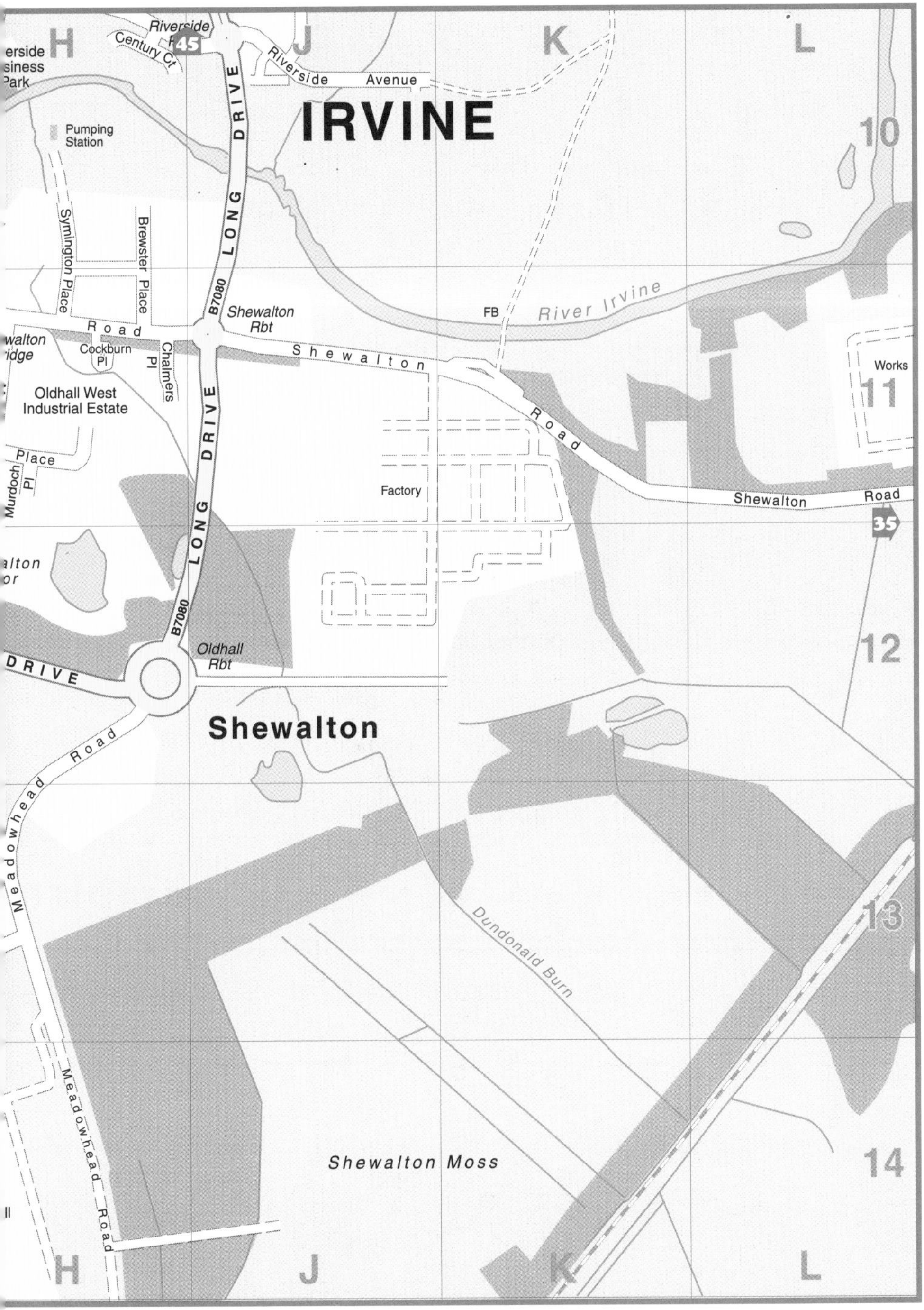

H
J
K
L
Riverside
Century Ct
45
erside
siness
Park
Riverside Avenue
IRVINE
Pumping Station
LONG DRIVE
10
Symington Place
Brewster Place
B7080
Shewalton Rbt
River Irvine
FB
Road
walton
ridge
Cockburn Pl
Chalmers Pl
Shewalton Road
Works
11
Oldhall West Industrial Estate
Place
Murdoch Pl
Factory
Shewalton Road
35
alton
or
LONG DRIVE
B7080
Oldhall Rbt
12
DRIVE
Shewalton
Meadowhead Road
13
Dundonald Burn
Meadowhead Road
Shewalton Moss
14
ll
H
J
K
L

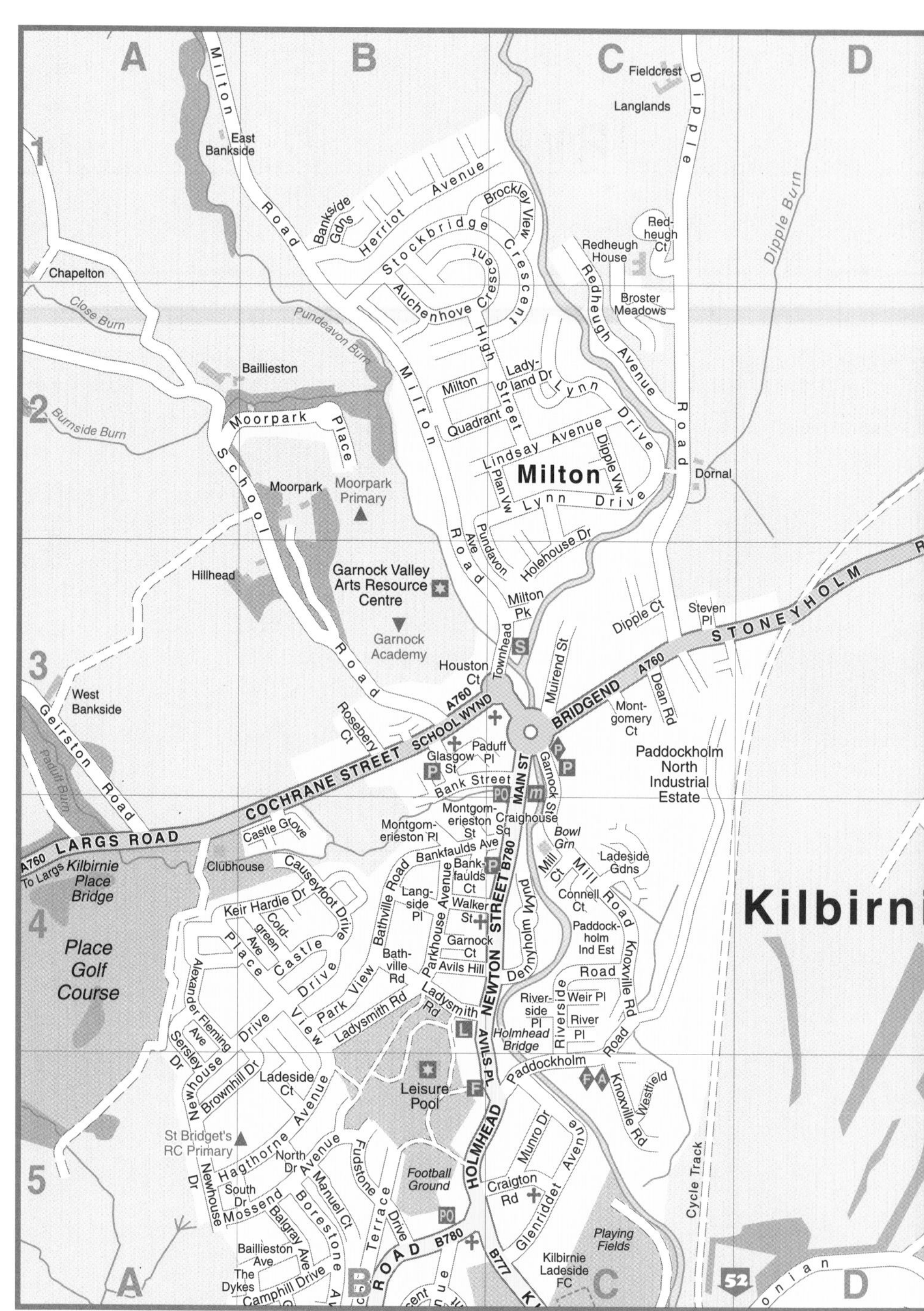

A
B
C
D
1
2
3
4
5
Milton Road
East Bankside
Chapelton
Close Burn
Pundeavon Burn
Bankside Gdns
Herriot Avenue
Brockley View Crescent
Stockbridge Crescent
Auchenhove Crescent
High Street
Fieldcrest
Langlands
Dipple Road
Dipple Burn
Redheugh Ct
Redheugh House
Broster Meadows
Redheugh Avenue
Baillieston
Burnside Burn
Moorpark Place
School Road
Moorpark
Moorpark Primary
Milton Quadrant
Ladyland Dr
Lynn Drive
Lindsay Avenue
Dipple Vw
Plan Vw
Milton
Dornal
Pundavon Ave
Holehouse Dr
Hillhead
Garnock Valley Arts Resource Centre
Garnock Academy
Milton Pk
Townhead
Houston Ct
Dipple Ct
Steven Pl
Stoneyholm
Muirend St
A760
Bridgend
Dean Rd
Montgomery Ct
West Bankside
Geirston Road
Paduff Burn
Rosebery Ct
School Wynd
Paduff Pl
Glasgow St
Bank Street
Cochrane Street
Main St
Garnock St
Paddockholm North Industrial Estate
Largs Road
To Largs
Castle Grove
Montgomerieston Pl
Montgomerieston St
Craighouse Sq
Bowl Grn
Ladeside Gdns
Kilbirnie Place Bridge
Clubhouse
Causeyfoot Drive
Bankfaulds Ave
Bankfaulds Ct
Newton Street B780
Mill Ct
Mill Road
Kilbirnie
Bathville Road
Langside Pl
Parkhouse Avenue
Walker St
Connell Ct
Paddockholm Ind Est
Keir Hardie Dr
Coldgreen Ave
Place Golf Course
Castle Drive
Garnock Ct
Avils Hill
Dennyholm Wynd
Knoxville Rd
Place
Alexander Fleming Ave
Park View
Bathville Rd
Ladysmith Rd
Riverside Pl
Weir Pl
River Pl
Sersley Dr
Drive
View
Holmhead Bridge
Avils Pl
Newhouse Dr
Brownhill Dr
Ladeside Ct
Ladeside Avenue
Leisure Pool
Paddockholm Road
Westfield
St Bridget's RC Primary
Hagthorne Avenue
North Dr
Fudstone Terrace
Holmhead
Munro Dr
Glenriddet Avenue
Manuel Ct
Football Ground
Cycle Track
South Dr
Mossend
Borestone Ave
Balgray Ave
Craigton Rd
Playing Fields
Drive
Baillieston Ave
The Dykes
Camphill Drive
Road B780
B777
Kilbirnie Ladeside FC
52

Index to Kilbirnie

Alexander Fleming Avenue A4
Auchenhove Crescent B2
Avils Hill B4
Avils Place C5
Baillieston Avenue B5
Balgray Avenue B5
Balgray Road C6
Bank Street B3
Bankfaulds Avenue B4
Bankfaulds Court B4
Bankside Gardens C1
Barony Terrace B5
Bathville Road B4
Beith Road D7
Borestone Avenue B6
Bridgend C3
Briery Court B6
Brockley View B1
Broster Meadows C1
Brownhill Drive A5
Burnside Street C7
Caledonian Place C6
Caledonian Road D6
Camphill Drive B5
Castle Drive B4
Castle Grove B4
Causeyfoot Drive B4
Central Avenue B6
Cochrane Street B4
Coldgreen Avenue B4
Connell Court C4
Craigends Road C7
Craighouse Square C4
Craigton Road C5
Daisybank D7
Dalry Road B6
Davidson Avenue E7
Dean Road C3
Dennyholm Wynd C4
Dipple Court C3
Dipple Road C2
Dipple View C2
Dykes, The B5
Eastern Crescent B6
Fudstone Drive B5
Garnock Court B4
Garnock Street C3
Garnock View C6
Garnockside C7
Geirston Road A3
Glasgow Street B3
Glebe Road C6
Glenriddet Avenue C5
Grahamston Avenue C6
Greenside Avenue B6
Hagthorne Avenue B5
Herriot Avenue B1
High Street C2
Holehouse Drive C3
Holmhead B5
Holms Road C7
Houston Court B3
Janefield Place C6
Keir Hardie Drive B4
Kersland Place D7
Kersland Road D7
Kerswinning Avenue B6
Kirkland Road C5
Knoxville Road C4, C5
Ladeside Court B5
Ladeside Gardens C4
Ladyland Drive C2
Ladysmith Road B4
Langside Place B4
Largs Road A4
Lindsay Avenue C2
Loadingbank Court B6
Loadingbank B6
Lochend Road D6
Longbar Avenue E7
Lynn Drive C2
Main Road C7
Main Street C4
Manuel Court B5
Mill Court C4
Mill Road C4
Milton Park C3
Milton Quadrant B2
Milton Road B2
Montgomerieston Place B4
Montgomerieston Street B4
Montgomery Court C3
Moorpark Place A2
Mossend Avenue B5
Muirend Street C3
Munro Drive C5
Newhouse Drive A5
Newton Street C4
North Drive B5
Paddockholm Road C5
Paduff Place B3
Park View B4
Parkhouse Avenue B4
Place View B4
Plan View C2
Pundavon Avenue B2
Redheugh Avenue C1
Redheugh Court C1
Redheugh House C1
River Place C4
Riverside Place C4
Riverside Road C4
Rosebery Court B3
St Brennans Court B6
School Road A2
School Wynd B3
Sersley Drive A4
Smith Avenue E7
South Drive B5
South Neuk B6
Station Court D7
Steven Place C3
Stockbridge Crescent B1
Stoneyholm Road C3
Sunderland Court B6
Townhead C3
Walker Street B4
Weir Place C4
Western Crescent B6
Westfield C5

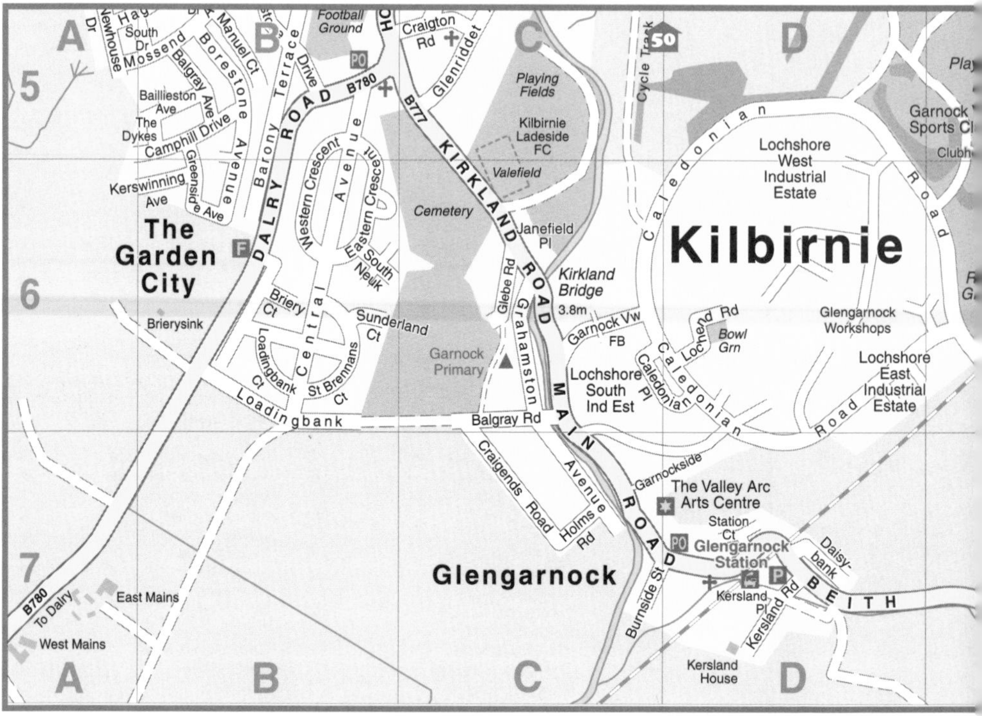

Kilbirnie
The Garden City
Glengarnock
Playing Fields
Kilbirnie Ladeside FC
Valefield
Cemetery
Garnock Primary
Lochshore West Industrial Estate
Lochshore South Ind Est
Lochshore East Industrial Estate
Glengarnock Workshops
Garnock Sports Cl
The Valley Arc Arts Centre
Glengarnock Station
Kirkland Bridge
3.8m
Football Ground
Brierysink
East Mains
West Mains
Kersland House
B780 To Dalry
DALRY ROAD
KIRKLAND ROAD
MAIN ROAD
BEITH
Caledonian Road
Cycle Track
Loadingbank
Balgray Rd
Craigends Road
Holms Rd
Avenue
Burnside St
Kersland Rd
Kersland Pl
Daisybank
Station Ct
Garnockside
Garnock Vw
Lochend Rd
Bowl Grn
Caledonia Pl
Grahamston
Glebe Rd
Janefield Pl
Craigton Rd
Glenriddet
Barony Terrace
Western Crescent
Eastern Crescent
Central Avenue
South Neuk
Briery Ct
Sunderland Ct
Loadingbank Ct
St Brennans Ct
Central Ct
Kerswinning Ave
Greenside Ave
Campbill Drive
The Dykes
Bailleston Ave
Balgray Ave
Borestone Avenue
Mossend
South Dr
Newhouse Dr
Manuel Ct

Index to street names in Kilbirnie can be found on page 51

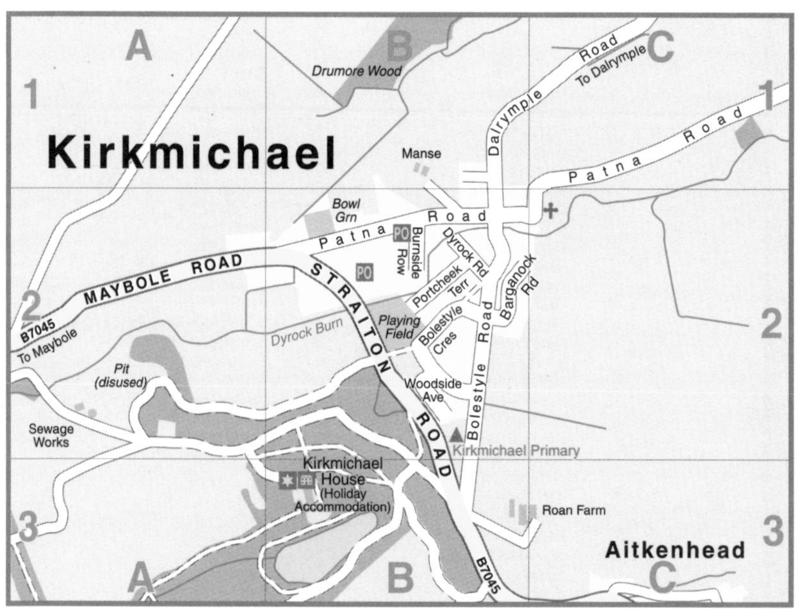

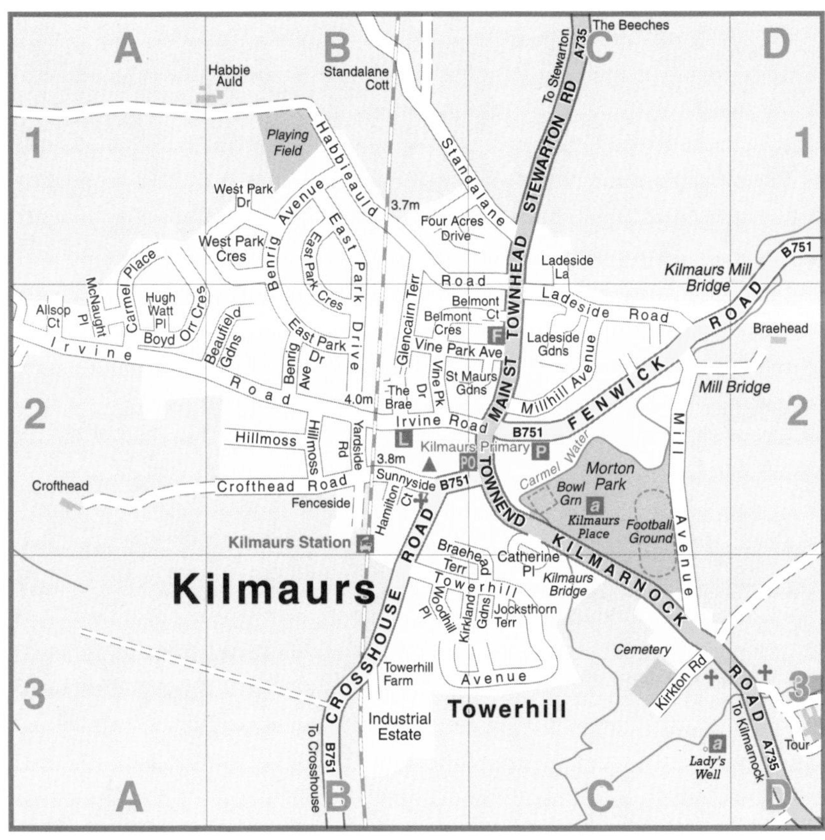

Index to Kilmaurs

Allsop Court	A2
Beaufield Gardens	B2
Belmont Court	C2
Belmont Crescent	C2
Benrig Avenue	B2
Boyd Orr Crescent	A2
Brae, The	B2
Braehead Terrace	B2
Carmel Place	A2
Catherine Place	C3
Crofthead Road	B2
Crosshouse Road	B3
East Park Crescent	B1
East Park Drive	B1
Fenwick Road	C2
Four Acres Drive	B1
Glencairn Terrace	B2
Habbieauld Road	B1
Hamilton Court	B2
Hillmoss	B2
Hugh Watt Place	A2
Irvine Road	B2
Jocksthorn Terrace	C3
Kilmarnock Road	C2
Kirkland Gardens	B3
Kirkton Road	C3
Ladeside Gardens	C2
Ladeside Lane	C1
Ladeside Road	C2
McNaught Place	A2
Main Street	C2
Mill Avenue	C2
Millhill Avenue	C2
St Maurs Gardens	C2
Standalane	B1
Stewarton Road	C1
Sunnyside	B2
Towerhill Avenue	B3
Townend	C2
Townhead	C2
Vine Park Avenue	B2
Vine Park Drive	B2
West Park Crescent	B1
West Park Drive	B1
Woodhill Place	B3
Yardside Road	B2

Index to Kirkmichael

Barganock Road	B2
Bolestyle Crescent	B2
Bolestyle Road	B2
Burnside Row	B2
Dalrymple Road	B1
Dyrock Road	B2
Maybole Road	A2
Patna Road	B2
Portcheek Terrace	B2
Straiton Road	B2
Woodside Avenue	B2

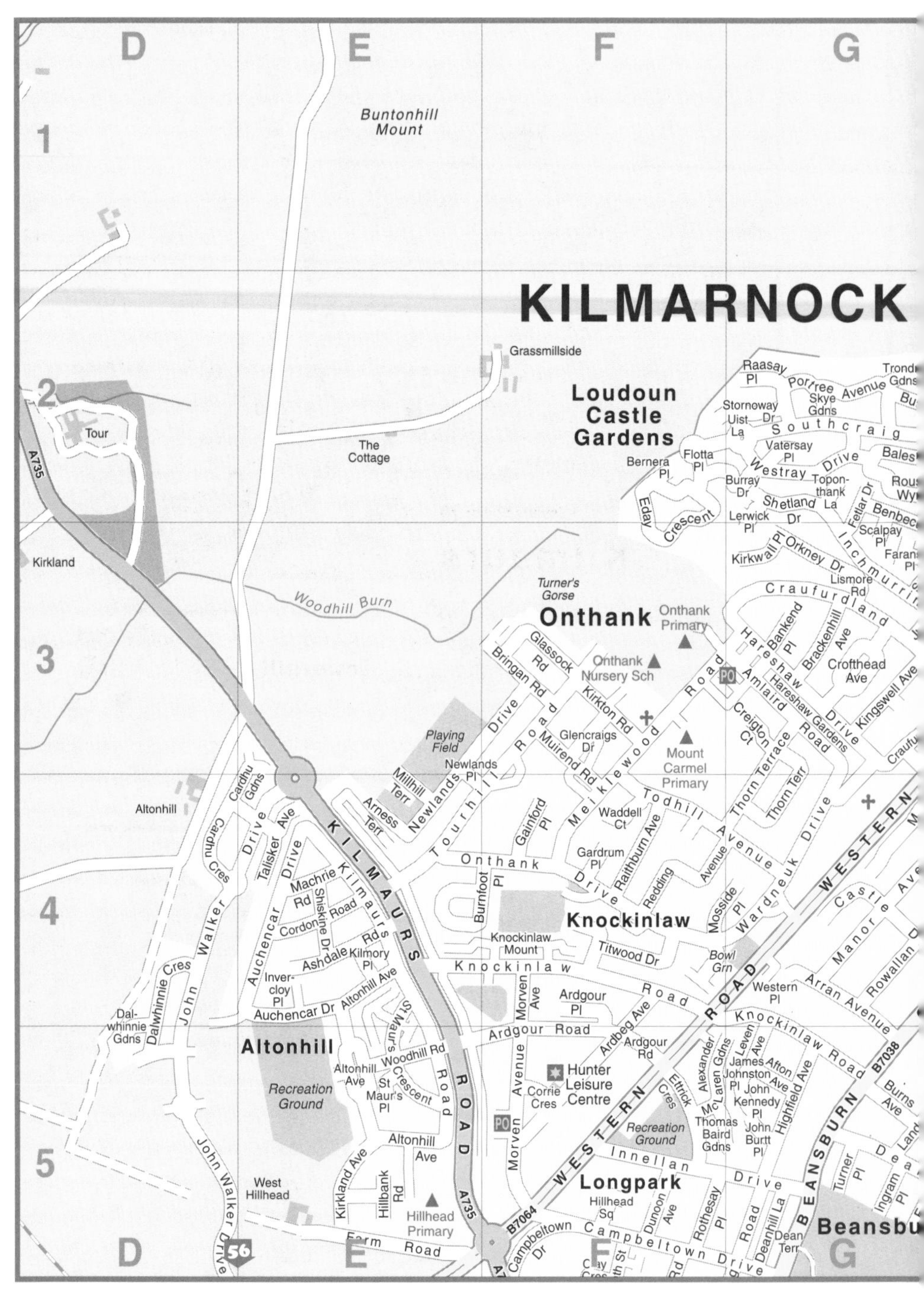

KILMARNOCK
Buntonhill Mount
Grassmillside
Loudoun Castle Gardens
Tour
The Cottage
A735
Kirkland
Woodhill Burn
Turner's Gorse
Onthank
Onthank Primary
Onthank Nursery Sch
Playing Field
Altonhill
Mount Carmel Primary
Knockinlaw
Knockinlaw Mount
Bowl Grn
Altonhill
Recreation Ground
Hunter Leisure Centre
Recreation Ground
Longpark
West Hillhead
Hillhead Primary
Beansburn
Kilmaurs Road
Western Road
Beansburn
B7064
B7038
John Walker Drive
Farm Road
Campbeltown Drive
Knockinlaw Road
Ardgour Road
Onthank Drive
Tourhill Road
Meiklewood Road
Todhill Avenue
Wardneuk Drive
Southcraig Drive
Westray Drive
Craufurdland Road
Hareshaw Drive
Arran Avenue
Innellan Drive

56

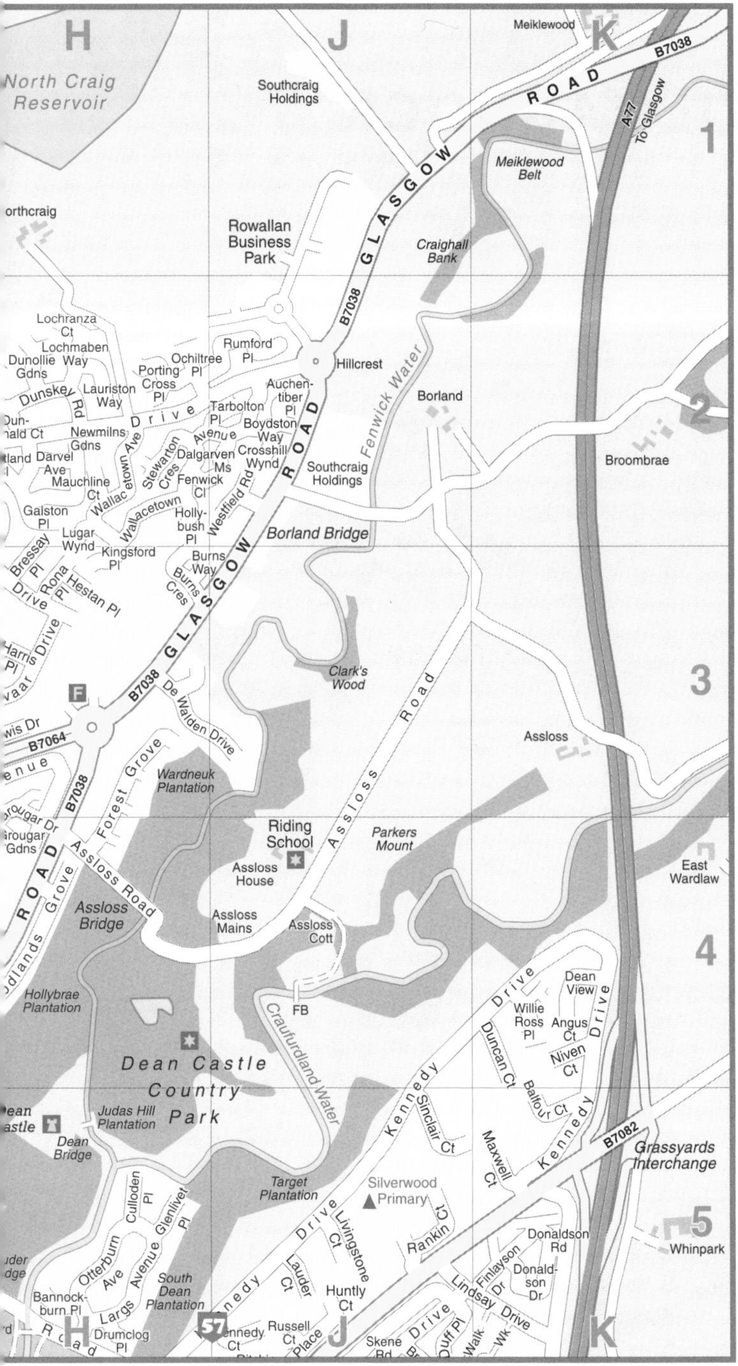

Index to Kilmarnock

continued on page 58....

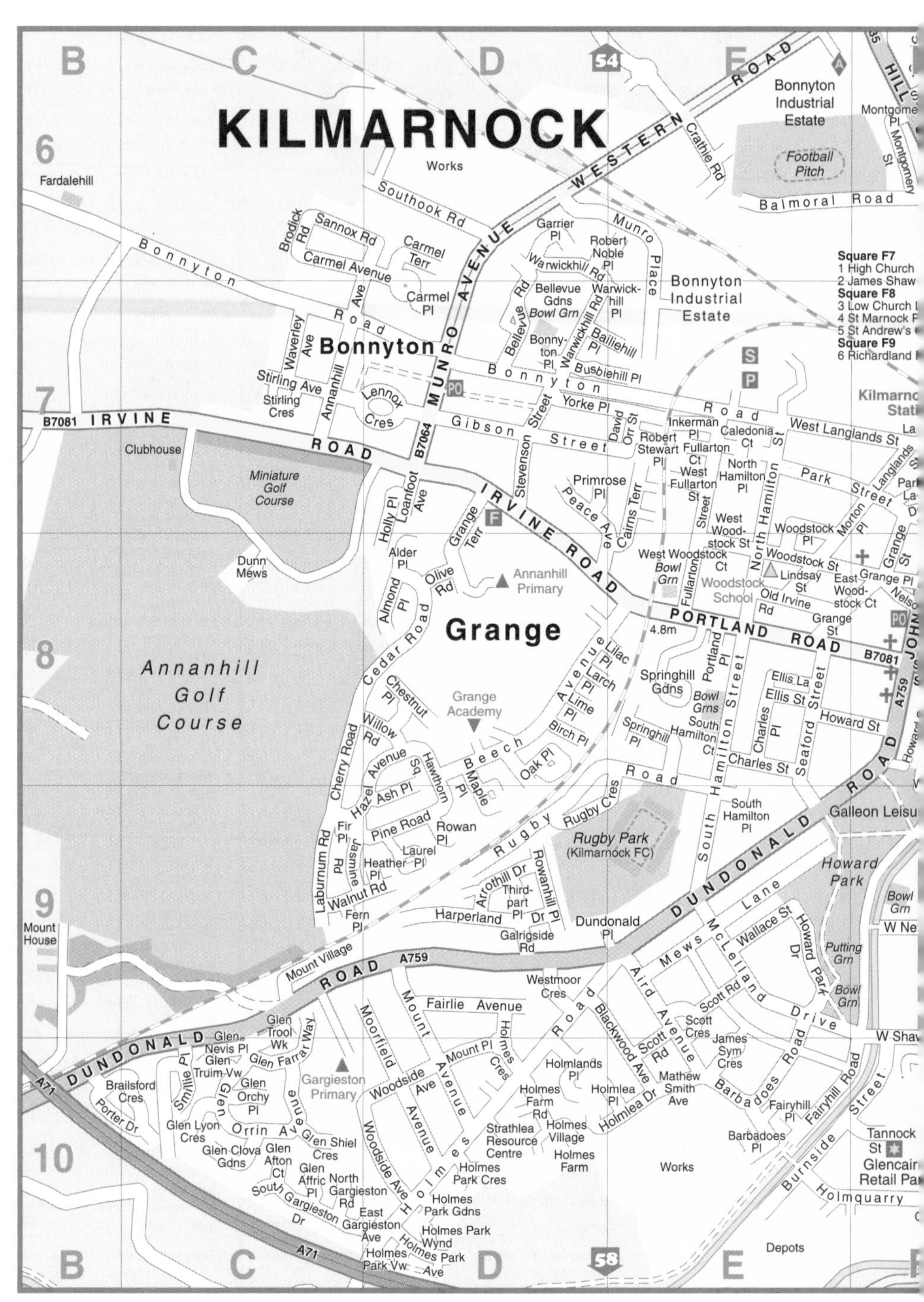
KILMARNOCK
Bonnyton
Grange
Annanhill Golf Course
Bonnyton Industrial Estate
Square F7
1 High Church
2 James Shaw
Square F8
3 Low Church
4 St Marnock
5 St Andrew's
Square F9
6 Richardland
Rugby Park (Kilmarnock FC)
Howard Park
Annanhill Primary
Grange Academy
Gargieston Primary
Woodstock School
Miniature Golf Course
Strathlea Resource Centre
Western Road
Irvine Road
Portland Road
Dundonald Road
Munro Avenue
Bonnyton Road
Southook Rd
Gibson Street
Cedar Road
Rugby Road
Fairlie Avenue
Holmes Farm
Glencairn Retail Park

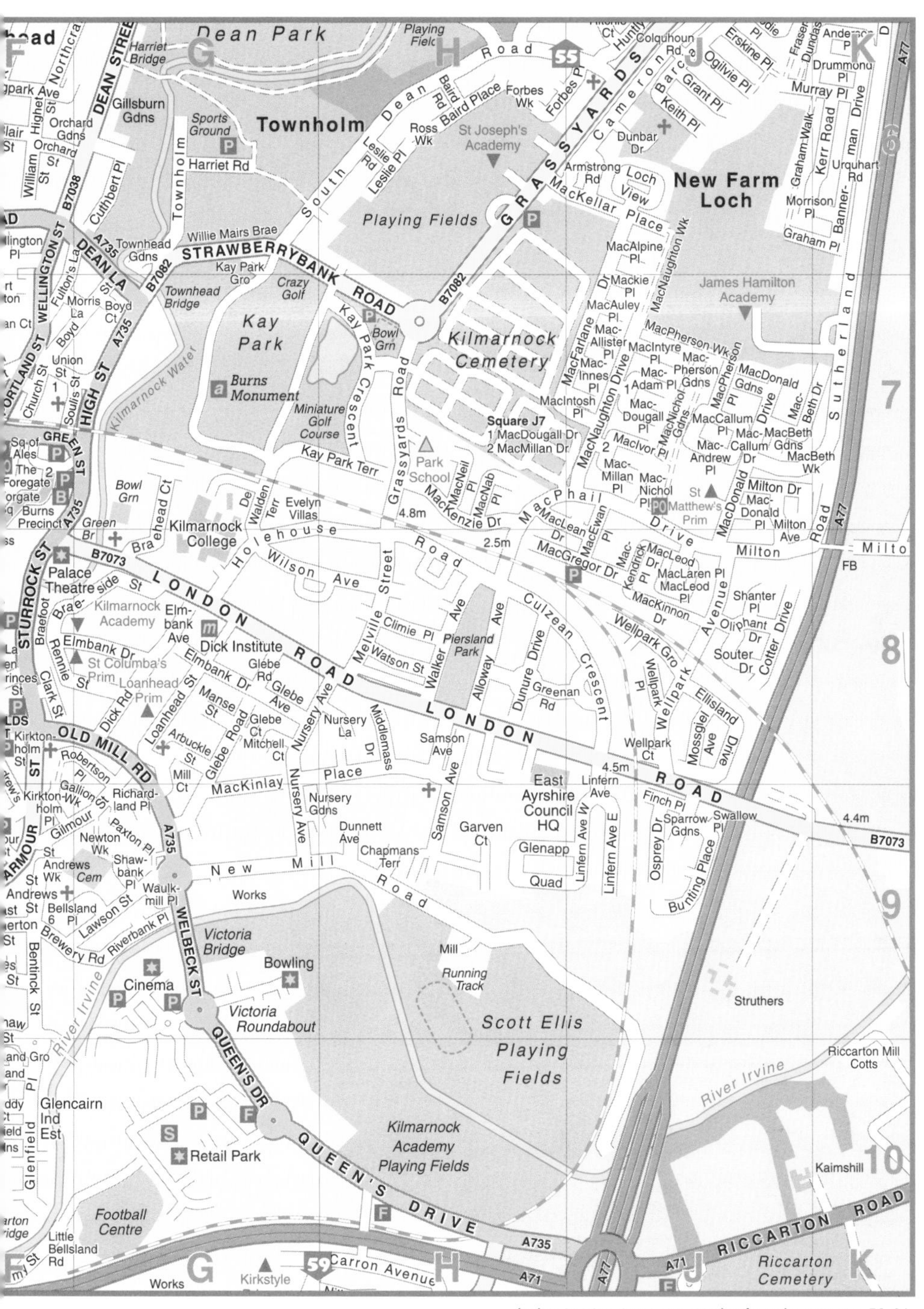

Dean Park
Townholm
Harriet Bridge
Gillsburn Gdns
Sports Ground
Harriet Rd
Playing Fields
St Joseph's Academy
South Dean Road
Baird Place
Forbes Wk
Ross Wk
Leslie Pl
GRASSYARDS
Cameron
Colquhoun Rd
Erskine Pl
Ogilvie Pl
Grant Pl
Keith Pl
Dunbar Dr
Armstrong Rd
Loch View
MacKellar Place
New Farm Loch
Murray Pl
Drummond Pl
Kerr Road
Graham Walk
Urquhart Rd
Morrison Pl
Graham Pl
Bannerman Drive
James Hamilton Academy
Sutherland Drive
DEAN STREET
Orchard Gdns
Orchard St
Cuthbert Pl
B7038
Willie Mairs Brae
Townhead Gdns
STRAWBERRYBANK ROAD
Kay Park Gro
Townhead Bridge
Crazy Golf
Kay Park
Burns Monument
Kilmarnock Water
Miniature Golf Course
Bowl Grn
Kay Park Crescent
Grassyards Road
B7082
Kilmarnock Cemetery
MacAlpine Pl
MacKie Pl
MacAuley Pl
MacNaughton Wk
MacPherson Wk
MacFarlane
MacAllister Pl
MacIntyre Pl
MacPherson Gdns
MacDonald Gdns
MacInnes Pl
MacAdam Pl
MacIntosh Pl
MacNaughton Drive
MacDougall Pl
MacCallum Drive
MacBeth Dr
MacBeth Gdns
MacBeth Wk
Square J7
1 MacDougall Dr
2 MacMillan Dr
MacIvor Pl
MacAndrew Pl
MacMillan Pl
MacNichol Pl
St Matthew's Prim
Milton Dr
MacDonald Pl
Milton Ave
Milton Road
Park School
MacNeil Pl
MacNab Pl
MacKenzie Dr
MacPhail Drive
MacLean Dr
MacEwan Pl
MacKendrick Pl
MacLeod Dr
MacLaren Pl
MacLeod Pl
MacGregor Dr
MacKinnon Dr
Avenue
Shanter Pl
Oliphant Dr
Souter Dr
Cotter Drive
Wellpark Gro
Wellpark Pl
Ellisland Drive
Mossgiel Ave
Wellpark Ct
Kay Park Terr
Walden Terr
Evelyn Villas
Holehouse Road
Kilmarnock College
Braehead Ct
Wilson Ave
Street
4.8m
2.5m
Green Br
B7073
Palace Theatre
LONDON ROAD
Kilmarnock Academy
Elmbank Ave
Dick Institute
Elmbank Dr
Glebe Rd
Glebe Ave
Climie Pl
Watson St
Melville St
Walker Ave
Piersland Park
Alloway Ave
Culzean Crescent
Dunure Drive
Greenan Rd
St Columba's Prim
Loanhead Prim
Loanhead St
Manse St
Glebe Road
Mitchell Ct
Nursery Ave
Nursery La
Middlemass Dr
Samson Ave
Arbuckle St
Mill Ct
MacKinlay Place
Nursery Gdns
Dunnett Ave
Chapmans Terr
Garven Ct
East Ayrshire Council HQ
Glenapp Quad
Linfern Ave
Linfern Ave W
Linfern Ave E
4.5m
Finch Pl
Sparrow Gdns
Swallow Pl
Osprey Dr
Bunting Place
4.4m
FB
STURROCK ST
HIGH ST
WELLINGTON ST
DEAN LA
A735
OLD MILL RD
Robertson Pl
Gallion Pl
Richardland Pl
Kirkton-holm St
Gilmour
Paxton Pl
Newton Wk
Shawbank Pl
St Andrews Wk
Cem
Waulkmill Pl
Bellsland Pl
Lawson St
Riverbank Pl
Brewery Rd
Bentinck St
New Mill Road
Works
Victoria Bridge
Bowling
Cinema
WELBECK ST
Victoria Roundabout
Mill
Running Track
Scott Ellis Playing Fields
Struthers
Riccarton Mill Cotts
River Irvine
QUEEN'S DR
QUEEN'S DRIVE
Glencairn Ind Est
Retail Park
Kilmarnock Academy Playing Fields
Football Centre
Little Bellsland Rd
Kirkstyle
Carron Avenue
A735
A71
A77
Kaimshill
RICCARTON ROAD
Riccarton Cemetery

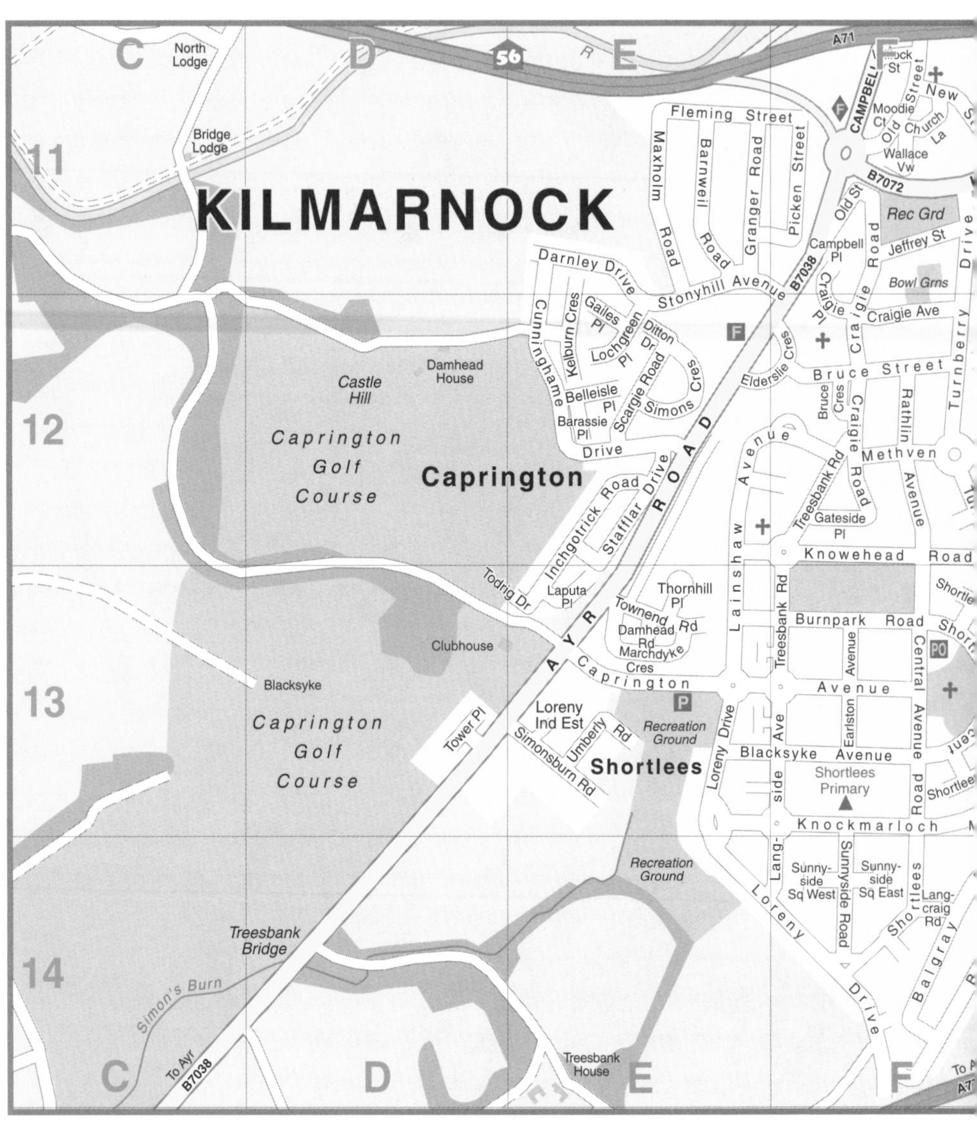

continued from page 55...

Bonnyton Road	D7
Boyd Court	G7
Boyd Street	G7
Boydston Way	J2
Brackenhill Avenue	G3
Braefoot	F8
Braehead Court	G8
Braeside Street	G8
Brailsford Crescent	C10
Bressay Place	H3
Brewery Road	F9
Bridge Lane	F8
Bridgehouse Court	G14
Bridgehousehill Road	F14
Bringan Road	F3
Brodick Road	C6
Brodie Place	J6
Broom Place	H11
Broomhill Quadrant	G12
Broomhill Road East	G12
Broomhill Road West	F12
Bruce Crescent	F12
Bruce Street	F12
Buchanan Place	G11
Bunting Place	J9
Burnfoot Place	E4
Burnpark Road	F13
Burns Avenue	G5
Burns Crescent	H3
Burns Precinct	F7
Burns Way	H3
Burnside Street	E10
Burra Drive	G2
Burray Drive	G2
Busbiehill Place	D7
Bussiehead Cottages	A3
Cairngorm Road	H13
Cairns Terrace	E7
Calder Place	G11
Caledonia Court	E7
Cameron Drive	J6
Campbell Place	F11
Campbell Street	F11
Campbeltown Drive	F5
Campsie Road	G13
Caprington Avenue	E13
Caprington Avenue	F13
Cardhu Crescent	D4
Cardhu Gardens	D4
Carmel Avenue	C6
Carmel Place	
Carmel Terrace	
Carron Avenue	G
Carron Avenue	H
Castle Drive	
Cedar Road	
Central Avenue	F
Cessock Place	H
Chapmans Terrace	
Charles Place	
Charles Street	
Cheapside Street	
Cherry Road	
Chestnut Place	
Cheviot Place	G
Church Lane	F
Church Street	

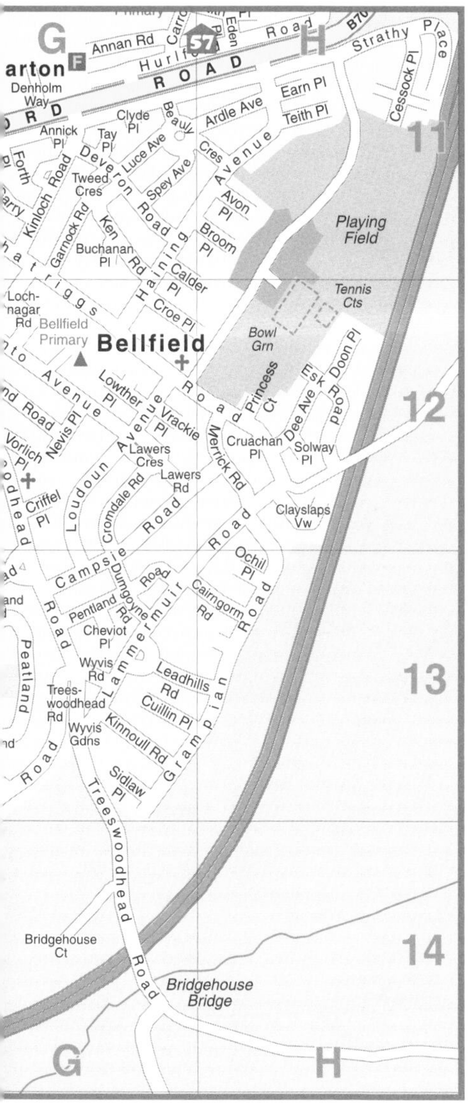

k Street	F8
Crescent	F5
slaps View	H12
ie Place	H8
e Place	G11
ege Wynd	F8
nsay Place	H2
uhoun Road	J6
monhead Road	F13
don Road	E4
ie Crescent	F5
er Drive	J8
ans Row	K9
gie Avenue	F12
gie Place	F12
gie Road	F12
hie Road	E6
Craufurdland Road	G3
Creigton Court	G3
Criffel Place	G12
Croe Place	G12
Croft Street	F7
Crofthead Avenue	G3
Cromdale Road	G12
Cross, The	F8
Crosshill Wynd	J2
Crosshouse Road	A4
Cruachan Place	H12
Cuillin Place	G13
Culloden Place	H5
Culzean Crescent	J8
Cumbrae Drive	H3
Cunninghame Drive	E12
Cuthbert Place	G6
Dalgarven Mews	J2
Dalwhinnie Crescent	D5
Dalwhinnie Gardens	D5
Damhead Road	E13
Darnley Drive	E11
Darvel Avenue	H2
Davaar Drive	H3
David Orr Street	E7
De Walden Drive	H3
De Walden Terrace	G7
Dean Court	F7
Dean Lane	G6
Dean Road	G5
Dean Street	G6
Dean Terrace	G5
Dean View	K4
Deanhill Lane	G5
Dee Avenue	H12
Denholm Way	G11
Deveron Road	G11
Dick Road	G8
Ditton Drive	E12
Dollars Row	J11
Donaldson Drive	K5
Donaldson Road	K5
Doon Place	H12
Douglas Street	F9
Drumclog Place	H5
Drummond Place	K6
Duff Place	J5
Dumgoyne Road	G13
Dunbar Drive	J6
Duncan Court	K4
Dundas Walk	J6
Dundonald Court	H2
Dundonald Place	E9
Dundonald Road	B10
Dundonald Road	E9
Dungavel Road	G12
Dunlop Street	F7
Dunn Mews	C8
Dunnett Avenue	H9
Dunollie Gardens	H2
Dunoon Avenue	F5
Dunskey Road	H2
Dunure Drive	H8
Dunure Place	H2
Earlston Avenue	F13
Earn Place	H11
East Gargieston Avenue	D10
East Netherton Street	F9
East Shaw Street	F9
East Woodstock Court	E8
Eday Crescent	F2
Eden Place	H11
Elderslie Crescent	F12
Ellis Lane	E8
Ellis Street	E8
Ellisland Drive	J8
Elmbank Avenue	G8
Elmbank Drive	G8
Eriskay Place	H3
Erskine Place	J6
Esk Road	H12
Esson Place	G5
Ettrick Crescent	F5
Evelyn Villas	G7
Failford Place	H4
Fair Isle Place	G2
Fairlie Avenue	D9
Fairyhill Place	E10
Fairyhill Road	E10
Faransay Place	G3
Farm Road	E5
Fenwick Close	J2
Fern Place	C9
Fetlar Drive	G2
Finch Place	J9
Finlayson Drive	K5
Fir Place	C9
Fleming Street	E11
Flotta Place	F2
Forbes Place	J6
Forbes Walk	H6
Foregate, The	F7
Forest Grove	H3
Forgate Square	F7
Forge Street	E7
Forth Place	G11
Fowlds Street	F8
Fraser Walk	J6
Fullarton Court	E7
Fullarton Street	E8
Fulton's Lane	F7
Furnace Court	K10
Gailes Place	E12
Gainford Place	F4
Gallion Walk	G8
Galrigside Road	D9
Galston Place	H2
Garden Street	F7
Gardrum Place	F4
Garnock Road	G11
Garrier Place	D6
Garry Place	G11
Garven Court	H9
Gateside Place	F12
Gibson Street	D7
Gillsburn Gardens	G6
Gilmour Street	F9
Glasgow Road	G4
Glasgow Road	H3
Glasgow Road	J1
Glassock Road	F3
Glebe Avenue	G8
Glebe Court	G8
Glebe Road	G8
Glen Affric Place	C10
Glen Afton Court	C10
Glen Clova Gardens	C10
Glen Farrar Way	C10
Glen Lyon Crescent	C10
Glen Nevis Place	C10
Glen Orchy Place	C10
Glen Orrin Avenue	C10
Glen Shiel Crescent	C10
Glen Trool Walk	C9
Glen Truim View	C10
Glenapp Quadrant	H9
Glencairn Square	F9
Glencraigs Drive	F3
Glenfield Gardens	F10
Glenfield Place	F10
Glenlivet Place	H5
Graham Place	J6
Graham Walk	J6
Grampian Road	H13
Grange Place	F8
Grange Street	F8
Grange Terrace	D7
Granger Road	E11
Grant Place	J6
Grassyards Road	H6
Grassyards Road	H7
Green Street	F7
Greenan Road	H8
Greenholm Street	F10
Grougar Drive	H3
Grougar Gardens	H4
Grougar Road	K8
Haining Avenue	G11
Hareshaw Drive	G3
Hareshaw Gardens	G3
Harperland Drive	D9
Harriet Road	G6

continued overleaf....

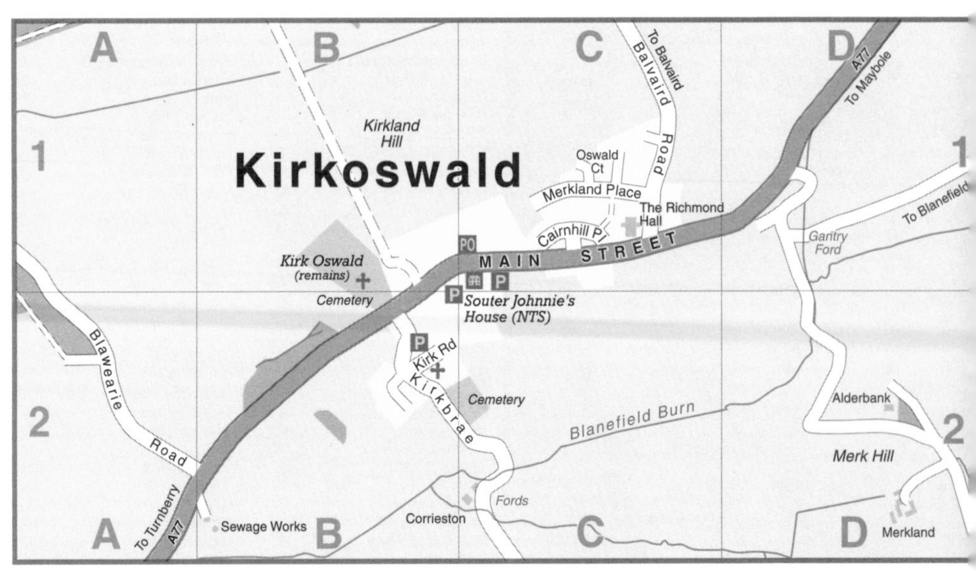

continued from page 59...

Harris Place H3
Hawthorn Square D8
Hazel Avenue D9
Heather Place D9
Hestan Place H3
High Church Lane (1) F7
High Glencairn Street F9
High Street G7
Highet Street F6
Highfield Avenue G5
Hill Street F6
Hillbank Road E5
Hillhead Square F5
Hillpark Drive F6
Holehouse Road G8
Holly Place D7
Hollybush Place H2
Holmes Crescent D9
Holmes Farm Road D10
Holmes Park Avenue D10
Holmes Park Crescent D10
Holmes Park Gardens D10
Holmes Park View D10
Holmes Park Wynd D10
Holmes Road D10
Holmes Village D10
Holmlands Place D10
Holmlea Drive E10
Holmlea Place E10
Holmquarry Road F10
Howard Court F8
Howard Park Drive E9
Howard Street E8
Huntly Court J5
Huntly Place J6
Hurlford Road F11
Hurlford Road G11
Inchgotrick Road E12
Inchmurrin Drive G3
Ingram Place G5
Inkerman Place E7
Innellan Drive F5
Invercloy Place E4
Iona Place G3
Irvine Road B7
Islay Place H3
James Johnston Place G5
James Little Street F9
James Shaw Lane (2) F7
James Sym Crescent E10
Jasmine Road C9
Jeffrey Street F11
John Burtt Place G5
John Dickie Street F7
John Finnie Street F8
John Kennedy Place G5
John Walker Drive D4, D5
Jura Road G3
Kaimshill Cottages K10
Katrine Court G11
Kay Park Crescent H7
Kay Park Grove G6
Kay Park Terrace G7
Keith Place J6
Kelburn Crescent E12
Ken Road G11
Kennedy Court J5
Kennedy Drive J5, K5
Kennedy Street F10
Kerr Road K6
Kilmarnock Road A7
Kilmaurs Road E4
Kilmory Place E4
King Street F8
Kingsford Place H3
Kingswell Avenue G3
Kinloch Road G11
Kinnoull Road G13
Kirkland Avenue E5
Kirkton Road F3
Kirktonholm Place F9
Kirktonholm Street F8
Kirkwall Place G3
Kirn Road F6
Knockinlaw Mount F4
Knockinlaw Road F4
Knockmarloch Drive F13
Knowehead Road F12
Laburnum Road C9
Lainshaw Avenue E13
Lammermuir Road G13
Landsborough Drive G5
Langcraig Road F14
Langlands Brae F7
Langlands Street F7
Langside Avenue F13
Laputa Place E13
Larch Place D8
Largs Avenue H5
Lauder Court J5
Laurel Place D9
Lauriston Way H2
Lawers Crescent G12
Lawers Road G12
Lawson Street G9
Leadhills Road G13
Lennox Crescent D7
Lerwick Place G2
Leslie Place H6
Leslie Road H6
Leven Avenue G5
Lewis Drive H3
Lilac Place E8
Lime Place D8
Lindsay Drive J5
Lindsay Street E8
Linfern Avenue East J10
Linfern Avenue West J10
Linfern Avenue J8
Lismore Road G3
Lister Street A7
Little Bellsland Road F10
Livingstone Court J5
Loanfoot Avenue D7
Loanhead Street G8
Loch View J6
Lochgreen Place E12
Lochmaben Wynd H2
Lochnagar Road G12
Lochranza Court H2
Lomond Road G12
London Road G8
Longpark Avenue F6
Loreny Drive E14
Loudoun Avenue G12
Low Church Lane (3) F8
Low Glencairn Street F10
Lowther Place G12
Luce Avenue G11
Lugar Wynd H2
MacAdam Place
MacAllister Place
MacAlpine Place
MacAndrew Place
MacAuley Place
MacBeth Drive
MacBeth Gardens
MacBeth Walk
MacCallum Drive
MacCallum Place
MacDonald Drive
Macdonald Gardens
MacDonald Place
MacDougall Drive (1)
MacDougall Place
MacEwan Place
MacFarlane Drive
MacGregor Drive
MacNichol Gardens
MacNichol Place
MacInnes Place
MacIntosh Place
MacIntyre Place
MacIvor Place
MacKellar Place
MacKendrick Place
MacKenzie Drive
MacKinlay Place
MacKinnon Drive
MacLaren Place
MacLean Drive
MacLeod Drive
MacLeod Place
MacMillan Drive (2)
MacMillan Place
MacNab Place
MacNaughton Drive
MacNaughton Walk
MacNeil Place
MacNichol Gardens
MacNichol Place
MacPhail Drive
MacPherson Gardens
MacPherson Place
MacPherson Walk
McLelland Drive
Machrie Road

kie Place J7
Road K9
or Avenue G4
se Street G8
le Place D8
chdyke Crescent E13
iew Smith Avenue E10
chllne Court H2
nolm Road E11
well Court K5
lewood Road F4
ille Street H8
ick Road H12
ven Avenue F12
ven Place G12
's Lane E9
llemass Drive H8
on Road F13
Court G9
Street F9
ill Terrace E3
n Avenue J7
n Drive J7
n Road J8
hell Court G8
tgomery Place F6
tgomery Street F6
die Court F11
rfield Avenue D10
is Lane G7
ison Place J6
on Place F7
en Avenue F5
sgiel Avenue J8
shead Road F13
side Place F4
nt Avenue D10
nt Place D10
nt Village C9
end Road F3
o Avenue D7
o Place E6
e Avenue G4
ay Place J6
on Street F8
s Place G12
Mill Road G9
Street F11
ands Drive E4
ands Place E4
milns Gardens H2
ton Walk G9
Place H11
n Court K4
n Gargieston Road C10
n Hamilton Place E7
n Hamilton Street E8
ncraig Road F6
ery Avenue G8
ery Gardens H9
ery Lane H8
ery Street F9
Place D8
Place H13
tree Place H2
ie Place J6
rvine Road E8
Mill Road G8
Street F11
ant Drive J8
Road D8
ank Drive E4
ard Gardens F6
ard Street F6
ey Drive G3
ey Drive J9
burn Avenue H5
Lane F7
Park Street E7
Paxton Place G9
Peace Avenue D7
Peatland Quadrant G13
Peatland Road G13
Pentland Road G13
Picken Street F11
Pine Road D9
Porter Drive C10
Porting Cross Place H2
Portland Place E8
Portland Road E8
Portland Street F7
Portree Avenue G2
Pottery Place F6
Priestland Close H2
Primrose Place D7
Princes Street F8
Princess Court H12
Queen Street F8
Queen's Drive H10
Raasay Place G2
Raithburn Avenue F4
Ralston Drive K8
Rankin Court J5
Rathlin Avenue F12
Redding Avenue F4
Rennie Street F8
Riccarton Road J10
Richardland Place G9
Richardland Road (6) F9
Ritchie Court J6
Riverbank Place G9
Robert Creighton Place F7
Robert Noble Place D6
Robert Stewart Place E7
Robertson Place G8
Rona Place H3
Rosebank Place F6
Ross Walk H6
Rothesay Place F5
Rousay Wynd G2
Rowallan Drive G4
Rowan Place D9
Rowanhill Place D9
Rugby Crescent D9
Rugby Road D9
Rumford Place J2
Russell Court J5
St Andrew's Court (5) F8
St Andrew's Street F8
St Andrews Street F9
St Andrew's Walk F9
St Marnock Place (4) F8
St Marnock Street F8
St Maur's Crescent E5
St Maur's Place E5
Samson Avenue H8
Sanda Place G3
Sandbed Lane F8
Sandbed Street F8
Sannox Road C6
Scalpay Place G3
Scargie Road E12
Scott Crescent E9
Scott Road E10
Scott Road E9
Seaford Street E8
Seright Crescent K9
Seright Square K8
Shanks Court F6
Shanter Place J8
Shawbank Place G9
Shetland Drive G2
Shiskine Drive E4
Shortlees Crescent F13
Shortlees Road F14
Sidlaw Place G13
Silverwood Road K8
Simons Crescent E12
Simonsburn Road E13
Simpson Street A6
Sinclair Court J5
Skene Road J5
Skye Gardens G2
Smiddy Court F10
Smillie Place C10
Solway Place H12
Soulis Street F7
Souter Drive J8
South Dean Road G6
South Gargieston Drive C10
South Hamilton Court E8
South Hamilton Place E9
South Hamilton Street E9
Southcraig Drive G2
Southook Road D6
Sparrow Gardens J9
Spey Avenue G11
Springhill Gardens E8
Springhill Place E8
Square of Ales F7
Stafflar Drive E12
Stafford Street F6
Station Drive K10
Stevenson Street D7
Stewarton Crescent H2
Stirling Avenue C7
Stirling Crescent C7
Stonyhill Avenue E11
Stornoway Drive G2
Strand Street F7
Strawberrybank Road G6
Stronsay Place G3
Struthers Avenue K8
Sturrock Street F8
Sunnyside Road F14
Sunnyside Square East F14
Sunnyside Square West F14
Sutherland Drive K7
Swallow Place J9
Talisker Avenue E4
Tannock Street F10
Tarbolton Place J2
Tay Place G11
Teith Place H11
Thirdpart Place D9
Thomas Baird Gardens F5
Thomson Street F6
Thorn Terrace G4
Thornhill Place E13
Tinto Avenue G12
Titchfield Street F9
Titwood Drive F4
Todhill Avenue F4
Todrig Drive E13
Toponthank Lane G2
Tourhill Road E4
Tower Place D13
Townend Road E13
Townhead Gardens G6
Townholm G6
Treesbank Road F12
Treesbank Road F13
Treeswoodhead Road G12
Trondra Gardens G2
Turnberry Drive F12
Turner Place G5
Tweed Crescent G11
Uist Lane G2
Umberly Road E13
Underwood Place F13
Union Street F7
Urquhart Road K6
Vatersay Place G2
Vorlich Place G12
Vrackie Place G12
Waddell Court F4
Walker Avenue H8
Wallace Street E9
Wallace View F11
Wallacehill Road F12
Wallacetown Avenue H2
Walnut Road C9
Wardneuk Drive G4
Wards Place F9
Warwickhill Place E7
Warwickhill Road D7
Water Lane F8
Waterside Court F8
Waterside Street F8
Watson Street H8
Waulkmill Place G9
Waverley Avenue C7
Welbeck Street G9
Wellington Avenue K8
Wellington Place F6
Wellington Street F7
Wellpark Avenue J8
Wellpark Court J8
Wellpark Grove J8
Wellpark Place J8
West Fullarton Street E7
West George Street F7
West Langlands Street E7
West Netherton Street F9
West Shaw Street F9
West Woodstock Court E8
West Woodstock Street E8
Western Place G4
Western Road F5
Westfield Road J2
Westmoor Crescent D9
Westray Drive G2
Whatriggs Road G11
William Street F6
Willie Mairs Brae G6
Willie Ross Place K4
Willock Street F11
Willow Road D8
Wilson Avenue G8
Witch Road F6
Witchill Place F6
Witchknowe Avenue F11
Witchknowe Court F12
Witchknowe Road F12
Woodhill Road E5
Woodlands Grove H4
Woodlands Place G4
Woodside Avenue D10
Woodstock Place E7
Woodstock Street E8
Wyvis Gardens G13
Wyvis Road G13
Yorke Place D7

Index to Kirkoswald

Balvaird Road C1
Blawearie Road A2
Cairnhill Place C1
Kirk Road B2
Kirkbrae B2
Oswald Court C1
Main Street C1
Merkland Place C1

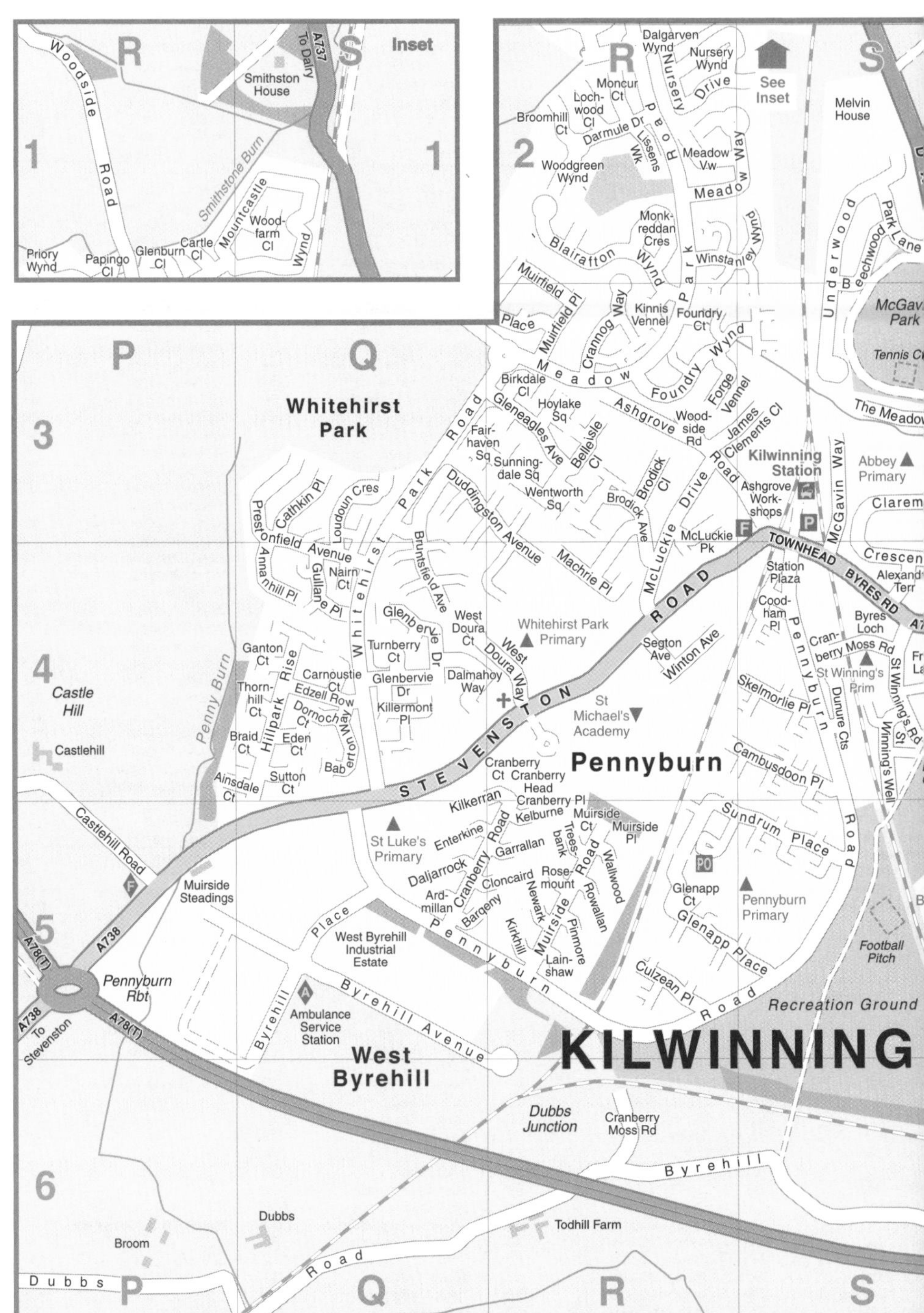
Inset
Woodside Road
Smithston House
A737 To Dalry
Smithstone Burn
Mountcastle
Wood-farm Cl
Wynd
Priory Wynd
Papingo Cl
Glenburn Cl
Cartle Cl
See Inset
Melvin House
Whitehirst Park
Kilwinning Station
Pennyburn
Castle Hill
Castlehill
Penny Burn
Stevenston Road
Townhead
Byres Rd
McGavin Park
Abbey Primary
Whitehirst Park Primary
St Michael's Academy
St Luke's Primary
Pennyburn Primary
St Winning's Prim
Muirside Steadings
West Byrehill Industrial Estate
Ambulance Service Station
West Byrehill
Pennyburn Rbt
To Stevenston
KILWINNING
Recreation Ground
Football Pitch
Dubbs Junction
Cranberry Moss Rd
Byrehill
Todhill Farm
Dubbs
Broom
Dubbs Road

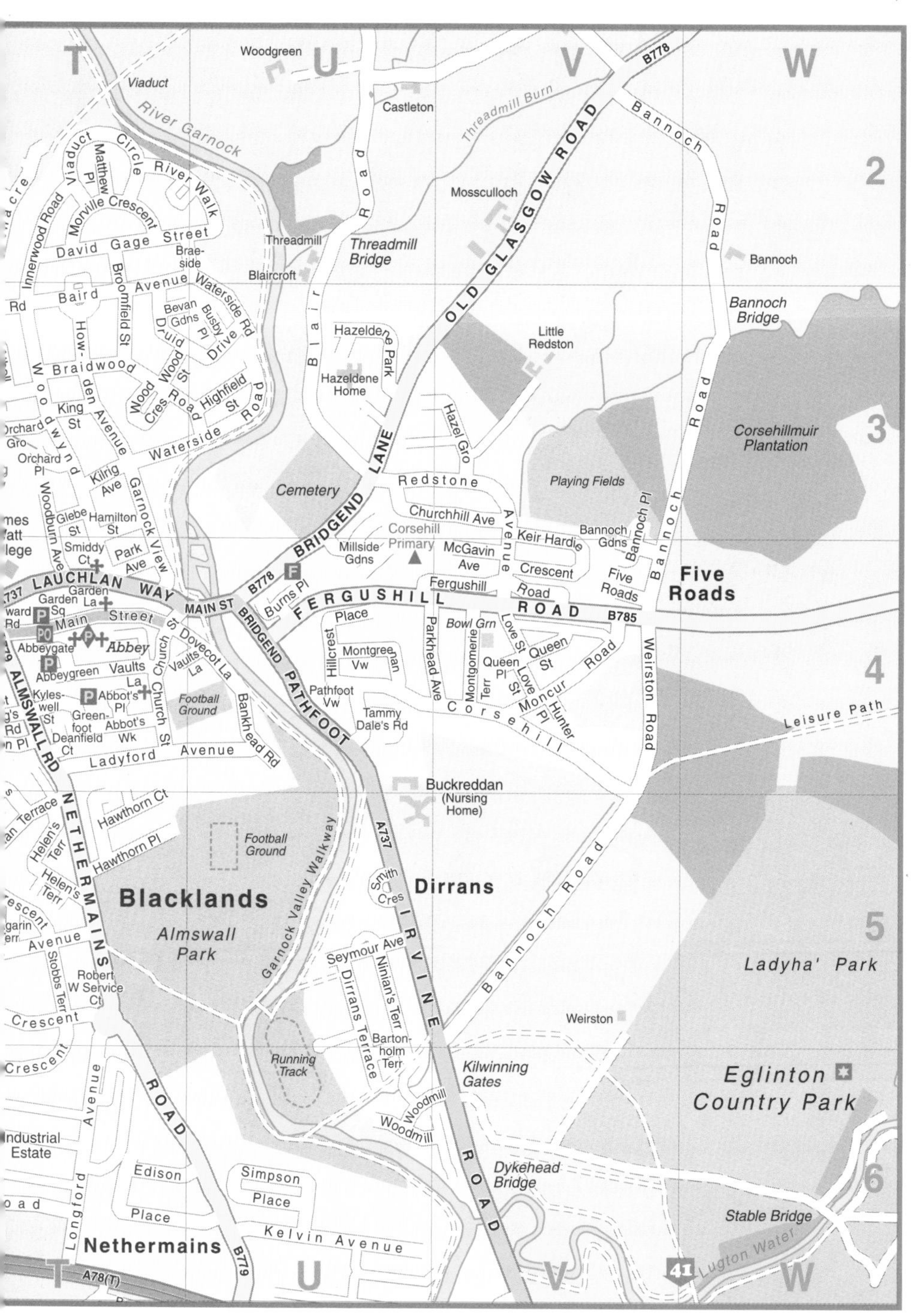

Index to street names can be found starting on page 98

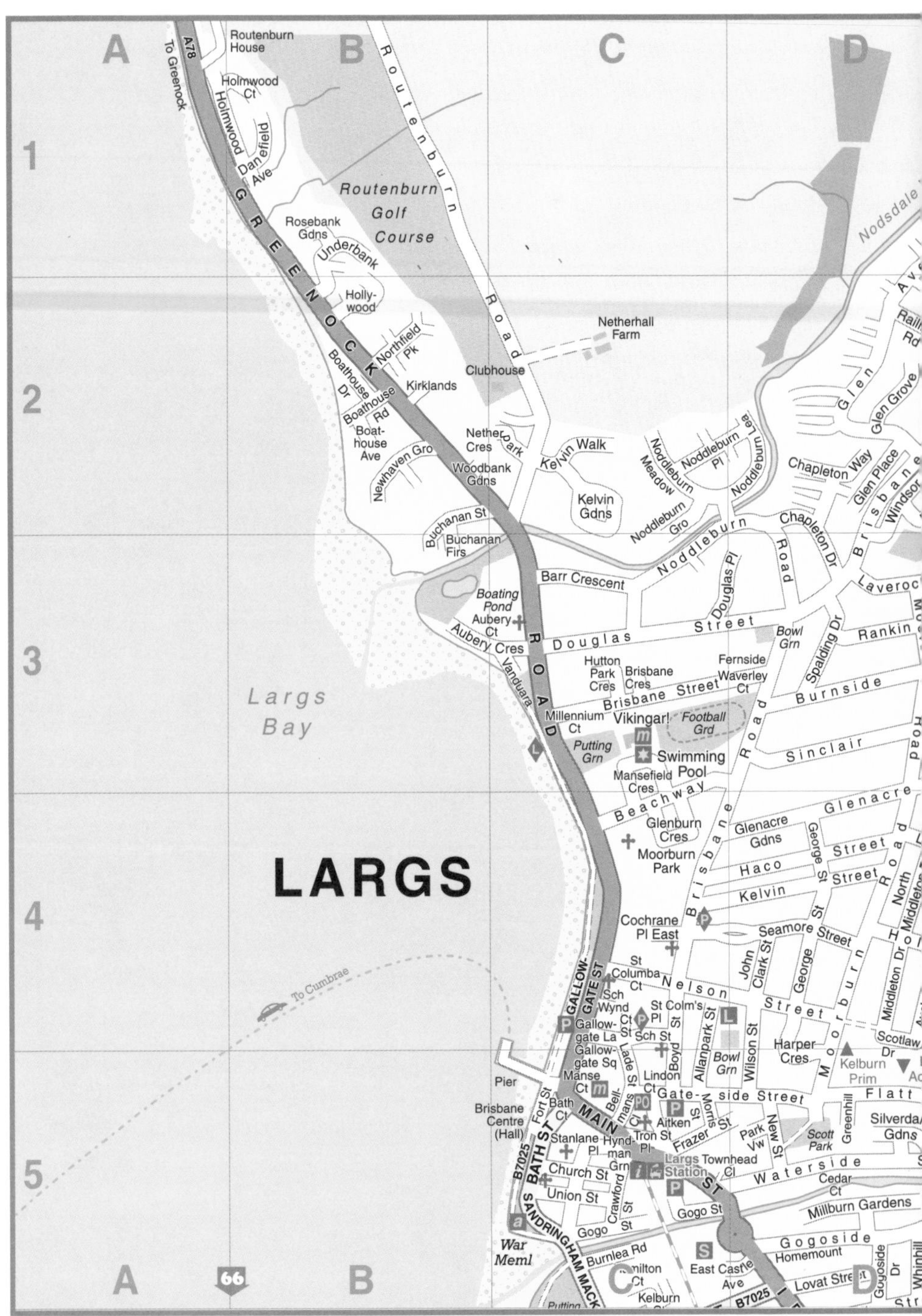
LARGS
Largs Bay
Routenburn Golf Course
Greenock Road
Routenburn Road
A78
To Greenock
Routenburn House
Holmwood Ct
Danefield Ave
Rosebank Gdns
Underbank
Hollywood
Northfield Pk
Kirklands
Boathouse Dr
Boathouse Rd
Boathouse Ave
Newhaven Gro
Nether Cres
Nether Park
Woodbank Gdns
Clubhouse
Netherhall Farm
Kelvin Walk
Kelvin Gdns
Noddleburn Meadow
Noddleburn Pl
Noddleburn Lea
Noddleburn Gro
Noddleburn
Buchanan St
Buchanan Firs
Barr Crescent
Boating Pond
Aubery Ct
Aubery Cres
Douglas Street
Douglas Pl
Chapleton Way
Chapleton Road
Chapleton Dr
Glen Place
Glen Grove
Glen
Nodsdale
Brisbane
Windsor
Laveroc
Hutton Park Cres
Brisbane Cres
Brisbane Street
Fernside
Waverley Ct
Bowl Grn
Spalding Dr
Rankin
Burnside
Millennium Ct
Vikingar!
Football Grd
Putting Grn
Swimming Pool
Mansefield Cres
Beachway
Vanduara
Sinclair
Glenburn Cres
Glenacre Gdns
Glenacre
George St
Street
Moorburn Park
Haco Street
Kelvin Street
North
Middleton
Cochrane Pl East
Seamore Street
John Clark St
George St
Moorburn
Middleton Dr
St Columba Ct
Nelson Street
Sch Wynd
St Colm's Pl
Gallowgate St
Gallowgate La
Gallowgate Sq
Sch St
Lade St
Boyd St
Allanpark St
Wilson St
Harper Cres
Kelburn Prim
Scotlaw Dr
Manse Ct
Lindon Ct
Gateside Street
Flatt
Pier
Brisbane Centre (Hall)
Fort St
Bath Ct
Bellmans Cl
Aitken St
Morris St
Frazer St
Tron St
Tron Pl
Park Vw
New St
Scott Park
Greenhill
Silverdale Gdns
Stanlane Pl
Hyndman Grn
Main St
Largs Station
Townhead Cl
Waterside
Cedar Ct
B7025
Bath St
Church St
Union St
Crawford St
Gogo St
Millburn Gardens
Gogoside
Homemount
Gogoside Dr
Whinhill
Sandringham
Mack
War Meml
Burnlea Rd
Hamilton Ct
Kelburn
East Castle Ave
Lovat Street
Putting
To Cumbrae
A B C D
1 2 3 4 5
66

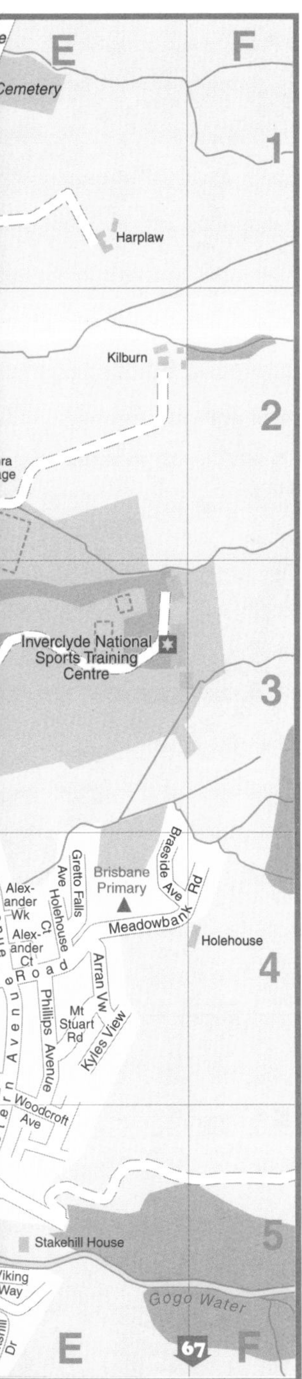

Index to Largs

Acre Avenue D7
Aitken Street C5
Alexander Avenue E3
Alexander Court E4
Alexander Walk E4
Allanpark Street C4
Anthony Court D7
Anthony Road D7
Arran View E4
Aubery Court B3
Aubery Crescent B3
Auchenmaid Drive D4
Bankhouse Avenue D6
Bankhouse Crescent D6
Bankhouse Grove E6
Barr Crescent C3
Bath Court C5
Bath Street C5
Beachway C4
Bellmans Close C5
Bellsdale Avenue E5
Blackdales Avenue D6
Blythswood Crescent D6
Boathouse Avenue B2
Boathouse Drive B2
Boathouse Road B2
Bowen Craig Walk D8
Bowen Craig D7
Boyd Street C4
Braeside Avenue E4
Brisbane Crescent C3
Brisbane Glen Road D3
Brisbane Road C4
Brisbane Street C3
Broom Court D6
Broomfield Crescent C6
Broomfield Place C6
Broomfield C6
Buchanan Firs B3
Buchanan Street B2
Burnlea Road C5
Burnside Road D3
Burnside Way E3
Carlton Court E2
Castle Bay Court C6
Castlehill Drive D5
Cathcart Road D6
Cedar Court D5
Chapelton Drive D2
Chapelton Way D2
Charles Street C6
Church Street C5
Cochrane Place East C4
Court Street C4
Crawford Street C5
Cunningham Drive D6
Curlinghall D6
Dalry Road E7
Danefield Avenue B1
Douglas Place C3
Douglas Street C3
Duffield Drive D7
East Castle Avenue C5
Eastern Avenue E5
Fernside D3
Flatt Road D5
Fort Street C5
Frazer Street C5
Gallowgate Lane C4
Gallowgate Square C4
Gallowgate Street C4
Gateside Street C5
George Street D4
Glen Avenue D2
Glen Grove D2
Glen Place D2
Glenacre Drive D4
Glenacre Gardens D4
Glenburn Crescent C4
Gogo Street C5
Gogoside Drive D5
Gogoside Road D5
Greenhill D5
Greenock Road B1
Greeto Falls Avenue E4
Haco Street D4
Halkshill Drive E5
Hamilton Court C5
Hamilton Drive D6
Harper Crescent D4
Haylie Brae E7
Haylie Gardens D6
Haylie Neuk D6
Hill Street C6
Holehouse Court E4
Holehouse Road D4
Hollywood B2
Holmwood Court B1
Holmwood A1
Homemount D5
Hutcheson Drive D7
Hutton Park Crescent C3
Hyndman Green C5
Inverclyde View D2
Irvine Road D5
Irvine Road E8
John Clark Street D4
John Street C6
Kelburn Court C6
Kelvin Gardens C2
Kelvin Street D4
Kelvin Walk C2
Kilburn Water E1
Kirklands B2
Kyles View E4
Lade Street C5
Laverock Drive D3
Lindsay Crescent D4
Lindon Court C5
Linn Avenue E4
Lovat Street D5
Mackerston Place C6
Main Street C5
Manse Court C5
Mansefield Crescent C3
May Street D6
Meadowbank Road E4
Middleton Drive D4
Milburn Gardens D5
Millennium Court C3
Moorburn Park C4
Moorburn Road D3
Morris Street C5
Mount Stuart Road E4
Nelson Street C4
Netherhall C2
Netherpark Crescent C2
New Street D5
Newhaven Grove B2
Noddleburn Grove C3
Noddleburn Lea D2
Noddleburn Meadow C2
Noddleburn Place C2
Noddleburn Road C3
North Middleton Drive D4
Northfield Park B2
Park View D5
Paton Quadrant E4
Pencil View D8
Phillips Avenue E4
Queens Avenue D4
Raillies Avenue D2
Raillies Road D2
Rankin Drive D3
Rockland Park D8
Rosebank Gardens B1
Roundel, The E4
Routenburn Road B1
Royal Avenue D4
St Colm's Place C4
St Columba Court C4
Sandringham C5
School Street C4
School Wynd C4
Scotlaw Drive D4
Scott Crescent E6
Scott Drive E5
Scott Street D6
Seabank Avenue D7
Seamore Street D4
Seaway Court D7
Silverae Court D6
Silverdale Gardens D5
Sinclair Drive D3
Sinclair Terrace E3
Spalding Drive D3
Springfield Gardens D6
Stakehill D5
Stanlane Place C5
Townhead Close C5
Trigoni Court D7
Tron Place C5
Underbank B1
Union Street C5
Vanduara C3
Viking Way E5
Walkerston Avenue D7
Warren Park Mews D7
Warrenpark Road D7
Waterside Street D5
Waverley Court D3
Whinhill Avenue D5
Wilson Street D4
Windsor Gardens D2
Woodbank Gardens B2
Woodcroft Avenue E5

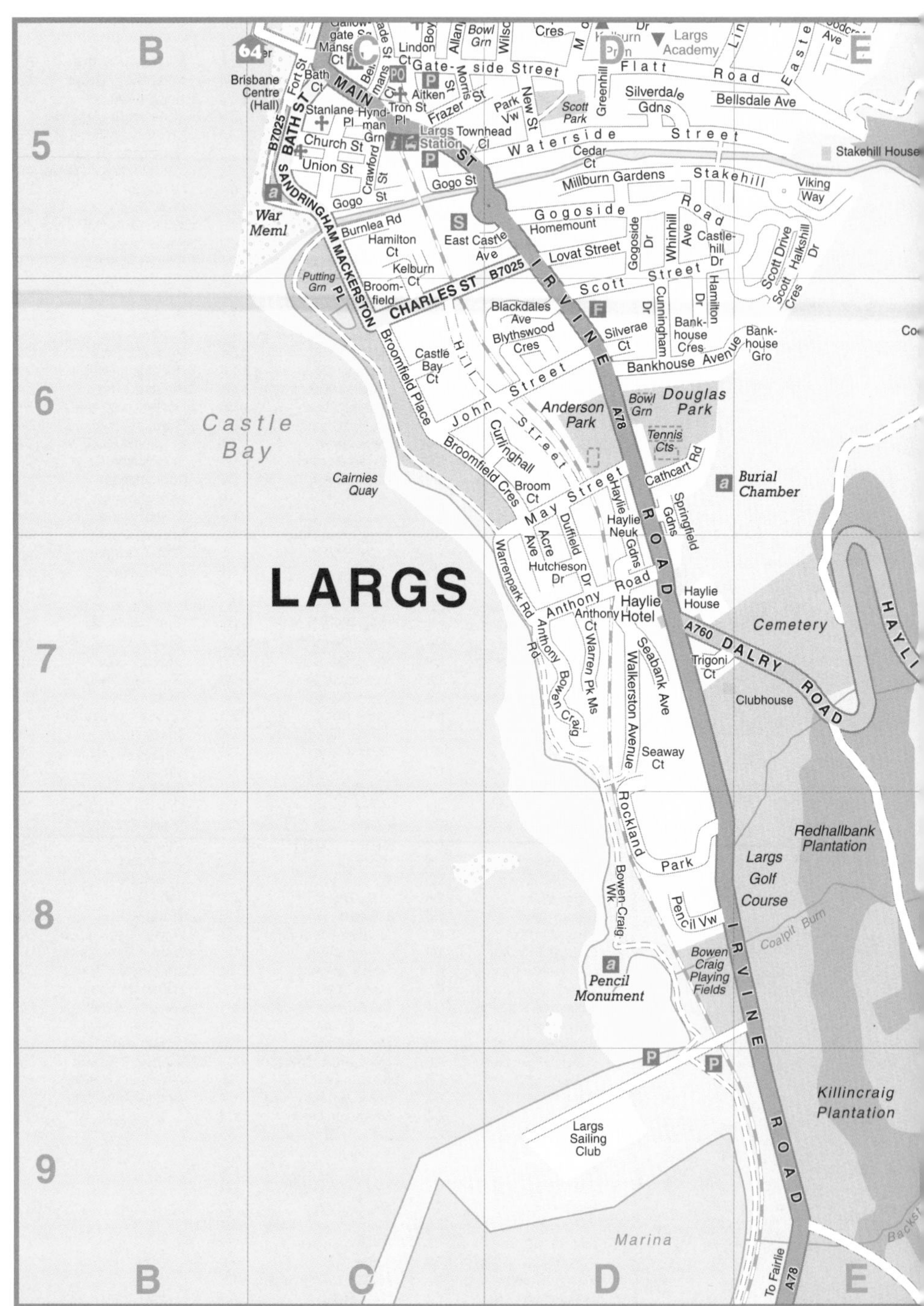

Index to street names can be found on page 65

Index to Logan & Lugar

Baillie Drive	C3	Park Terrace	B2
Boswell Crescent	B3	Paterson Avenue	B3
Braehead Place	C2	Peesweep Brae	B2
Bryce Avenue	C3	Rigg Road	B1
Craigston Square	C2	River View	C2
Dixton Avenue	B3	Thornwood Drive	B2
Eglinton Drive	C3		
Glen Avenue	B3		
Glenmuir Crescent	B3		
Glenmuir Road	B4		
Glenmuir Water Road	D4		
Holmhead Crescent	B3		
Logan Avenue	B4		
Logangate Terrace	B4		
Loganhill Road	C4		
Muirkirk Road	C1		

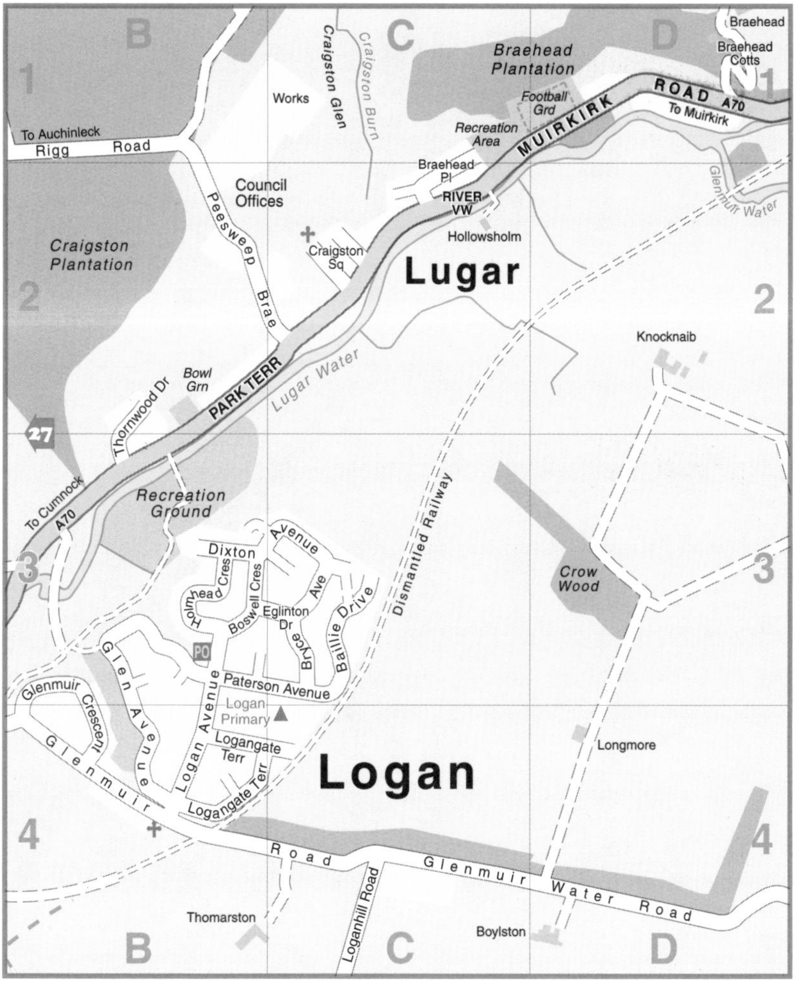

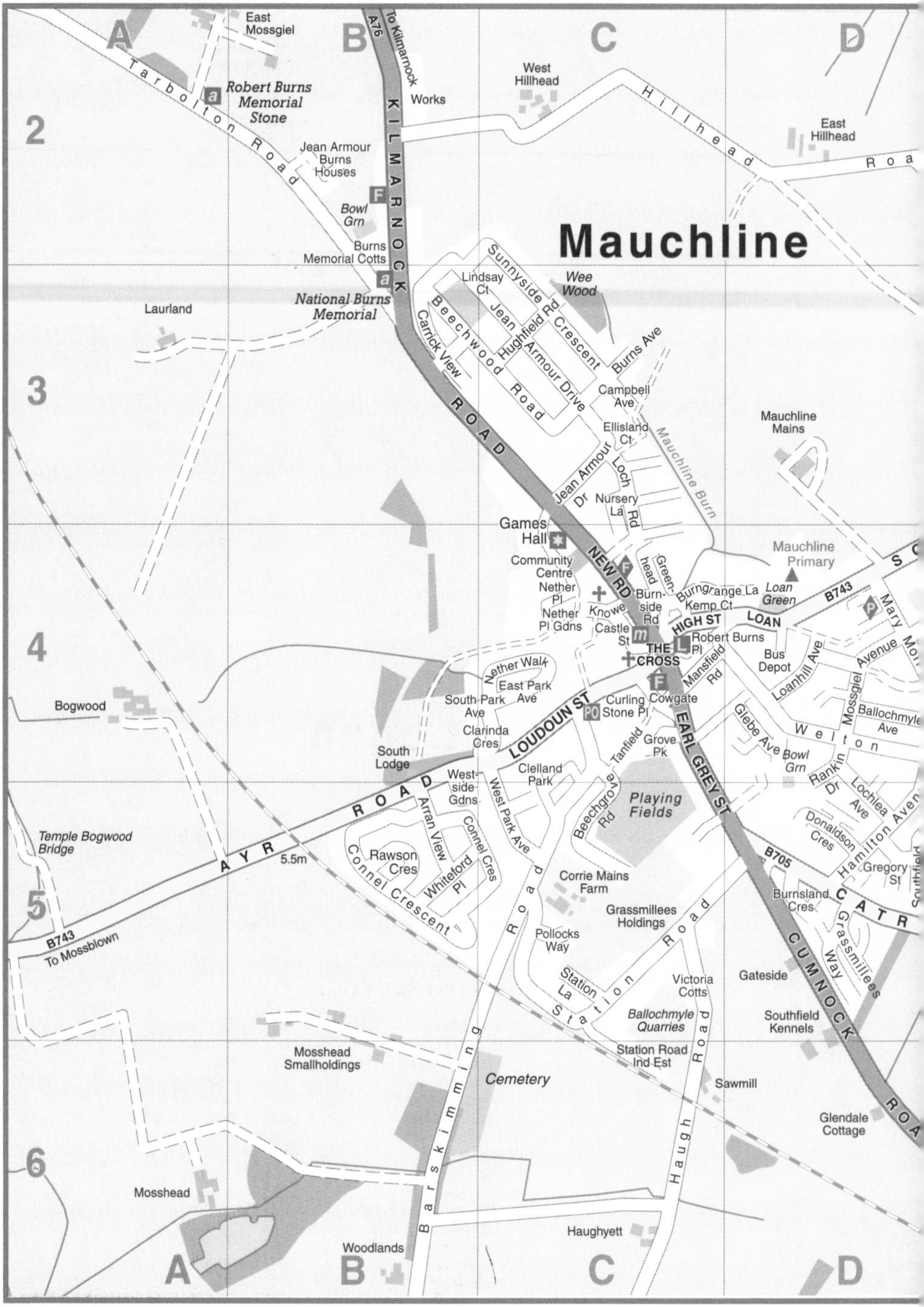

A B C D

2 3 4 5 6

Mauchline

East Mossgiel
To Kilmarnock
A76
West Hillhead
Tarbolton Road
Robert Burns Memorial Stone
Works
Hillhead Road
East Hillhead
Jean Armour Burns Houses
KILMARNOCK ROAD
Bowl Grn
Burns Memorial Cotts
Sunnyside Crescent
Lindsay Ct
Wee Wood
National Burns Memorial
Laurland
Beechwood Road
Jean Armour Drive
Hughfield Rd
Carrick View
Burns Ave
Campbell Ave
Ellisland Ct
Mauchline Mains
Mauchline Burn
Jean Armour Dr
Loch Rd
Nursery La
Games Hall
Community Centre
NEW RD
Green-head
Mauchline Primary
Nether Pl
Burn-side Rd
Burngrange La
Loan Green
B743
Nether Pl Gdns
Knowe
Kemp Ct
HIGH ST
LOAN
Mary
Castle St
Robert Burns Pl
THE CROSS
Bus Depot
Loanhill Ave
Avenue
Mossgiel Avenue
Nether Walk
East Park Ave
Mansfield Rd
Bogwood
South Park Ave
Curling Stone Pl
Cowgate
Ballochmyle Ave
LOUDOUN ST
Clarinda Cres
Tanfield
Glebe Ave
Welton
Grove Pk
Bowl Grn
South Lodge
Clelland Park
EARL GREY ST
Rankin Dr
Lochlea Ave
West-side Gdns
West Park Ave
Playing Fields
Hamilton Ave
Beechgrove Rd
Arran View
Connel Cres
Donaldson Cres
Temple Bogwood Bridge
AYR ROAD
5.5m
Rawson Cres
B705
Gregory St
Southfield
Whiteford Pl
Corrie Mains Farm
Burnsland Cres
CATR
Connel Crescent
Grassmillees Holdings
Grassmillees Way
B743
To Mossblown
Pollocks Way
Station Road
CUMNOCK ROAD
Gateside
Station La
Victoria Cotts
Station
Ballochmyle Quarries
Southfield Kennels
Barskimming Road
Mosshead Smallholdings
Station Road Ind Est
Cemetery
Sawmill
Haugh Road
Glendale Cottage
Mosshead
Haughyett
Woodlands

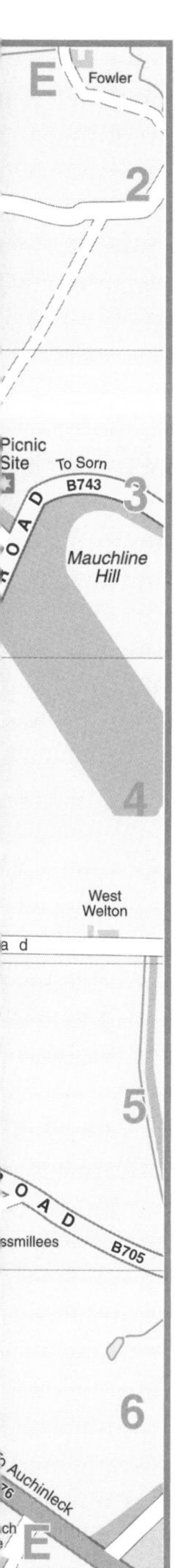

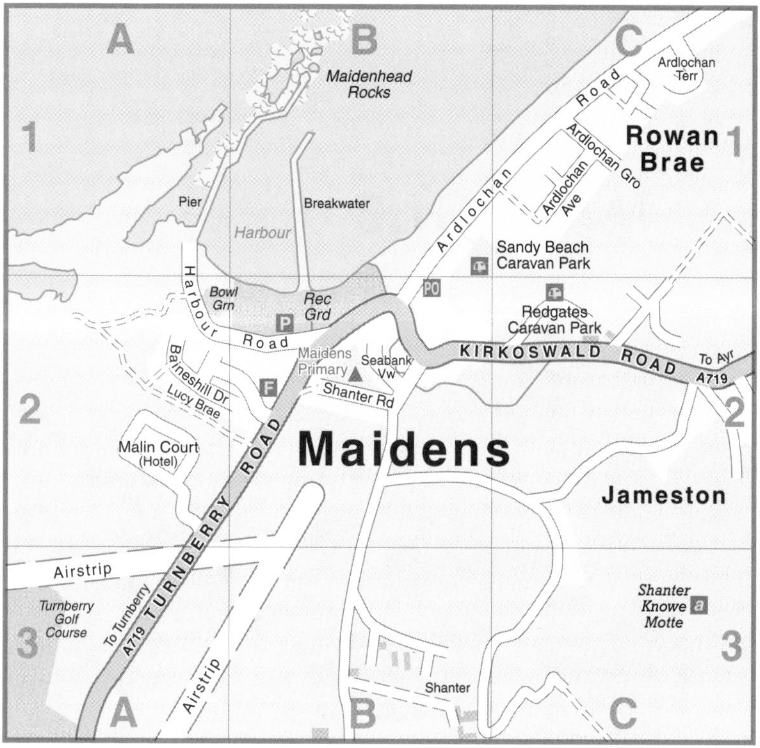

A B C
1
Maidenhead Rocks
Ardlochan Terr
Rowan Brae
Ardlochan Road
Ardlochan Gro
Ardlochan Ave
Pier
Breakwater
Harbour
Sandy Beach Caravan Park
Harbour Road
Bowl Grn
Rec Grd
PO
Redgates Caravan Park
Maidens Primary
Seabank Vw
KIRKOSWALD ROAD
To Ayr A719
2
Baineshill Dr
Lucy Brae
Shanter Rd
Malin Court (Hotel)
Maidens
Jameston
TURNBERRY ROAD
Airstrip
Turnberry Golf Course
To Turnberry A719
Shanter Knowe Motte
Shanter
3
A B C

Index to Mauchline

Alexander Terrace D4
Arran View B5
Auld Avenue D4
Ayr Road B5
Ballochmyle Avenue D4
Barskimming Road B6
Beechgrove Road C5
Beechwood Road B3
Burngrange Lane C4
Burns Avenue C3
Burns Memorial Cottages B2
Burnside Road C4
Burnsland Crescent D5
Campbell Avenue C3
Carrick View B3
Castle Street C4
Catrine Road D5
Clarinda Crescent C4
Clelland Park C5
Connel Crescent B5
Cowgate C4
Cross, The C4
Cumnock Road D5
Curling Stone Place C4
Donaldson Crescent D5
Earl Grey Street C4
East Park Avenue C4
Ellisland Court C3
Fernlea Avenue D5
Glebe Avenue D4
Grassmillees Way D5
Greenhead C4
Gregory Street D5
Grove Park C4
Hamilton Avenue D5
Haugh Road C6
High Street C4
Hillhead Road D2
Hughfield Road C3
Jean Armour Burns Houses B2
Jean Armour Drive C3
Kemp Court C4
Kilmarnock Road B2
Knowe C4
Lindsay Court C3
Loan D4
Loanhill Avenue D4
Loch Road C3
Lochlea Avenue D4
Loudoun Street C4
Mansfield Road C4
Mary Morrison Drive D4
Mossgiel Avenue D4
Nether Place C4
Nether Place Gardens C4
Nether Walk C4
New Road C4
Nursery Lane C3
Pollocks Way C5
Rankin Drive D4
Rawson Crescent B5
Robert Burns Place C4
Sorn Road D4
South Park Avenue B4
Southfield Avenue D5
Station Lane C5
Station Road C5
Sunnyside Crescent C3
Tanfield C4
Tarbolton Road A2
Victoria Cottages C5
Waterside Gardens B5
Welton Road D4
West Park Avenue C5
Whiteford Place B5

Index to Maidens

Ardlochan Avenue C1
Ardlochan Grove C1
Ardlochan Road B1
Ardlochan Terrace C1
Baineshill Drive A2
Harbour Road A1
Kirkoswald Road C2
Lucy Brae A2
Seabank View B2
Shanter Road B2
Turnberry Road A3

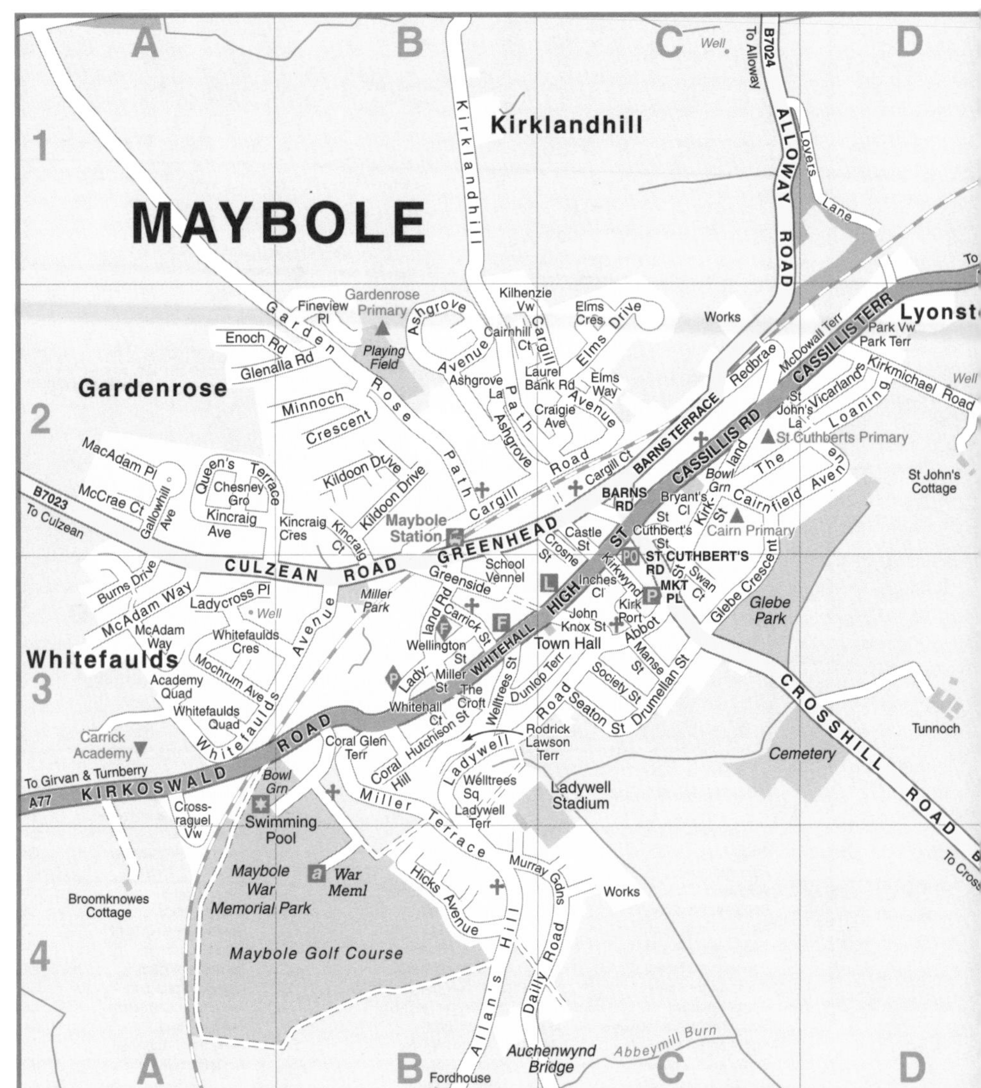
MAYBOLE
Kirklandhill
Gardenrose
Whitefaulds
Lyonst
A
B
C
D
1
2
3
4
To Alloway
B7024
ALLOWAY ROAD
Lovers Lane
Well
Kirklandhill
Gardenrose Primary
Playing Field
Fineview Pl
Enoch Rd
Glenalla Rd
Garden Rose Path
Minnoch Crescent
Ashgrove Avenue
Ashgrove La
Ashgrove Path
Kilhenzie Vw
Cairnhill Ct
Cargill Road
Laurel Bank Rd
Craigie Ave
Elms Cres
Elms Drive
Elms Way
Elms Avenue
Works
Redbrae
McDowall Terr
CASSILLIS TERR
Park Vw
Park Terr
Kirkmichael Road
Vicarland
Loaning
St John's La
St Cuthberts Primary
St John's Cottage
MacAdam Pl
Queen's Terrace
Chesney Gro
Kincraig Ave
McCrae Ct
Gallowhill Ave
B7023
To Culzean
Kildoon Drive
Kildoon Dr
Kincraig Cres
Kincraig Ct
Maybole Station
Cargill Ct
BARNS TERRACE
CASSILLIS RD
BARNS RD
Bryant's Cl
Bowl Grn
Kirkland
The Cairnfield Avenue
Cairn Primary
CULZEAN ROAD
GREENHEAD
Castle St
Crosne St
School Vennel
Greenside
St Cuthbert's St
ST CUTHBERT'S RD
Kirk St
Swan Ct
Glebe Crescent
Glebe Park
Burns Drive
McAdam Way
Ladycross Pl
Well
Miller Park
Avenue
Inches Cl
Kirkwynd
MKT PL
Kirk Port
HIGH ST
John Knox St
Abbot
Carrick St
Ladyland Rd
Wellington St
WHITEHALL
Town Hall
Manse St
Drumellan St
CROSSHILL ROAD
McAdam Way
Whitefaulds Cres
Mochrum Ave
Academy Quad
Whitefaulds Quad
Whitefaulds Avenue
Miller St
The Croft
Whitehall Ct
Welltrees St
Dunlop Terr
Society St
Seaton St
Road
Rodrick Lawson Terr
Cemetery
Tunnoch
Carrick Academy
To Girvan & Turnberry
A77
KIRKOSWALD ROAD
Coral Glen Terr
Hutchison St
Coral Hill
Ladywell
Welltrees Sq
Ladywell Terr
Ladywell Stadium
Bowl Grn
Crossraguel Vw
Swimming Pool
Miller Terrace
Murray Gdns
Works
ROAD
To Cross
Maybole War Memorial Park
War Meml
Hicks Avenue
Broomknowes Cottage
Maybole Golf Course
Allan's Hill
Dailly Road
Auchenwynd Bridge
Abbeymill Burn
Fordhouse

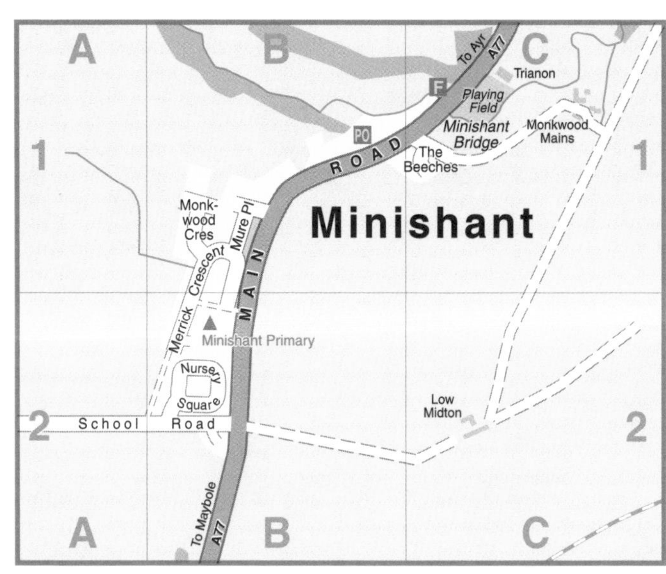

Index to Maybole

Street	Grid
Abbot Street	C3
Academy Quadrant	A3
Allan's Hill	B4
Alloway Road	C1
Ashgrove	B2
Ashgrove Avenue	B2
Ashgrove Lane	B2
Barns Road	C2
Barns Terrace	C2
Bryant's Close	C2
Burns Drive	A3
Cairnfield Avenue	C2
Cairnhill Court	B2
Cargill Avenue	C2
Cargill Court	C2
Cargill Road	B2
Carrick Street	B3
Cassillis Road	C2
Cassillis Terrace	D2
Castle Street	C2
Chesney Grove	A2
Coral Glen Terrace	B3
Coral Hill	B3
Craigie Avenue	C2
Croft, The	B3
Crosne Street	C2
Crosshill Road	D3
Crossraguel View	A3
Culzean Road	B3
Dailly Road	C4
Drumellan Street	C3
Dunlop Terrace	B3
Elms Crescent	C2
Elms Drive	C2
Elms Way	C2
Enoch Road	A2
Fineview Place	B2
Gallowhill Avenue	A2
Garden Rose Path	B2
Glebe Crescent	C3
Glenalla Road	A2
Greenhead	B3
Greenside	B3
Hicks Avenue	B4
High Street	C3
Hutchison Street	B3
Inches Close	C3
John Knox Street	C3
Kildoon Drive	B2
Kilhenzie View	B2
Kincraig Avenue	A2
Kincraig Court	B2
Kincraig Crescent	B2
Kirkland Street	C2
Kirklandhill Path	B1
Kirkmichael Road	D2
Kirkoswald Road	A3
Kirk Port	C3
Kirk Wynd	C3
Ladycross Place	A3
Ladyland Road	B3
Ladywell Road	B3
Ladywell Terrace	B3
Laurel Bank Road	B2
Loaning, The	D2
Lovers Lane	D1
MacAdam Place	A2
McAdam Way	A3
McCrae Court	A2
McDowall Terrace	D2
Manse Street	C3
Market Place	C3
Miller Street	B3
Miller Terrace	B3
Minnoch Crescent	B2
Mochrum Avenue	A3
Murray Gardens	C4
Park Terrace	D2
Park View	D2
Queen's Terrace	A2
Redbrae	C2
Rodrick Lawson Terrace	B3
St Cuthberts Road	C3
St Cuthberts Street	C2
St John's Cottages	D2
St John's Lane	D2
School Vennel	B3
Seaton Street	C3
Society Street	C3
Swan Court	C3
Vicarlands	D2
Wellington Street	B3
Welltrees Square	B3
Welltrees Street	B3
Whitefaulds Avenue	A3
Whitefaulds Crescent	A3
Whitefaulds Quadrant	A3
Whitehall	B3
Whitehall Court	B3

Index to Minishant

Street	Grid
Beeches, The	C1
Merrick Crescent	B2
Monkwood Crescent	B1
Mure Place	B1
Nursery Square	B2
School Road	A2

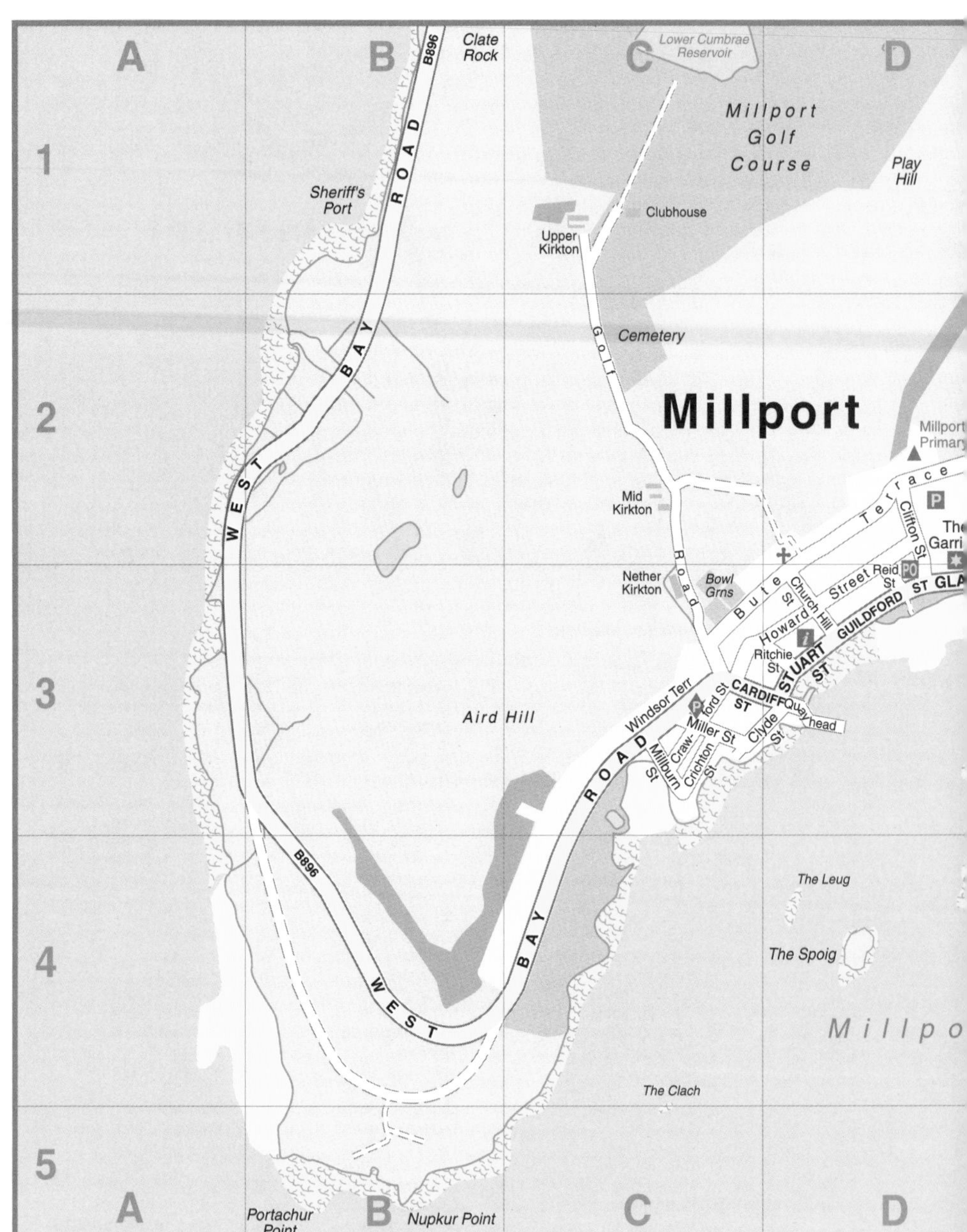
A
B
C
D
1
2
3
4
5
Clate Rock
Lower Cumbrae Reservoir
Millport Golf Course
Play Hill
B896
WEST BAY ROAD
Sheriff's Port
Clubhouse
Upper Kirkton
Cemetery
Golf Road
Millport
Millport Primary
Mid Kirkton
Nether Kirkton
Bowl Grns
Terrace
Clifton St
The Garri
Bute St
Church Hill
Street
Reid St
GUILDFORD ST
GLA
Howard St
Ritchie St
STUART ST
CARDIFF ST
Quayhead
Windsor Terr
Crawford St
Miller St
Clyde St
Millburn St
Craw- Crichton St
Aird Hill
The Leug
The Spoig
Millpo
The Clach
Portachur Point
Nupkur Point

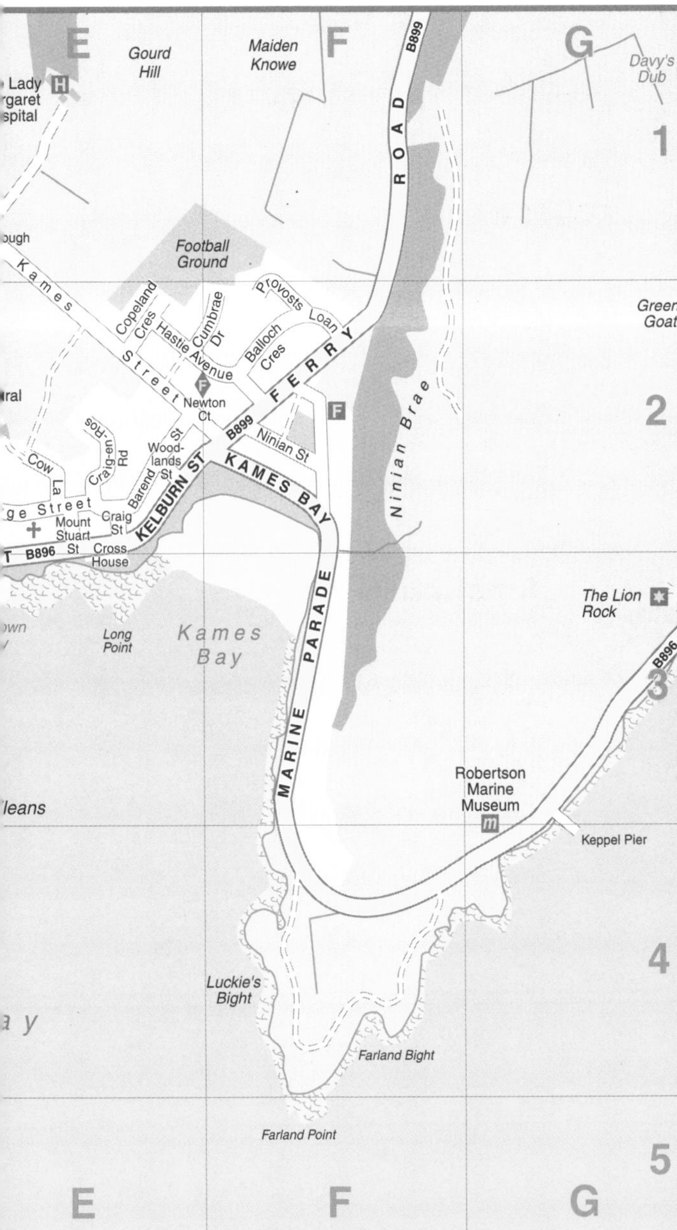

Index to Millport

Street	Grid
Balloch Crescent	F2
Barend Street	E2
Bute Terrace	C3
Cardiff Street	C3
Church Hill Street	D3
Clifton Street	D2
Clyde Street	D3
College Street	D1, D2
Copeland Crescent	E2
Cow Lane	E2
Craig Street	E2
Craig-en-Ros Road	E2
Crawford Street	C3
Crichton Street	C3
Cross House	E3
Cumbrae Drive	F2
Cumbrae Drive	F2
Ferry Road	F2
George Street	E2
Glasgow Street	D3
Golf Road	C2
Guildford Street	D3
Hastie Avenue	E2
Howard Street	C3
Kames Bay	F2
Kames Street	E1
Kelburn Street	E2
Marine Parade	F3
Millburn Street	C3
Miller Street	C3
Mount Stuart Street	E2
Newton Court	F2
Ninian Street	F2
Provosts Loan	F2
Quayhead	D3
Reid Street	D3
Ritchie Street	D3
Stuart Street	D3
West Bay Road	A2
West Bay Road	D4
Windsor Terrace	C3
Woodlands Street	E2

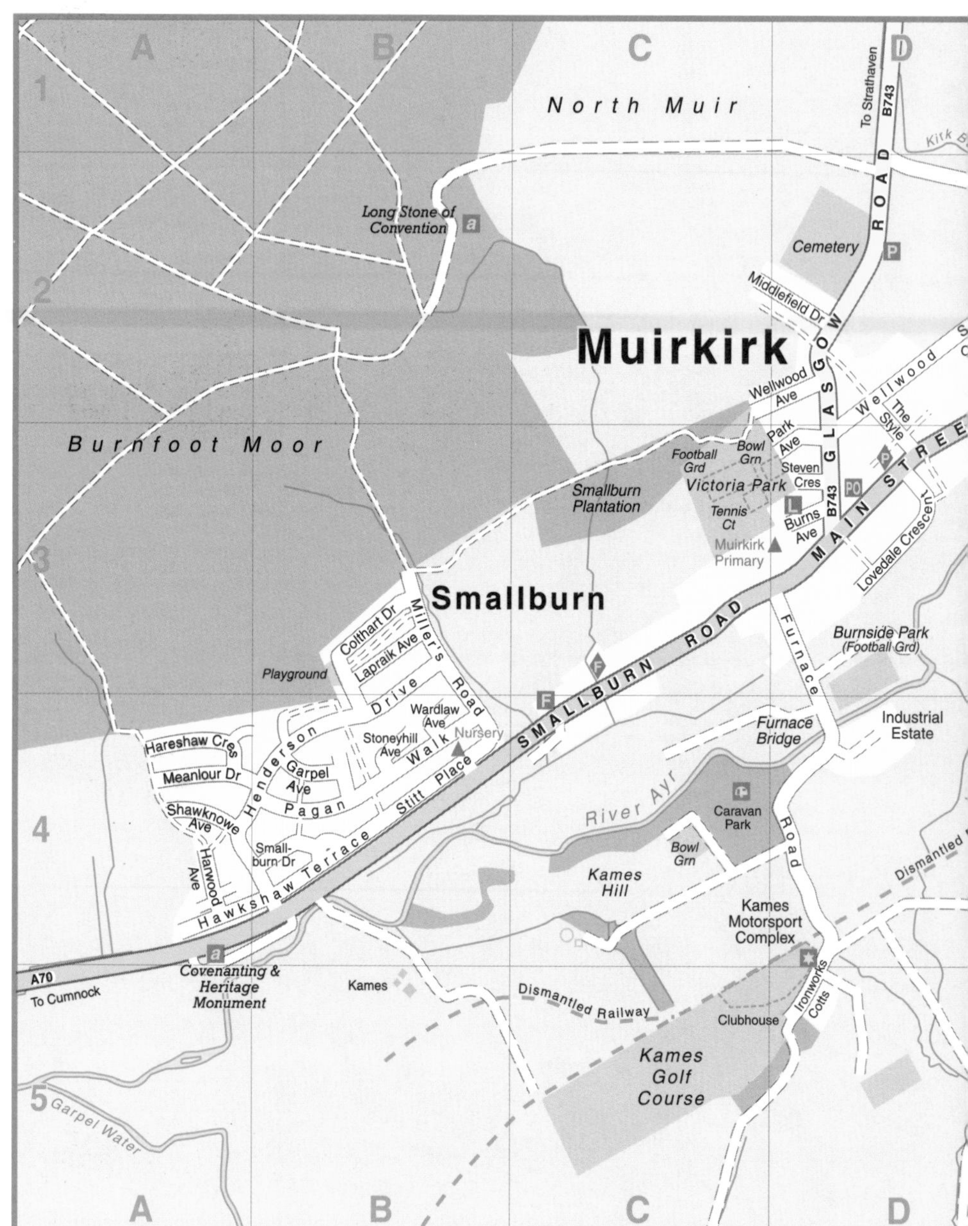
North Muir
To Strathaven
B743
Kirk B
Long Stone of Convention
Cemetery
ROAD
Middlefield Dr
Muirkirk
GLASGOW
Wellwood Ave
Wellwood
The Style
Burnfoot Moor
Park Ave
Football Grd
Bowl Grn
Steven Cres
Victoria Park
Smallburn Plantation
Tennis Ct
B743
Burns Ave
MAIN STREET
Lovedale Crescent
Muirkirk Primary
Smallburn
Colthart Dr
Miller's Road
Lapraik Ave
Furnace Road
Burnside Park (Football Grd)
Playground
Drive
Wardlaw Ave
SMALLBURN ROAD
Industrial Estate
Furnace Bridge
Hareshaw Cres
Henderson
Stoneyhill Ave
Nursery
Walk
Meanlour Dr
Garpel Ave
Stitt Place
Pagan
River Ayr
Caravan Park
Shawknowe Ave
Road
Harwood Ave
Small-burn Dr
Hawkshaw Terrace
Bowl Grn
Kames Hill
Dismantled
Kames Motorsport Complex
A70
To Cumnock
Covenanting & Heritage Monument
Kames
Dismantled Railway
Clubhouse
Ironworks Cotts
Kames Golf Course
Garpel Water

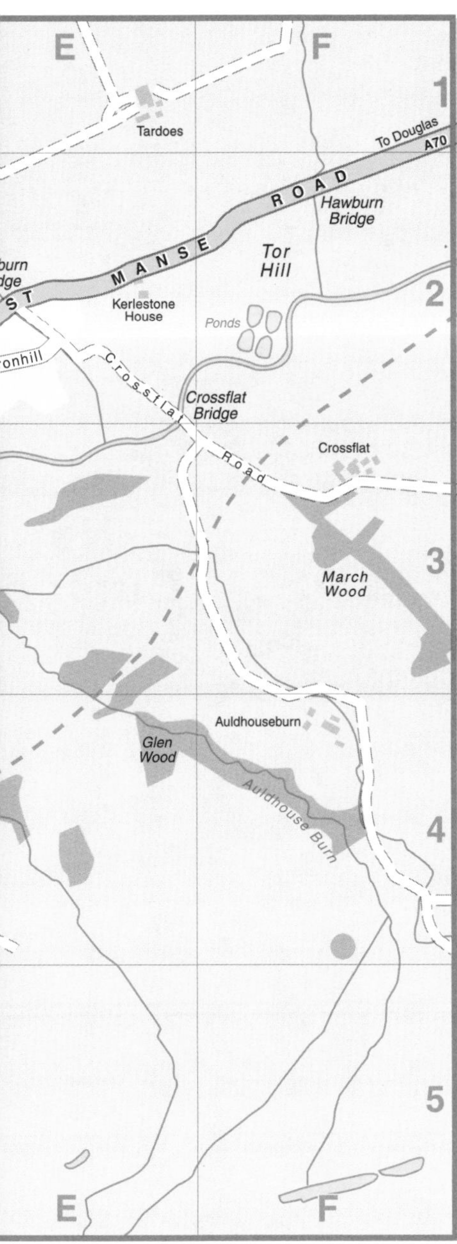

Index to Muirkirk

Bridge Street	E2
Burns Avenue	D3
Cairn View	D3
Carruthers Park	D2
Colthart Drive	B3
Crossflat Road	E2
Furnace Road	D3
Garpel Avenue	B4
Garronhill	E2
Glasgow Road	D3
Hareshaw Crescent	A4
Harwood Avenue	A4
Hawkshaw Terrace	B4
Henderson Drive	A4
Ironworks Cottages	D5
Kirk Green	E2
Lapraik Avenue	B3
Lovedale Crescent	D3
Main Street	D3
Manse Road	E2
Meanlour Drive	A4
Middlefield Drive	D2
Miller's Road	B3
Pagan Walk	B4
Park Avenue	D3
Shawknowe Avenue	A4
Smallburn Drive	B4
Smallburn Road	C4
Steven Crescent	D3
Stitt Place	B4
Stoneyhill Avenue	B4
Style, The	D3
Wardlaw Avenue	B4
Wellwood Avenue	D2
Wellwood Street	D2

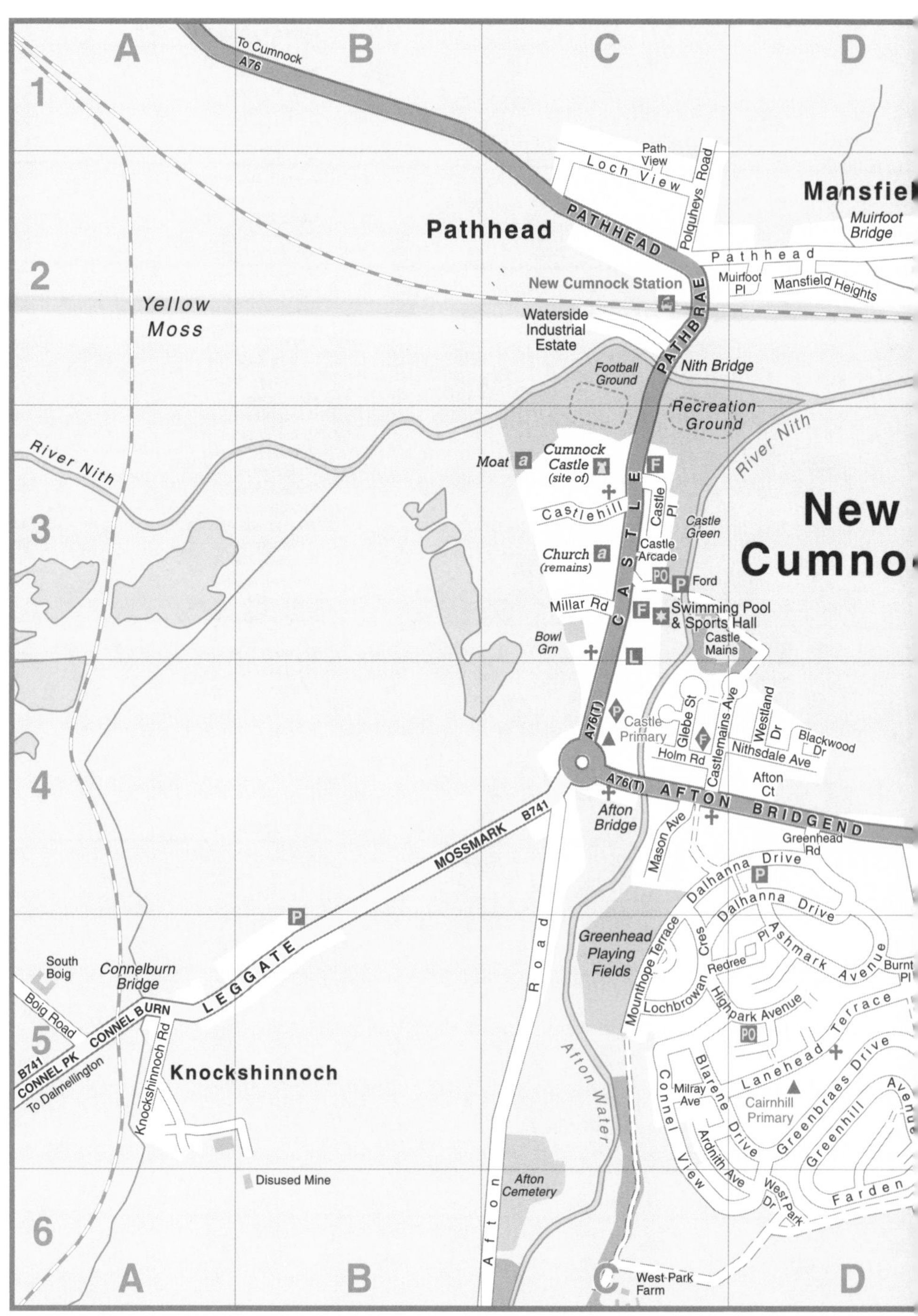
To Cumnock
A76
Path View
Loch View
Polquheys Road
Mansfield
Muirfoot Bridge
Pathhead
PATHHEAD
Pathhead
Muirfoot Pl
Mansfield Heights
New Cumnock Station
PATHBRAE
Yellow Moss
Waterside Industrial Estate
Football Ground
Nith Bridge
Recreation Ground
River Nith
River Nith
Moat
Cumnock Castle (site of)
Castlehill
Castle Pl
CASTLE
Castle Green
New Cumnock
Church (remains)
Castle Arcade
PO
Ford
Millar Rd
Swimming Pool & Sports Hall
Bowl Grn
Castle Mains
Glebe St
Castlemains Ave
Westland Dr
Blackwood Dr
Castle Primary
Holm Rd
Nithsdale Ave
A76(T)
Afton Ct
A76(T)
AFTON BRIDGEND
Afton Bridge
Mason Ave
Greenhead Rd
MOSSMARK
B741
Dalhanna Drive
Dalhanna Drive
Greenhead Playing Fields
Mounthope Terrace
Cres
Redree Pl
Ashmark Avenue
Burnt Pl
South Boig
Connelburn Bridge
LEGGATE
Road
Boig Road
CONNEL BURN
Lochbrowan
Highpark Avenue
PO
Lanehead Terrace
B741
CONNEL PK
To Dalmellington
Knockshinnoch Rd
Knockshinnoch
Afton Water
Connel View
Milray Ave
Blarene Drive
Cairnhill Primary
Greenbraes Drive
Avenue
Greenhill
Ardnith Ave
West Park Dr
Farden
Disused Mine
Afton Cemetery
Afton
West Park Farm
A B C D
1 2 3 4 5 6

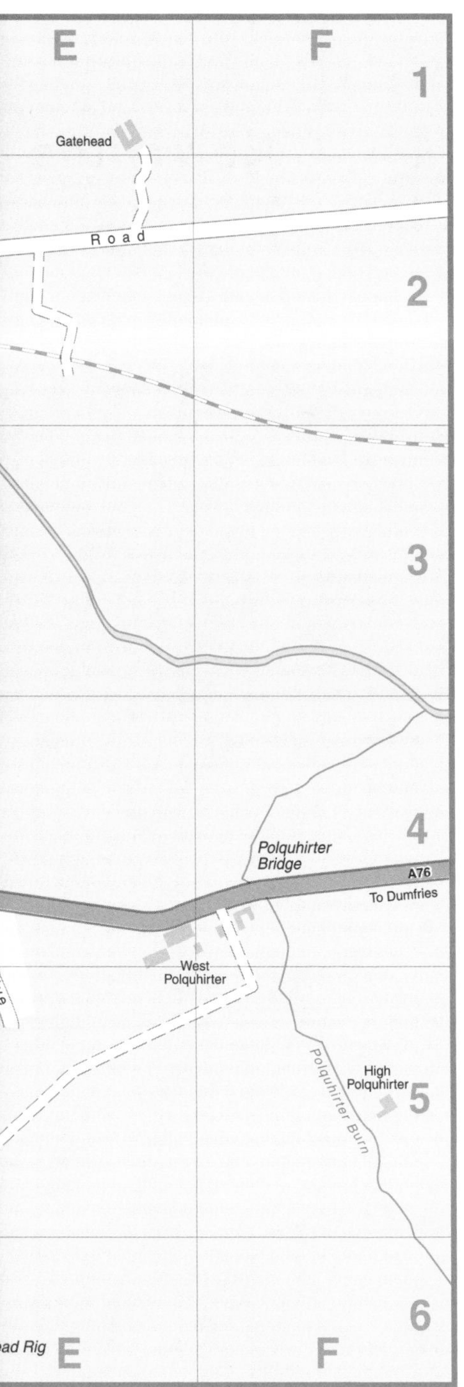

AaaIndex to New Cumnock

Afton Bridgend	C4
Afton Court	D4
Afton Road	C6
Ardnith Avenue	C5
Ashmark Avenue	D5
Blackwood Drive	D4
Blarene Drive	C5
Boig Road	A5
Burnton Place	D5
Cairnhill Place	D4
Castle Arcade	C3
Castle Place	C3
Castlehill	C3
Castlemains Avenue	C4
Connel Burn	A5
Connel Park	A5
Connell View	C5
Dalhanna Drive	D4
Farden Avenue	D6
Glebe Street	C4
Glenafton Drive	D5
Greenbraes Drive	D5
Greenhead Road	D4
Greenhill Avenue	D5
Hamilton Drive	E4
High Park Avenue	D5
Holm Road	C4
Knockshinnoch Road	A5
Lanehead Terrace	D5
Leggate	A5
Lime Road	D4
Loch View	C2
Lochbrowan Crescent	C5
Mansfield Court	D2
Mansfield Heights	D2
Mansfield Road	D2
Mason Avenue	C4
Millar Road	C3
Milray Avenue	C5
Mossmark	B4
Mounthope Terrace	C5
Muirfoot Place	D2
Nithsdale Avenue	D4
Pathbrae	C2
Pathhead	C2
Path View	C2
Polquheys Road	C2
Redree Place	D5
Stellhead Avenue	E5
West Park Drive	D6
Westland Drive	D4

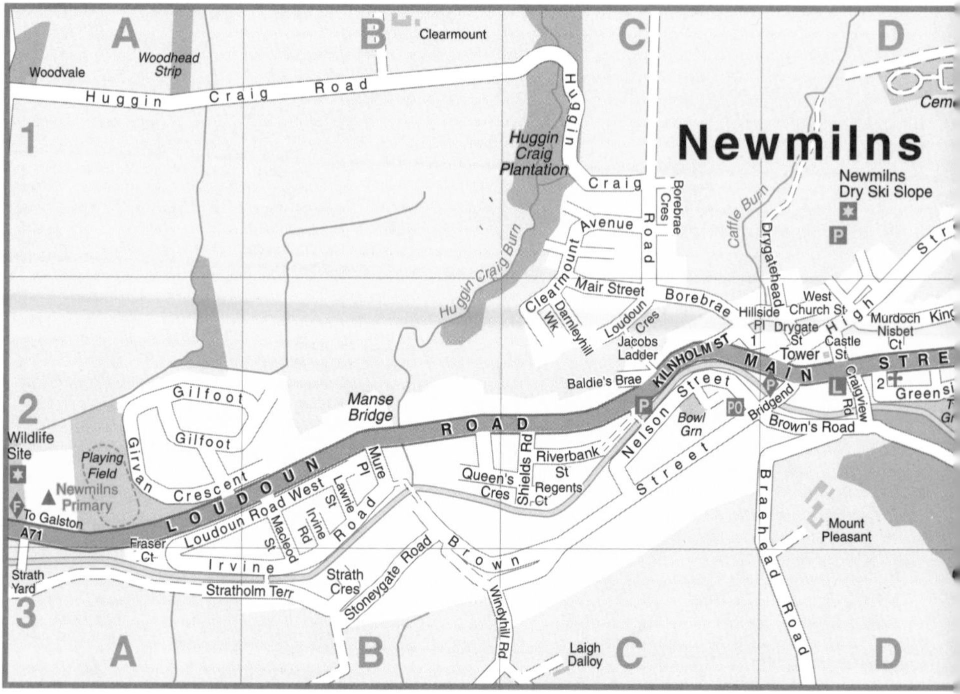

A B C D
1
2
3
Newmilns
Woodvale
Woodhead Strip
Clearmount
Huggin Craig Road
Huggin Craig Plantation
Huggin Craig
Borebrae Cres
Road
Newmilns Dry Ski Slope
Cem
Caffle Burn
Huggin Craig Burn
Avenue
Clearmount
Mair Street
Borebrae
Drygatehead
Hillside Pl
West Church St
Drygate St
High
Str
Murdoch Nisbet Ct
King
Clearmount Wk
Darnleyhill
Loudoun Cres
Jacobs Ladder
Kilnholm St
Tower
Castle St
Main Street
Baldie's Brae
Craigview Rd
Greensi
Gilfoot
Manse Bridge
Loudoun Road
Nelson Street
Bowl Grn
PO
Bridgend
Brown's Road
Wildlife Site
Playing Field
Girvan Crescent
Mure Pl
Shields Rd
Riverbank St
Queen's Cres
Regents Ct
Newmilns Primary
To Galston
A71
Loudoun Road West
Lawrie St
Irvine Rd
Macleod St
Road
Braehead Road
Mount Pleasant
Fraser Ct
Irvine
Brown
Strath Yard
Stratholm Terr
Strath Cres
Stoneygate Road
Windyhill Rd
Laigh Dalloy

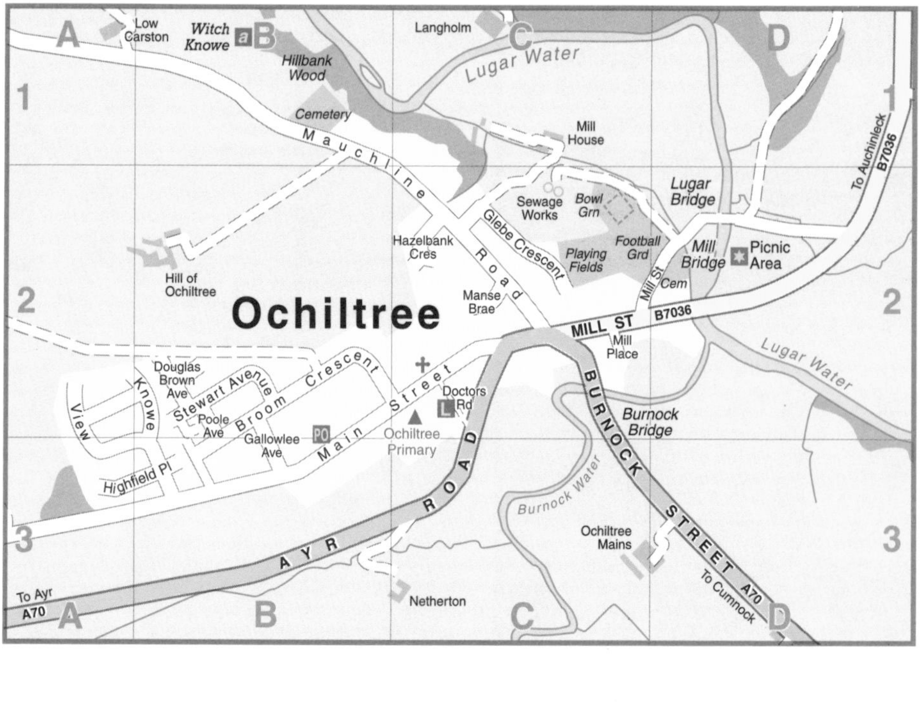

A B C D
1
2
3
Ochiltree
Low Carston
Witch Knowe
Langholm
Hillbank Wood
Lugar Water
Cemetery
Mill House
Mauchline Road
Glebe Crescent
Sewage Works
Bowl Grn
Lugar Bridge
To Auchinleck
B7036
Hazelbank Cres
Playing Fields
Football Grd
Mill Bridge
Picnic Area
Hill of Ochiltree
Manse Brae
Mill St
Cem
Mill St
B7036
Mill Place
Lugar Water
Douglas Brown Ave
Stewart Avenue
Crescent
Main Street
Doctors Rd
Knowe
View
Poole Ave
Broom
Gallowlee Ave
PO
Ochiltree Primary
Burnock Bridge
Burnock Street
Burnock Water
Highfield Pl
Ayr Road
Ochiltree Mains
To Ayr
A70
Netherton
To Cumnock
A70

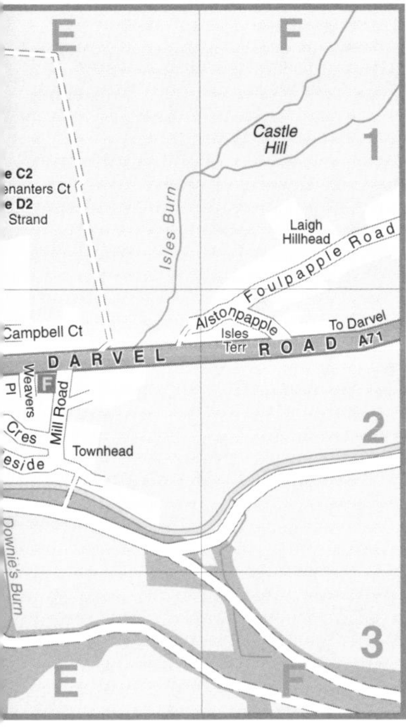

Index to Newmilns

Alstonpapple F2
Baldies Brae C2
Borebrae C2
Borebrae Crescent C1
Braehead Road D2
Bridgend D2
Brown Street B2
Browns Road D2
Burn Road D2
Campbell Court E2
Campbell Street E2
Castle Street D2
Clearmount Avenue C2
Covenanters Court (1) C2
Craigview Road D2
Dalwhatswood Road E1
Darnleyhill Walk C2
Darvel Road E2
Drygate Street D2
Drygatehead D1
East Church Court D1
East Strand (2) D2
Foulpapple Road F2
Fraser Court A3
Gilfoot A2
Girvan Crescent A2
Greenhead D2
Greenside D2
High Street D2
Hillside Place C2
Huggin Craig Road C1
Irvine Road A3
Isles Street E2
Isles Terrace F2
Jacobs Ladder C2
Kilnholm Street C2
Kings Crescent D2
King Street D2
Ladeside E2
Lawrie Street B2
Loudoun Crescent C2
Loudoun Road A2
Loudoun Road West A2
MacLeod Street B2
Main Street C2
Mair Street C2
Mill Crescent E2
Mill Road E2
Murdoch Nisbet Court D2
Mure Place B2
Nelson Street C2
Persian Sands D2
Queens Crescent B2
Regents Court C2
Riverbank Street C2
Shields Road C2
Stoneygate Road B3
Strath Crescent B3
Stratholm Terrace A3
Townhead E2
Union Street E2
Weavers Place E2
West Campbell Street D2
West Church Street D2
Windyhill Road C3

Index to Ochiltree

Ayr Road B3
Broom Crescent B2
Burnock Street C2
Doctor's Road C2
Douglas Brown Avenue B2
Gallowlee Avenue B3
Glebe Crescent C2
Hazelbank Crescent C2
Highfield Place A3
Knowe View B2
Main Street B3
Manse Brae C2
Mauchline Road B1
Mill Place C2
Mill Street C2
Poole Avenue B2
Stewart Avenue B2

Index to Sorn

Anderson Crescent B1
Dalgain Drive C2
Dalyearnoch Road B1
Fir Park B1
Main Street C2
Old Avenue B2
Treesbank Cottages B1
Woodlands Road C1

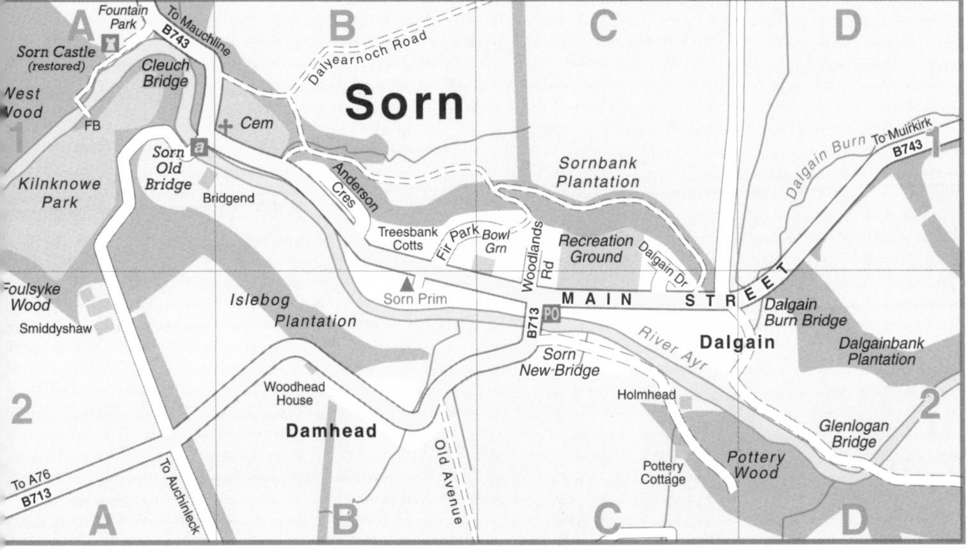

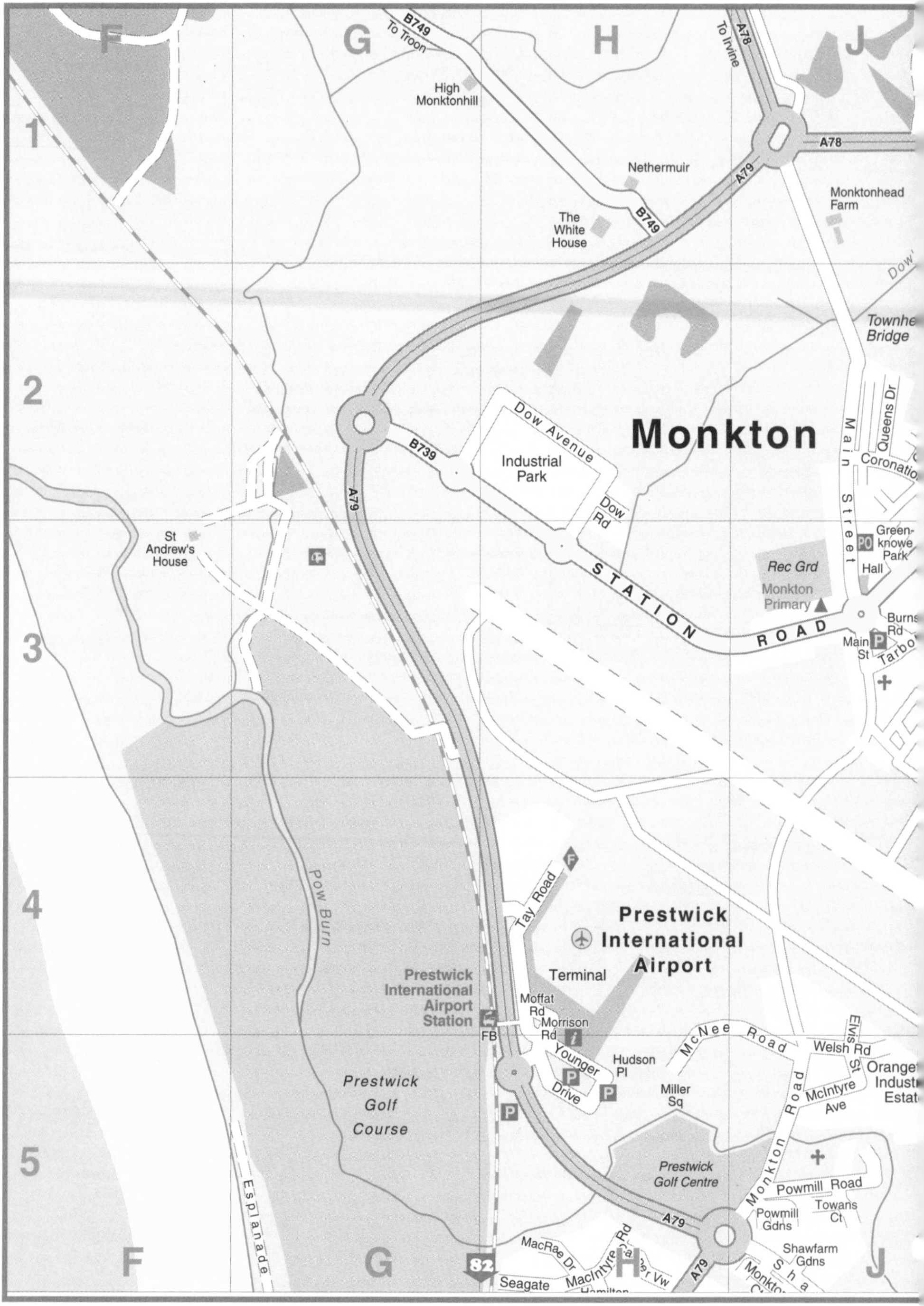

F G H J

1 2 3 4 5

B749
To Troon
To Irvine
A78
A79
High Monktonhill
Nethermuir
Monktonhead Farm
The White House
Dow
Townhead Bridge

Monkton

Queens Dr
Main Street
Coronation
B739
Dow Avenue
Industrial Park
Dow Rd
St Andrew's House
Green-knowe Park
PO
Hall
Rec Grd
Monkton Primary
STATION ROAD
Burns Rd
Main St
Tarbolton
Pow Burn
Tay Road

Prestwick International Airport

Terminal
Prestwick International Airport Station
FB
Moffat Rd
Morrison Rd
Younger Drive
Hudson Pl
Miller Sq
McNee Road
Welsh Rd
Elvis St
Orangefield Industrial Estate
McIntyre Ave
Monkton Road
Prestwick Golf Course
Prestwick Golf Centre
Powmill Road
Powmill Gdns
Towans Ct
Shawfarm Gdns
Shaw
Monkton Ct
Esplanade
MacRae Dr
MacIntyre Rd
Archer Vw
Seagate
MacIntyre
Hamilton

82

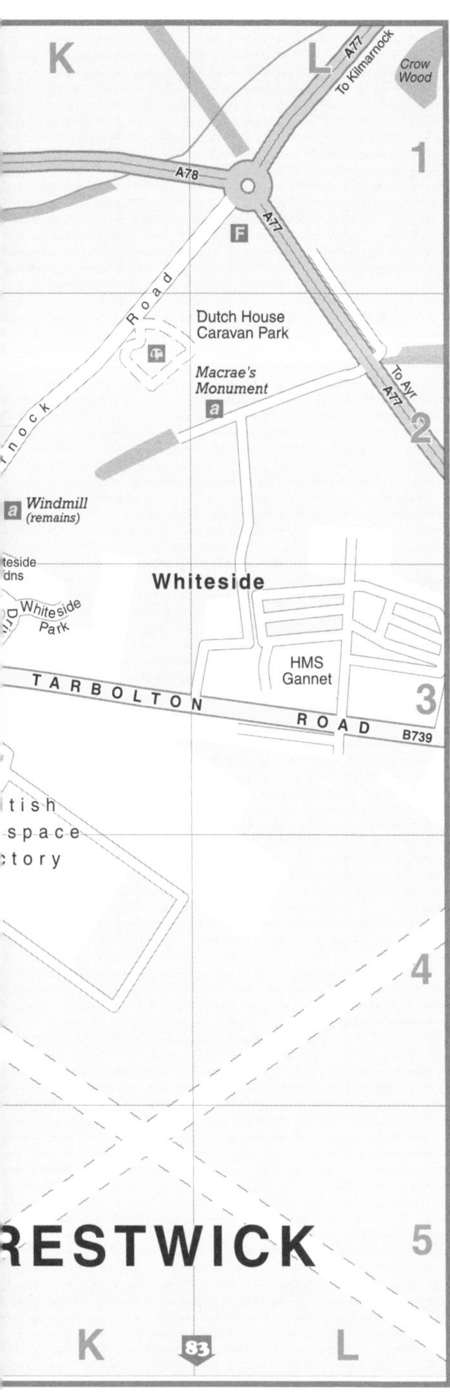

Index to Prestwick

Abbot Court	J10
Adamton Road North	J7
Adamton Road South	H9
Adamton Terrace	H8
Afton Avenue	H10
Ailsa Street	G7
Aitkenbrae Drive	J7
Alexandra Avenue	H6
Alexandra Court	H6
Allanvale Road	G7
Alvord Avenue	J6
Anderson Crescent	K8
Angus Avenue	J7
Annfield Road	G7
Annfield Terrace	G7
Ardayre Road	G7
Ardfin Court	H9
Ardfin Road	H10
Arran Park	G10
Auchincruive Avenue	H8
Ayr Road	G9
Baird Place	J3
Baird Road	J3
Bank Street	G7
Barnweil Avenue	H9
Barony Road	H9
Bellevue Crescent	H8
Bellevue Road	H7
Bellfield Lane	G7
Bellrock Avenue	G10
Bellrock Road	F10
Benmore	H10
Bennan House (1)	G10
Bennoch Place	J10
Bentfield Drive	G10
Berelands Avenue	J7
Berelands Gardens	J6
Berelands Road	J6
Biggart Road	H8
Blackford Crescent	K6
Blanefield Avenue	H9
Boyd Street	H7
Boydfield Avenue	H6
Boydfield Gardens	H6
Brandon Gardens	G8
Briarhill Court	J7
Briarhill Road	H7
Briarhill Street	H7
Bridge Street	G7
Broompark Avenue	H7
Broompark Crescent	H7
Bruce Avenue	G9
Bruce Lane	G9
Burgh Road	G7
Burnside Gardens	H6
Burnside Road	J3
Caerlaverock Avenue	H7
Caerlaverock Road	H7
Calvinston Road	J10
Cangillan Court	J10
Capper View	H5
Cargill Drive	J10
Carleton Gardens	H8
Carnell Crescent	J8
Carnell Terrace	J8
Carradale Drive	H10
Carrick Place	G8
Charles Avenue	J2
Clune Drive	J7
Cochrane Place	G7
Coila Avenue	H9
Colonsay House (11)	G10
Coronation Street	J2
Corrie House (2)	G10
Coulthard Drive	J9
Coylebank	H9
Craigfin Court	J10
Craigie Street	G7
Craigneil Drive	H8
Craigpark Avenue	G9
Craigskeen Place	J10
Crandleyhill Road	G9
Crawford Avenue	H9
Creran Court	H10
Crescent, The	H6
Crofthead Road	H6
Crosbie Terrace	J8
Cross, The	H6
Culzean Avenue	J8
Cumbrae House (12)	G10
Cunninghame Road	H8
Dalwood Road	G7
Devilla Court	H10
Doon Avenue	G10
Douglas Avenue	G9
Dow Avenue	H2
Dow Road	H2
Duart Avenue	H7
Duart Crescent	H8
Dundonald Terrace	J8
East Road	J9
East Road	H10
Edmiston Avenue	G8
Elvis Street	J5
Englewood Avenue	G10
Esperanto Road	K7
Esplanade	F8
Fairway View	J9
Farden Place	J9
Fearnoch	H10
Ferguson Avenue	J7
Fernbank	G10
Fernbank Court	G10
Fiddison Place	K10
Firhill Drive	J2
Fullarton Road	H9
Fulshaw Court	J10
Gardiner Street	H7
Garryhorn	J10
Glenburn Road	K7
Glenpark Avenue	J9
Grangemuir Court	G8
Grangemuir Road	G8
Gray Street	H7
Greenan Terrace (2)	J8
Greenknowe Park	J3
Greenside Avenue	J8
Gullin Drive	J10
Hamilton Way	H6
Hawthorn Avenue	H8
Hawthorn Gardens	H8
Heathfield Road	G10
Heathpark	H10
Highfield Avenue	J8
Hillside Crescent	J7
Hudson Place	H5
Hunter Street	H7
Indale Avenue	J8
James Street	G10

continued overleaf....

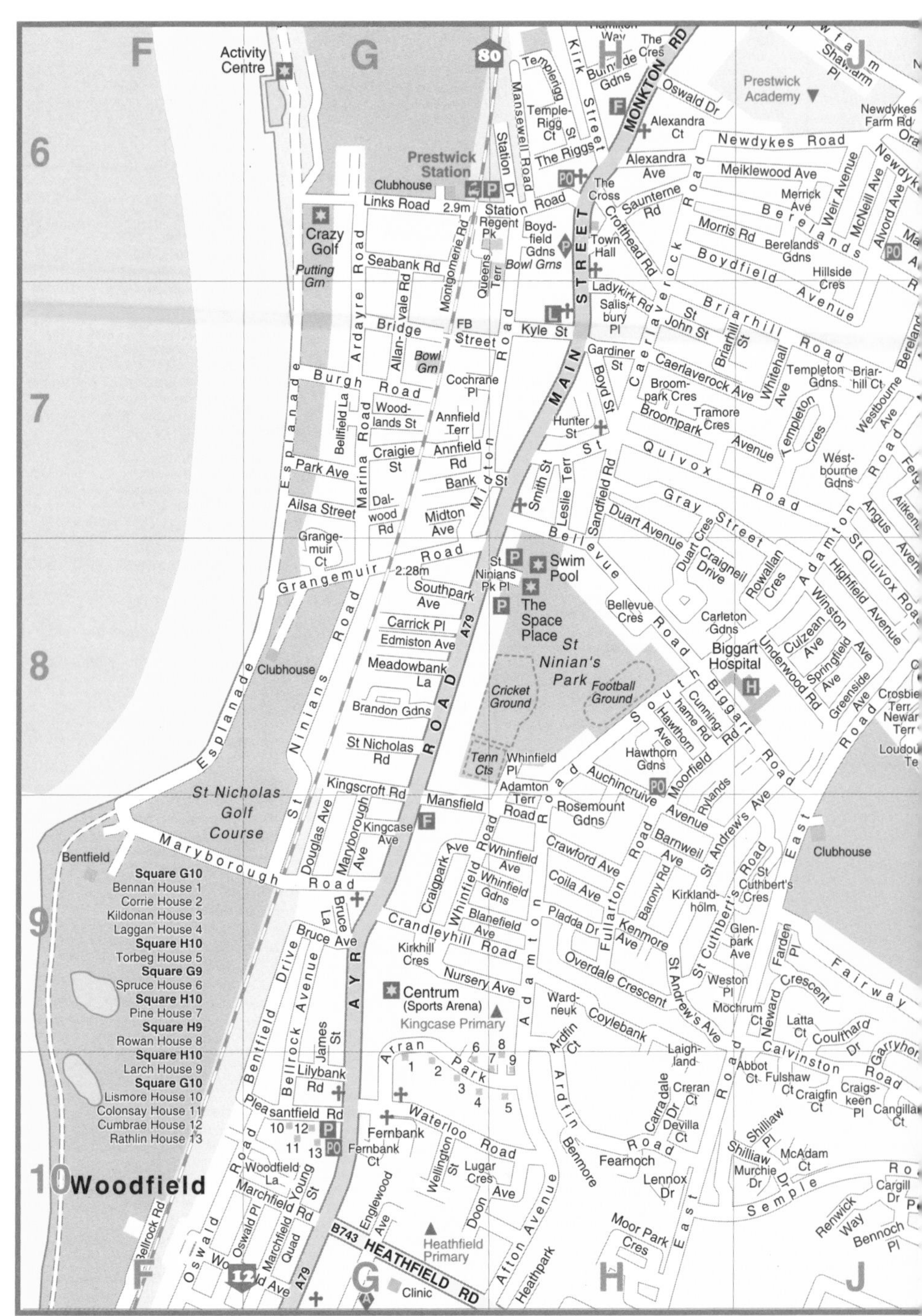
F
G
H
J
6
7
8
9
10
80
12
Activity Centre
Prestwick Station
Clubhouse
Links Road
2.9m
Station Road
Station Dr
Mansewell Road
Templerigg Ct
The Riggs
Kirk Street
Burnside Gdns
The Cres
Hamilton Way
MONKTON RD
Oswald Dr
Prestwick Academy
Newdykes Farm Rd
Newdykes Road
Alexandra Ct
Alexandra Ave
Meiklewood Ave
Merrick Ave
Weir Avenue
McNeill Ave
Alvord Ave
Berelands
Berelands Gdns
Morris Rd
Saunterne Rd
The Cross
Crofthead Rd
Town Hall
Crazy Golf
Putting Grn
Ardayre Road
Montgomerie Rd
Regent Pk
Boydfield Gdns
Bowl Grns
Queens Terr
Seabank Rd
Allanvale Rd
Boydfield Avenue
Hillside Cres
Ladykirk Rd
Salisbury Pl
Caerlaverock Road
Briarhill Road
Briarhill St
John St
Bridge Street
FB
Kyle St
Bowl Grn
Gardiner St
Boyd St
Caerlaverock Ave
Whitehall Ave
Templeton Gdns
Briar-hill Ct
Berelands
Burgh Road
Esplanade
Bellfield La
Woodlands St
Cochrane Pl
Broompark Cres
Tramore Cres
Broompark Avenue
Templeton Cres
Westbourne Ave
MAIN STREET
Annfield Terr
Annfield Rd
Hunter St
Marina Road
Craigie St
Midton Road
Quivox Road
Westbourne Gdns
Park Ave
Bank St
Smith St
Leslie Terr
Sandfield Rd
Ailsa Street
Dalwood Rd
Midton Ave
Gray Street
Duart Avenue
Duart Cres
Craigneil Drive
Rowallan Cres
Adamton Road
Angus Ave
St Quivox Road
Aitken
Grangemuir Ct
Grangemuir Road
2.28m
St Ninians Pk Pl
Swim Pool
The Space Place
Bellevue Road
Bellevue Cres
Southpark Ave
Carleton Gdns
Winston Ave
Highfield Avenue
Culzean Ave
Springfield Ave
Carrick Pl
Edmiston Ave
A79
St Ninians Road
St Ninian's Park
Biggart Hospital
Underwood Rd
Greenside Ave
Crosbie Terr
Newark Terr
Clubhouse
Meadowbank La
Cricket Ground
Football Ground
South Biggart Road
Cunninghame Rd
Hawthorn Ave
Hawthorn Gdns
Moorfield
Brandon Gdns
AYR ROAD
St Nicholas Rd
Tenn Cts
Whinfield Pl
Auchincruive Avenue
Rylands
St Andrew's Ave
Loudoun Te
St Nicholas Golf Course
Kingscroft Rd
Adamton Terr
Rosemount Gdns
Mansfield Road
Kingcase Ave
Douglas Ave
Maryborough Ave
Maryborough Road
Bentfield
Whinfield Road
Craigpark Ave
Whinfield Ave
Whinfield Gdns
Crawford Ave
Coila Ave
Barnweil Ave
Barony Rd
St Cuthbert's Road
St Cuthbert's Cres
East Road
Clubhouse
Kirklandholm
Square G10
Bennan House 1
Corrie House 2
Kildonan House 3
Laggan House 4
Square H10
Torbeg House 5
Square G9
Spruce House 6
Square H10
Pine House 7
Square H9
Rowan House 8
Square H10
Larch House 9
Square G10
Lismore House 10
Colonsay House 11
Cumbrae House 12
Rathlin House 13
Bruce La
Bruce Ave
Crandleyhill Road
Blanefield Ave
Pladda Dr
Fullarton Ave
Kenmore Ave
Glenpark Ave
Farden Pl
Fairway
Kirkhill Cres
Overdale Crescent
Weston Pl
Crescent
Bentfield Drive
Bellrock Avenue
Centrum (Sports Arena)
Nursery Ave
Kingcase Primary
Wardneuk
Coylebank
Mochrum Ct
Neward Cres
Latta Ct
Coulthard Dr
Garryhorn
James St
Arran Park
Ardfin Ct
Ardfin Road
Laighland
Abbot Ct
Calvinston Road
Lilybank Rd
Carradale Dr
Creran Ct
Fulshaw Ct
Craigfin Ct
Craigskeen Pl
Cangillan Ct
Pleasantfield Rd
Waterloo Road
Fernbank
Fernbank Ct
Devilla Ct
Shilliaw Pl
Shilliaw Dr
McAdam Ct
Woodfield
Woodfield La
Young St
Wellington St
Lugar Cres
Benmore
Fearnoch
Lennox Dr
Murchie Dr
Semple Road
Cargill Dr
Marchfield Rd
Oswald Pl
Bellrock Rd
Englewood Ave
Doon Ave
Afton Avenue
Moor Park Cres
Renwick Way
Bennoch Pl
Marchfield Quad
Oswald Road
Woodfield Ave
B743 HEATHFIELD RD
Heathfield Primary
Heathpark
Clinic

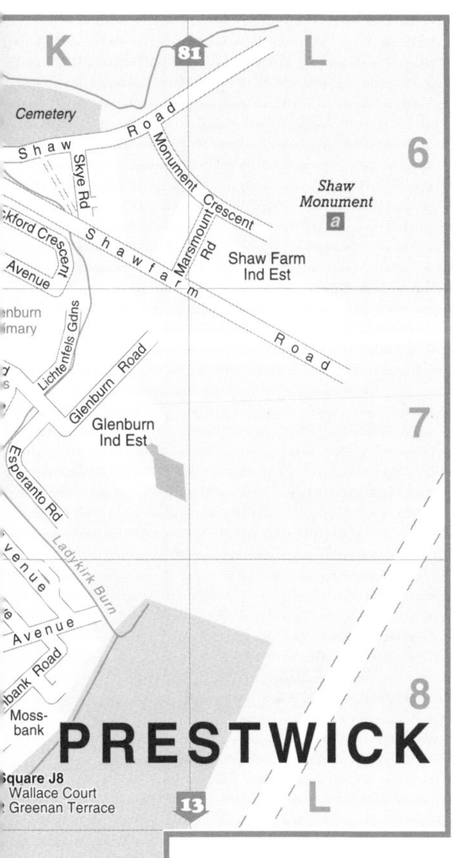

continued from overleaf....

Kenmore Avenue H9
Kildonan House (3) G10
Kilmarnock Road K2
Kingcase Avenue G9
Kingscroft Road G8
Kirk Street H6
Kirkhill Crescent G9
Kirklandholm H9
Kyle Street H7
Ladykirk Road H7
Laggan House (4) G10
Laighland H10
Langcroft Avenue K6
Larch House (9) H10
Latta Court J9
Lennox Drive H10
Leslie Terrace H7
Lichtenfels Gardens K7
Lilybank Road G10
Links Road G6
Lismore House (10) G10
Loudon Terrace J8
Lugar Crescent G10
MacIntyre Road H5
MacRae Drive H5
McAdam Court J10
McIntyre Avenue J5
McNee Road H5
McNeill Avenue J6
Main Street (Prestwick) H7
Main Street (Monkton) J2, J3
Mansewell Road H6
Mansfield Road G9
Manson Avenue J6
Marchburn Avenue K7
Marchfield Quadrant G10
Marchfield Road G10
Marina Road G7
Maryborough Avenue G9
Maryborough Road F9
Meadowbank Lane G8
Meiklewood Avenue H6
Merrick Avenue J6
Midton Avenue G7
Midton Road H7
Miller Square H5
Mochrum Court J9
Moffat Road H4
Monkton Court J5
Monkton Road H6
Monkton Road J5
Montgomerie Road G7
Monument Crescent K6
Monument Road L6
Moor Park Crescent H10
Moorfield Road H8
Morris Road H6
Morrison Road H4
Mossbank K8
Murchie Drive J10
Neward Crescent J9
Newark Terrace J8
Newdykes Court J6
Newdykes Farm Road J6
Newdykes Road J6
Nisbet Drive J10
Nursery Avenue G9
Obree Avenue J10
Orangefield Drive J6
Oswald Drive H6
Oswald Place F10
Oswald Road F10
Outdale Avenue K7
Overdale Crescent H9
Park Avenue G7
Pentland Drive J10
Pine House (7) H10
Pladda Drive H9
Pleasantfield Road G10
Powmill Gardens J5
Powmill Road J5
Queens Drive J2
Queens Terrace G6
Raith Avenue K8
Raith Terrace K8
Rathlin House (13) G10
Regent Park H6
Renwick Way J10
Riggs, The H6
Rosemount Gardens H9
Rowallan Crescent J8
Rowan House (8) H9
Rowanbank Road K8
Rylands H9
St Andrew's Avenue H9
St Cuthbert's Crescent J9
St Cuthbert's Road H9
St John Street H7
St Nicholas Road G8
St Ninians Park Place H8
St Ninians Road G9
St Quivox Road H7
Salisbury Place H7
Sandfield Road H7
Sanquhar Avenue K8
Saunterne Road H6
Seabank Road G6
Seagate H5
Semple Road J10
Shaw Road K6
Shawfarm Court J6
Shawfarm Gardens J5
Shawfarm Place J6
Shawfarm Road J5, K6
Sherwood Road K7
Shilliaw Drive J10
Shilliaw Place J10
Skye Road K6
Smith Street H7
Southpark Avenue G8
Springfield Avenue J8
Spruce House (6) G10
Station Drive H6
Station Road (Prestwick) H6
Station Road (Monkton) H3
Strang Place J10
Tarbolton Road K3
Tay Road H4
Templerigg Court H6
Templerigg Street H6
Templeton Crescent J7
Templeton Gardens J7
Torbeg House (5) H10
Towans Court J5
Tramore Crescent H7
Underwood Road J8
Wallace Court (1) J8
Wardneuk H9
Waterloo Road G10
Weir Avenue J6
Wellington Street G10
Welsh Road J5
Westbourne Avenue J7
Westbourne Gardens J7
Weston Place H9
Whinfield Avenue H9
Whinfield Gardens H9
Whinfield Place H8
Whinfield Road G9
Whitehall Avenue J7
Whiteside Drive K3
Whiteside Gardens K2
Whiteside Park K3
Whiteside Place K3
Whiteside Road J8
Winston Avenue J8
Wood Park H8
Woodfield Avenue F10
Woodfield Lane G10
Woodlands Street G7
Young Street G10
Younger Drive H5

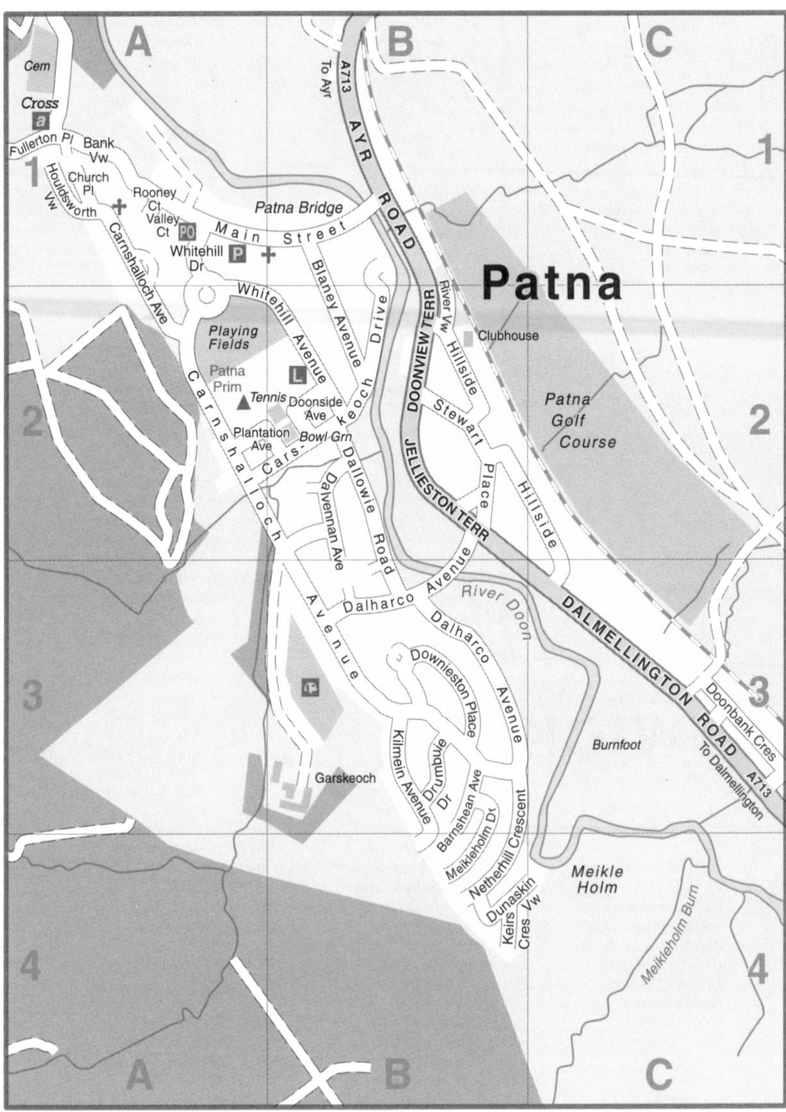

Index to Patna

Ayr Road	B1	Doonbank Crescent	C3	Kilmein Avenue	B3
Bank View	A1	Doonside Avenue	B2	Main Street	A1
Barnshean Avenue	B3	Doonview Terrace	B2	Meikleholm Drive	B4
Blaney Avenue	B2	Downieston Place	B3	Netherhill Crescent	B4
Carnshalloch Avenue	A2	Drumbuie Drive	B3	Plantation Avenue	A2
Carskeoch Drive	B2	Dunaskin View	B4	River View	B2
Church Place	A1	Fullerton Place	A1	Rooney Court	A1
Dalharco Avenue	B3	Hillside	B2	Stewart Place	B2
Dallowie Road	B2	Houldsworth View	A1	Valley Court	A1
Dalmellington Road	C3	Jellieston Terrace	B2	Whitehill Avenue	A2
Dalvennan Avenue	B2	Keirs Crescent	B4	Whitehill Drive	A1

Index to Skelmorlie

Annetyard Drive	C8
Annetyard Road	C8
Balnagowan Road	C7
Balvonie	B8
Beithglass Avenue	C7
Caskie Drive	C8
Chaseley Gardens	B9
Crescent, The	B7
Eglinton Drive	B6
Eglinton Gardens	B7
Eglinton Terrace	B8, B9
Fosterland	C8
Golf Course Road	C7
Halketburn Road	C8
Halketburn Terrace	C8
Heywood Gardens	B8
Highfield Court	B8
Hill View	C7
Innes Park Road	C7
Kilmory Gardens	B8
Lane, The	C7
Long Hill	B7
Montgomerie Drive	C6
Montgomerie Terrace	B7
Mount Stuart Drive	C2
Paddockdyke	C8
Redcliffe Manor	B8
Rothesay Court	B6
Sandybrae Road	C7
Seton Terrace	C7
Shore Road	B7
Shores, The	B10
Shuma Court	B10
Skelmorlie Castle Road	C7, C10
Skelmorlie Cross	C7
Station Road	B6
Strathclyde House	B9
Toward View	C7
Waters Edge	B7
Winton Drive	B6

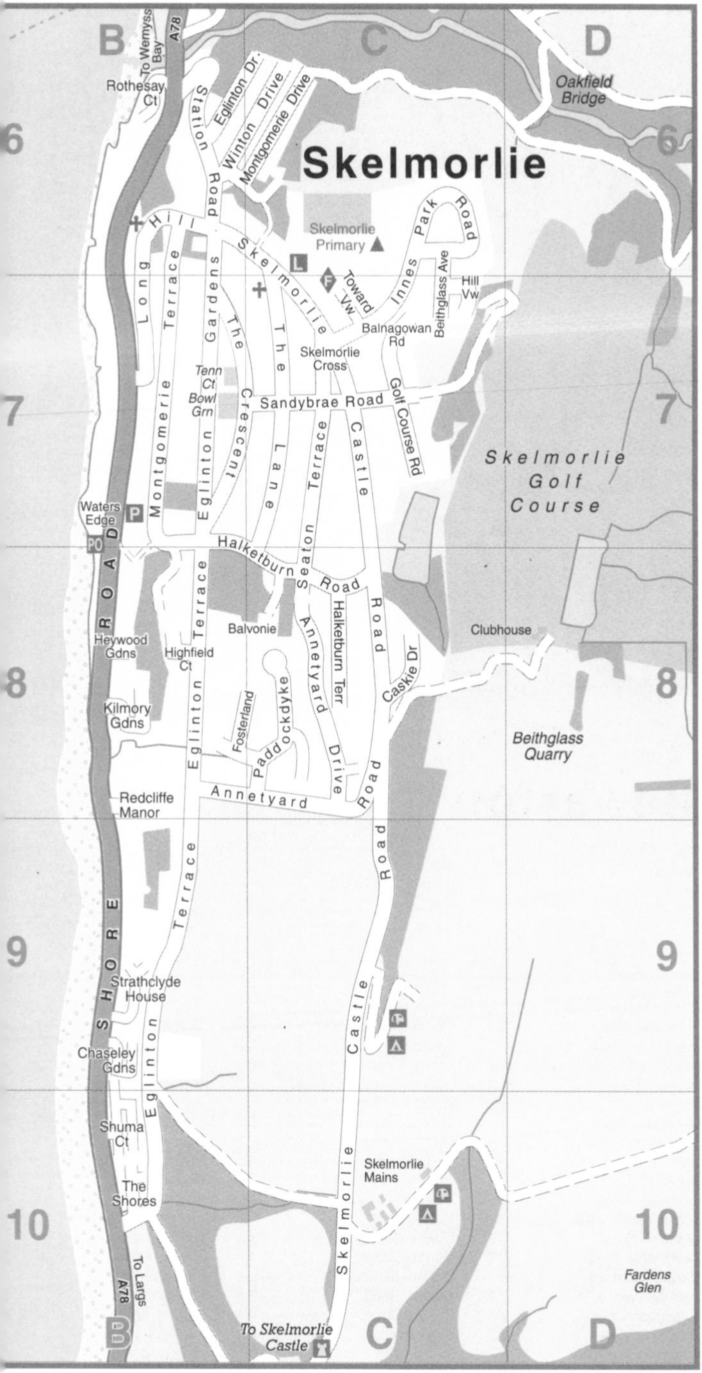

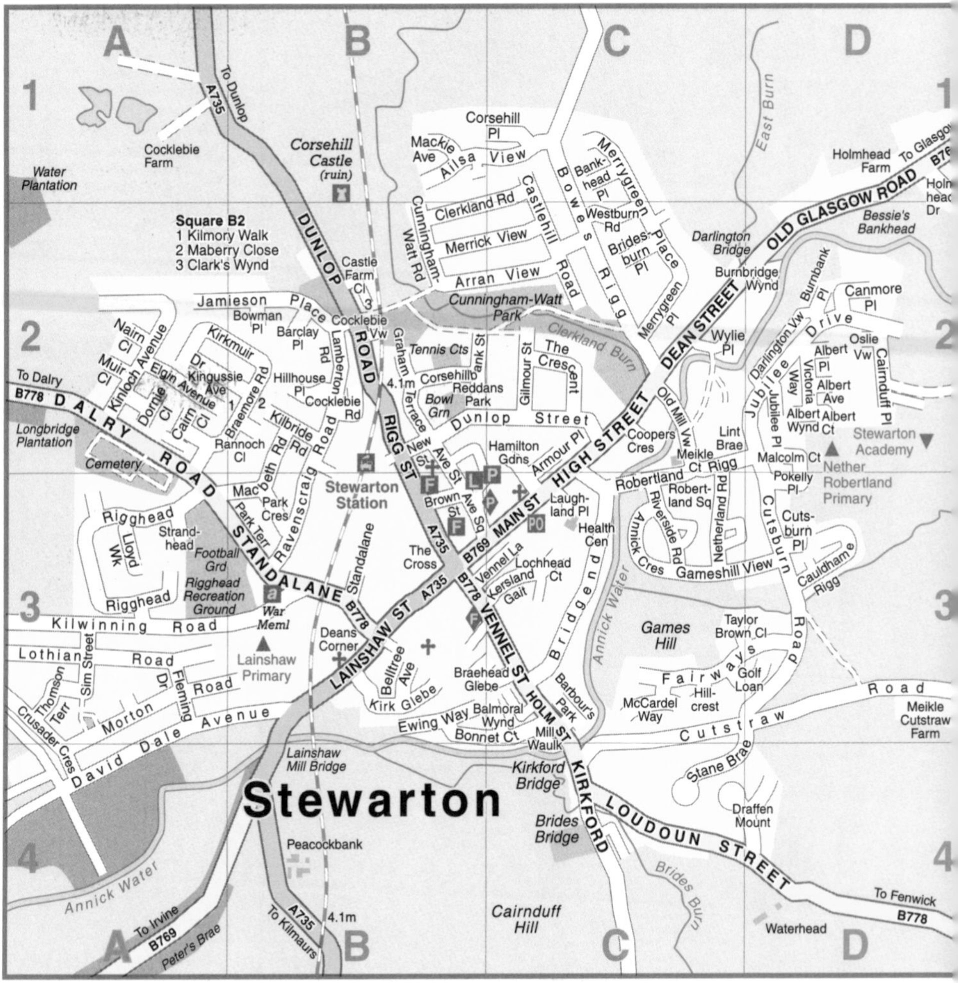

Square B2
1 Kilmory Walk
2 Maberry Close
3 Clark's Wynd

Stewarton

Index to Stewarton

Ailsa View B1
Albert Avenue D2
Albert Court D2
Albert Place D2
Albert Wynd D2
Annick Crescent C3
Armour Place C2
Arran View B2
Avenue Square B3
Avenue Street B2
Balmoral Wynd C3
Bankhead Place C1
Barbours Park C3
Barclay Place B2
Belltree Avenue B3
Bonnet Court B3
Bowes Rigg C1
Bowman Place B2
Braehead Glebe C3
Braemore Road A3
Bridesburn Place C2
Bridgend C3
Brown Street B3
Burnbank Place D2
Burnbridge Wynd C2
Cairn Close A2
Cairnduff Place D2
Canmore Place D2
Castle Farm Close B2
Castlehill Road C2
Cauldhame Rigg D3
Clark's Wynd (3) B2
Clerkland Road B2
Cocklebie Road B2
Cocklebie View B2
Coopers Crescent C2
Corsehillbank Street B2
Corsehill Place C1
Crusader Crescent A3
Crescent, The C2
Cross, The B3
Cunningham-Watt Road B2
Cutsburn Place D3
Cutsburn Road D3
Cutstraw Road C3
Dalry Road A2
Darlington View D2
David Dale Avenue A4
Dean Street C2
Deans Corner B3
Dornie Close A2
Draffen Mount D4
Dunlop Road B2
Dunlop Street B2
Elgin Avenue A2
Ewing Way B3
Fairways C3
Fleming Drive A3
Gameshill View
Gilmour Street
Golfloan
Graham Terrace
Hamilton Gardens
High Street
Hillcrest
Hillhouse Place
Holmhead Drive
Holm Street
Jamieson Place
Jubilee Drive
Jubilee Place
Kersland Gate
Kilbride Road
Kilmory Walk (1)
Kilwinning Road
Kingussie Avenue
Kinloch Avenue
Kirk Glebe

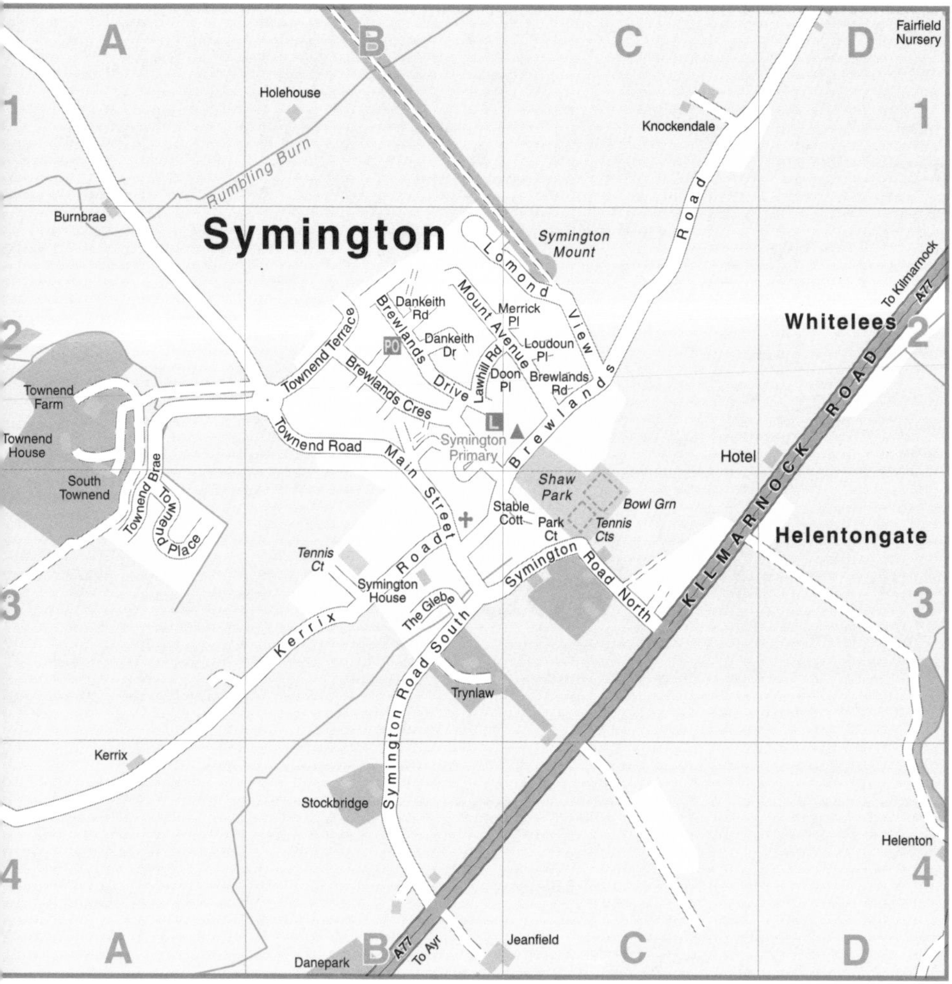

Symington

A B C D
1 2 3 4

Holehouse
Rumbling Burn
Burnbrae
Knockendale
Fairfield Nursery
Symington Mount
Lomond View
Road
Dankeith Rd
Brewlands
Mount Avenue
Merrick Pl
Dankeith Dr
Loudoun Pl
Lawhill Rd
Doon Pl
Brewlands Rd
Drive
Townend Terrace
Brewlands Cres
Brewlands
Whitelees
To Kilmarnock
A77
Kilmarnock Road
Townend Farm
Townend House
South Townend
Townend Road
Main Street
Symington Primary
Hotel
Shaw Park
Bowl Grn
Stable Cott
Park Ct
Tennis Cts
Helentongate
Townend Brae
Townend Place
Tennis Ct
Road
Symington House
Symington Road North
The Glebe
Kerrix
Symington Road South
Trynlaw
Kerrix
Stockbridge
Helenton
Jeanfield
Danepark
A77
To Ayr

kford	C4	Morton Road	A3	Springwell Place	C2	Dankeith Drive	B2
kmuir Drive	A2	Muir Close	A2	Standalane	B3	Dankeith Road	B2
inshaw Street	B3	Nairn Close	A2	Strandhead	A3	Doon Place	B2
mberton Road	B2	Netherland Road	C3	Stane Brae	C4	Glebe, The	B3
ughland Place	C3	New Street	B2	Taylor Brown Close	C3	Kerrix Road	B3
t Brae	C2	Old Glasgow Road	D2	Thomson Terrace	A3	Kilmarnock Road	C3
chhead Court	C3	Old Mill View	C2	Vennel Lane	C3	Lawhill Road	B2
yd Walk	A3	Oslie View	D2	Vennel Street	C3	Lomond View	B2
thian Road	A3	Park Crescent	B3	Victoria Way	D2	Loudoun Place	C2
udoun Street	C4	Park Terrace	B3	Westburn Road	C2	Main Street	B2
cBeth Road	B3	Pokelly Place	D3	Wylie Place	C2	Merrick Place	C2
ckie Avenue	B1	Rannoch Close (4)	B2			Mount Avenue	B2
Cardel Way	C3	Ravenscraig Road	B3			Park Court	C3
berry Close (2)	B2	Reddans Park	B2			Stable Cottage	C3
in Street	C3	Rigg Street	B2			Symington Road North	B3
lcolm Court	D2	Righead	A3	**Index to Symington**		Symington Road South	B4
ikle Court	C2	Riverside Road	C3			Townend Brae	A3
rrick View	B2	Robertland Rigg	C3	Brewlands Crescent	B2	Townend Place	A3
rrygreen Place	C2	Robertland Square	C3	Brewlands Drive	B2	Townend Road	B2
l Walk	C3	Sim Street	A3	Brewlands Road	C2	Townend Terrace	B2

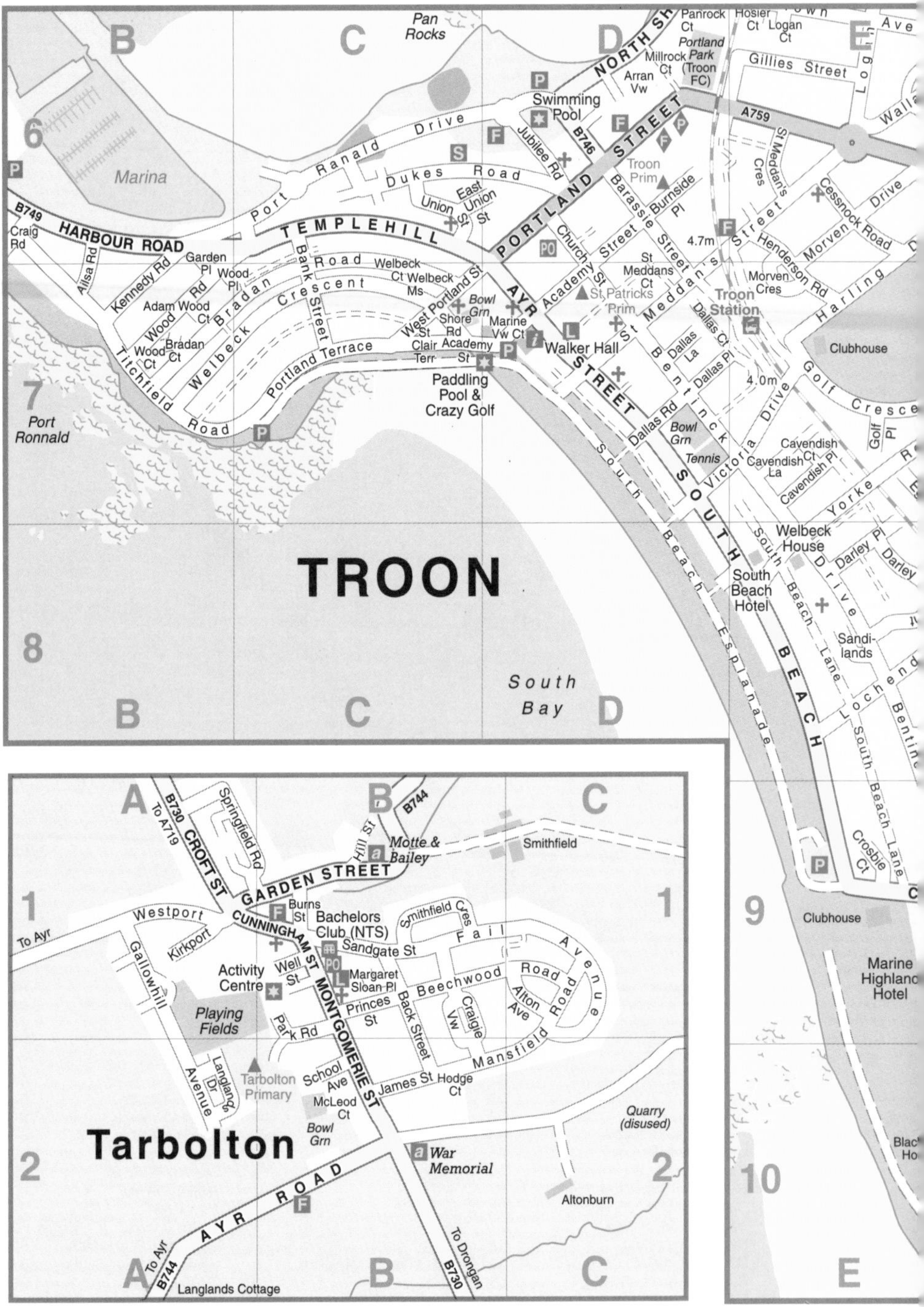

B
C
D
E
6
7
8
9
10
Pan Rocks
Marina
P
B749
HARBOUR ROAD
Craig Rd
Ailsa Rd
Kennedy Rd
Garden Pl
Wood Pl
Adam Wood Ct
Wood Rd
Wood Ct
Bradan Ct
Bradan Road
Welbeck Crescent
Titchfield Road
Port Ronnald
Port Ranald Drive
Dukes Road
Union St
East Union St
TEMPLEHILL
Bank Street
Welbeck Ct
Welbeck Ms
West Portland St
Portland Terrace
St Clair Terr
Shore Rd
Bowl Grn
Marine Vw Ct
Academy St
Paddling Pool & Crazy Golf
Swimming Pool
Jubilee Rd
B746
PORTLAND STREET
AYR STREET
NORTH SH
Arran Vw
Millrock Ct
Panrock Ct
Hosier Ct
Logan Ct
Portland Park (Troon FC)
Gillies Street
A759
Ave
Log
Walla
Troon Prim
Barassie Street
Burnside Pl
Church St
Academy Street
St Meddans Ct
St Patricks Prim
St Meddan's Street
St Meddan's Cres
Walker Hall
PO
L
4.7m
Henderson Rd
Cessnock Road
Morven Drive
Morven Cres
Harling
Troon Station
Dallas Ct
Dallas La
Dallas Pl
Dallas Rd
Bentinck
4.0m
Clubhouse
Golf Crescent
Golf Pl
Bowl Grn
Tennis
Victoria Drive
Cavendish Ct
Cavendish La
Cavendish Pl
Yorke
South Beach
SOUTH BEACH
South Beach Esplanade
Welbeck House
South Beach Hotel
Darley Pl
Darley
Drive
South Beach Lane
Sandilands
Lochend
Bentinck
Crosbie Ct
TROON
South Bay
Clubhouse
Marine Highland Hotel
Black Ho

A
B
C
1
2
B730
To A719
CROFT ST
Springfield Rd
B744
Hill St
Motte & Bailey
Smithfield
GARDEN STREET
Burns St
Westport
To Ayr
Kirkport
CUNNINGHAM ST
Bachelors Club (NTS)
Smithfield Cres
Fail Avenue
Sandgate St
Gallowhill Avenue
Activity Centre
Well St
Margaret Sloan Pl
Beechwood Road
Alton Ave
Road
Playing Fields
Princes St
Back Street
Craigie Vw
Park Rd
MONTGOMERIE ST
Mansfield
Langlands Dr
Tarbolton Primary
School Ave
James St
Hodge Ct
McLeod Ct
Quarry (disused)
Bowl Grn
Tarbolton
War Memorial
AYR ROAD
F
Altonburn
To Ayr
B744
To Drongan
B730
Langlands Cottage

Index to street names can be found on page 91

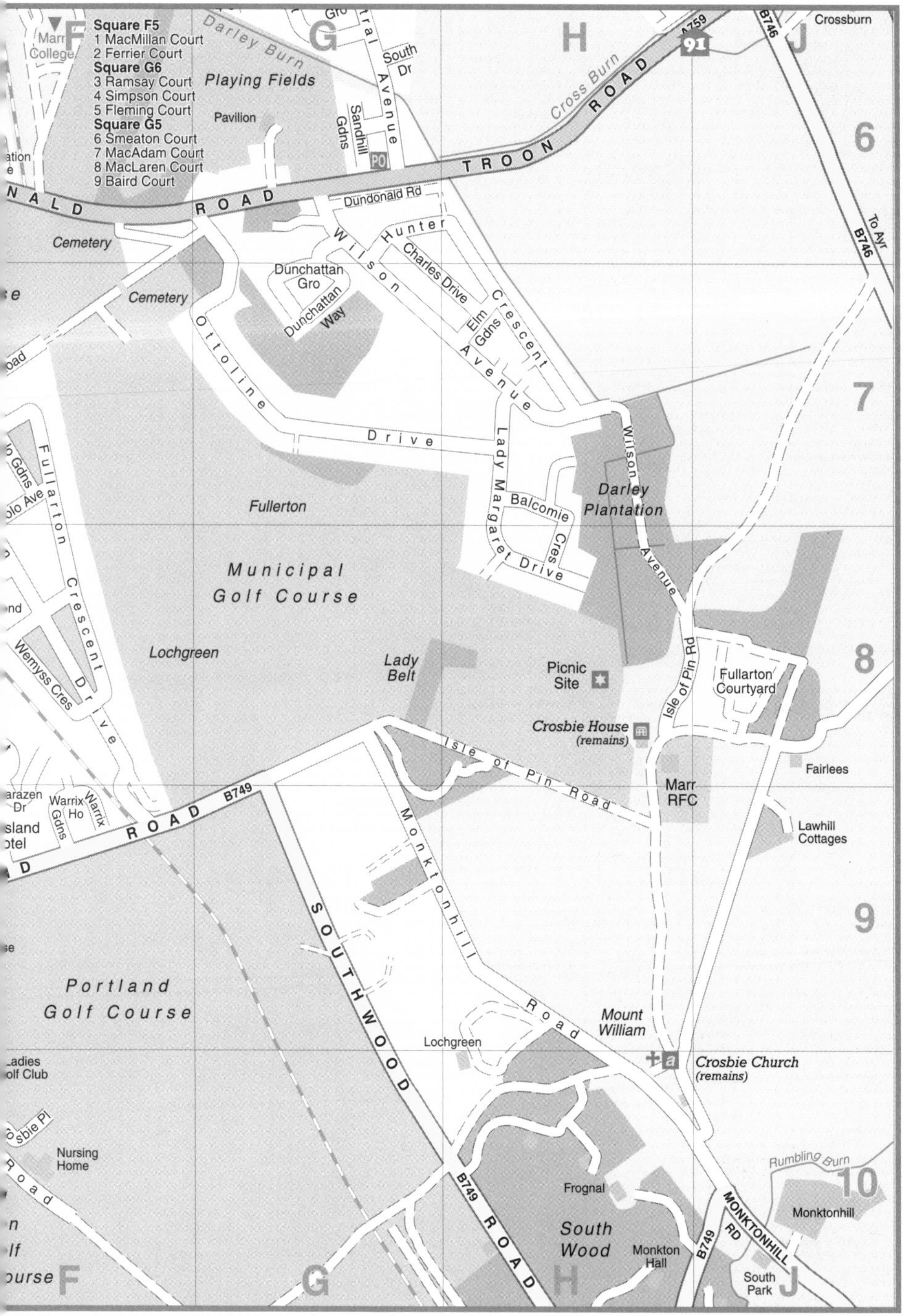

Square F5
1 MacMillan Court
2 Ferrier Court
Square G6
3 Ramsay Court
4 Simpson Court
5 Fleming Court
Square G5
6 Smeaton Court
7 MacAdam Court
8 MacLaren Court
9 Baird Court

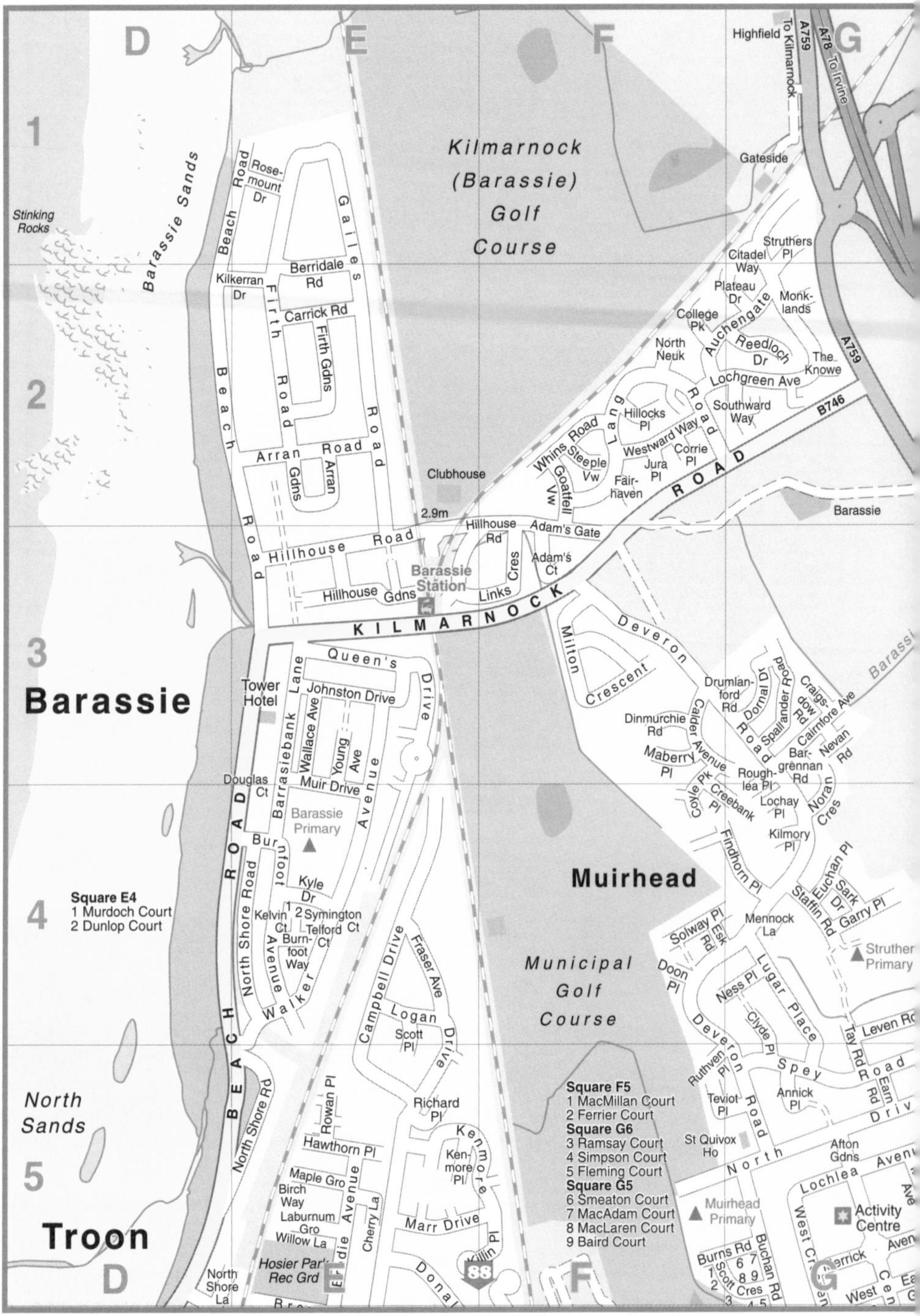

D E F G
1 2 3 4 5

Barassie
Troon
Muirhead
Kilmarnock (Barassie) Golf Course
Municipal Golf Course
Barassie Sands
Stinking Rocks
North Sands
Highfield
Gateside
Clubhouse
Barassie Station
Tower Hotel
Barassie Primary
Struthers Primary
Muirhead Primary
Activity Centre
St Quivox Ho
Hosier Park Rec Grd
To Kilmarnock A759
A78 To Irvine
A759
B746
2.9m
88

Beach Road
Rosemount Dr
Gailes Road
Berridale Rd
Kilkerran Dr
Firth Road
Carrick Rd
Firth Gdns
Arran Road
Arran Gdns
Hillhouse Road
Hillhouse Gdns
Hillhouse Rd
Links Cres
Adam's Gate
Adam's Ct
Kilmarnock Road
Queen's Drive
Johnston Drive
Barassiebank Lane
Wallace Ave
Young Ave
Muir Drive
Avenue
Douglas Ct
Burnfoot Avenue
Kyle Dr
Kelvin Ct
Symington Ct
Telford Ct
Burnfoot Way
Walker Avenue
North Shore Road
North Shore Rd
North Shore La
Beach Road
Campbell Drive
Fraser Ave
Logan Drive
Scott Pl
Richard Pl
Kenmore
Kenmore Pl
Marr Drive
Killin Pl
Donald
Rowan Pl
Hawthorn Pl
Maple Gro
Birch Way
Laburnum Gro
Willow La
Cherry La
Eddie Avenue
Citadel Way
Struthers Pl
Plateau Dr
Monklands
College Pk
Auchengate
Reedloch Dr
North Neuk
The Knowe
Lochgreen Ave
Southward Way
Lang Road
Hillocks Pl
Whins Road
Steeple Vw
Westward Way
Corrie Pl
Jura Pl
Fairhaven
Goatfell Vw
Barassie
Deveron Road
Milton Crescent
Drumlanford Rd
Dornal Dr
Spallander Road
Craigsdow Rd
Cairnfore Ave
Dinmurchie Rd
Calder Avenue
Maberry Pl
Bargrennan Rd
Nevan Rd
Roughlea Pl
Coyle Pk
Creebank Pl
Lochay Pl
Noran Cres
Kilmory Pl
Findhorn Pl
Euchan Pl
Sark Dr
Staffin Rd
Garry Pl
Solway Pl
Esk Rd
Mennock La
Doon Pl
Lugar Place
Ness Pl
Clyde Pl
Spey Road
Leven Rd
Tay Rd
Earn Rd
Ruthven Pl
Teviot Pl
Annick Pl
Drive
Afton Gdns
North Avenue
Lochlea Ave
West Crescent
Burns Rd
Scott Cres
Buchan Rd
Carrick
West Cen

Square E4
1 Murdoch Court
2 Dunlop Court

Square F5
1 MacMillan Court
2 Ferrier Court
Square G6
3 Ramsay Court
4 Simpson Court
5 Fleming Court
Square G5
6 Smeaton Court
7 MacAdam Court
8 MacLaren Court
9 Baird Court

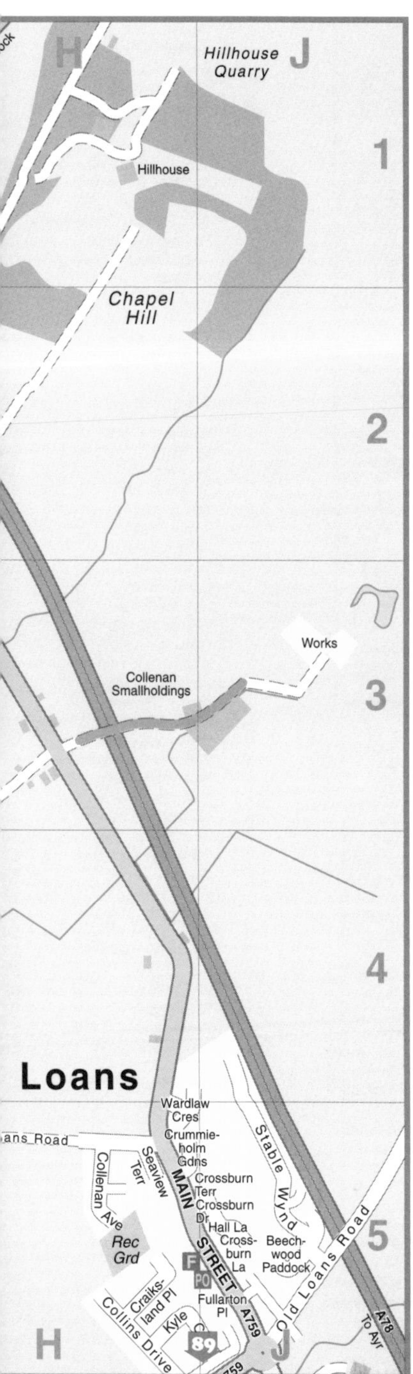

Index to Tarbolton

Street	Grid
Alton Avenue	C1
Ayr Road	A2
Back Street	B1
Beechwood Road	B1
Burns Street	B1
Craigie View	B1
Croft Street	A1
Cunningham Street	B1
Fail Avenue	B1
Gallowhill Avenue	A1
Garden Street	B1
Hill Street	B1
Hodge Court	B2
James Street	B2
Kirkport	A1
Langlands Drive	A2
Mcleod Court	B2
Mansefield Road	B2
Margaret Sloan Place	B1
Montgomerie Street	B1
Park Road	B1
Princes Street	B1
Sandgate Street	B1
School Avenue	B2
Smithfield Crescent	B1
Springfield Road	A1
Well Street	B1
Westport	A1

Index to Troon

Street	Grid
Academy Street	D7
Adams Court	F3
Adam's Gate	F3
Adam Wood Court	B7
Afton Gardens	G5
Ailsa Road	B7
Aldersyde Avenue	G5
Annick Place	G5
Arran Gardens	E2
Arran Road	E2
Arran View	D6
Auchengate	F2
Ayr Street	D7
Baird Court (9)	G5
Balcomie Crescent	H7
Bank Street	C7
Barassie Bank Lane	E3
Barassie Street	D6
Bargrennan Road	G3
Beach Road	D1, D5
Beechwood Paddock	J5
Bentinck Close	E9
Bentinck Crescent	F8
Bentinck Drive	D7, E8
Berriedale Road	E2
Birch Way	E5
Bradan Court	B7
Bradan Road	C7
Brodie Avenue	E5
Brown Avenue	E6
Buchan Road	G5
Burnfoot Avenue	E4
Burnfoot Way	E4
Burns Road	F5
Burnside Place	D6
Cairnfore Avenue	G3
Calder Avenue	F3
Campbell Drive	E4
Carrick Road	E2
Cavendish Court	E7
Cavendish Lane	E7
Cavendish Place	E7
Central Avenue	G5
Cessnock Road	E6
Charles Drive	G6
Cherry Lane	E5
Church Street	D6
Citadel Way	G1
Clyde Place	G4
College Park	F2
Collenan Avenue	H5
Collins Drive	H5
Corrie Place	F2
Coyle Park	F4
Craig Road	B6
Craigend Road	F9
Craigsdow Road	G3
Craiksland Place	H5
Creebank Place	F4
Crosbie Court	E9
Crosbie Place	F10
Crosbie Road	E9
Crossburn Drive	J5
Crossburn Lane	J5
Crossburn Terrace	J5
Crummieholm Gardens	H5
Dallas Court	D7
Dallas Lane	D7
Dallas Place	D7
Dallas Road	D7
Darley Crescent	E8
Darley Place	E8
Deveron Road	F3
Deveron Road	F4
Dinmurchie Road	F3
Donald Crescent	E6
Doon Place	F4
Dornal Drive	G3
Douglas Court	E3
Drumlanford Road	G3
Dukes Road	C6
Dunchattan Grove	G7
Dunchattan Way	G7
Dundonald Road	F6
Dunlop Court (2)	E4
Earn Road	G5
East Grove	G5
East Union Street	C6
Eglinton Crescent	E7
Eglinton Drive	F7
Elm Gardens	H7
Esk Road	F4
Euchan Place	G4
Fairhaven	F2
Ferrier Court (2)	F5
Findhorn Place	G4
Firth Gardens	E2
Firth Road	E2
Fleming Court (5)	G5
Fraser Avenue	E4
Fullarton Courtyard	J8
Fullarton Crescent	F7
Fullarton Drive	F8
Fullarton Place	J5
Gailes Road	E1
Garden Place	B6
Garry Place	G4
Gillies Street	E6

continued overleaf....

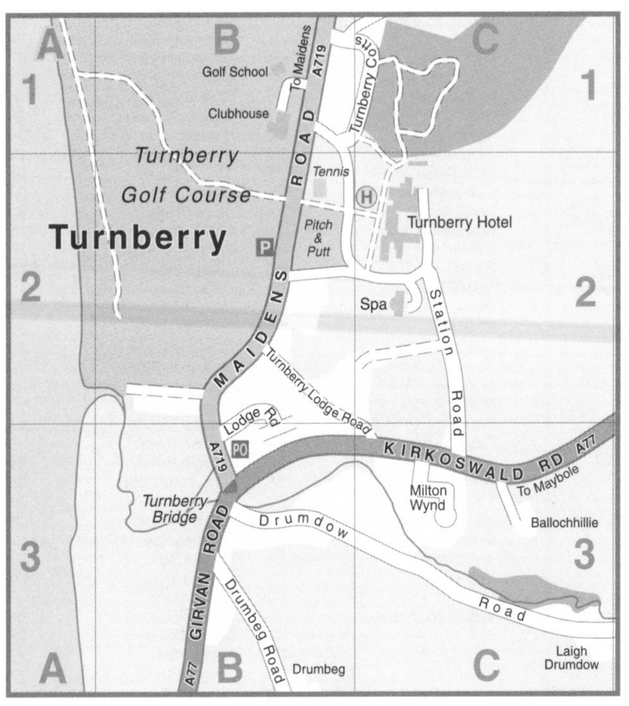

Index to Troon

continued from page 91

Goatfell View F2
Golf Crescent E7
Golf Place E7
Hall Lane J5
Harbour Road B6
Harling Drive E7
Hawthorn Place E5
Henderson Road E6
Hillhouse Gardens E3
Hillhouse Road E3
Hillocks Place F2
Hosier Court E6
Hunter Crescent G6
Isle of Pin Road H8
Johnston Drive E3
Jubilee Road D6
Jura Place F2
Kelvin Court E4
Kenmore Place E5
Kenmore E5
Kennedy Road B7
Kilkerran Drive E2
Killantrae House F8
Killin Place F5
Kilmarnock Road E3
Kilmory Place G4
Knowe, The G2
Kyle Crescent H5
Kyle Drive E4
Laburnum Grove E5
Lady Margaret Drive H7
Lang Road F2
Leven Road G4
Links Crescent F3
Lochay Place G4
Lochend Place F8
Lochend Road E8
Lochgreen Avenue G2
Lochlea Avenue G5
Logan Court E6
Logan Drive E4, E6
Lugar Place G4
MacAdam Court (7) G5
MacLaren Court (8) G5
MacMillan Court (1) F5
Maberry Place F3
Main Street J5
Maple Grove E5
Marine View Court D7
Marr Drive E5
Mennock Lane G4
Merrick Avenue G5
Millrock Court D6
Milton Crescent F3
Monklands G2
Monktonhill Road G9, J10
Morven Crescent E7
Morven Drive E6
Mossgiel Avenue G5
Muir Drive E4
Murdoch Court (1) E4
Ness Place G4
Nevan Road G3
Noran Crescent G4
North Drive G5
North Neuk F2
North Shore Lane D5
North Shore Road D6
Old Loans Road H5, J5
Old Station Brae F6
Old Station Wynd F6
Ottoline Drive G7
Panrock Court D6
Plateau Drive G2
Polo Avenue F7
Polo Gardens F7
Port Ranald Drive C6
Portland Street D6
Portland Terrace C7
Queens Drive E3
Ramsay Court (3) G5
Reedloch Drive G2
Richard Place E5
Rosemount Drive E1
Roughlea Place G4
Rowan Place E5
Ruthven Place F5
St Clair Terrace C7
St Quivox House G5
St Meddan's Court D7
St Meddan's Crescent E6
St Meddan's Street D7
Sandhill Gardens G6
Sandilands E8
Sarazen Drive F9
Sark Drive G4
Scott Crescent G5
Scott Place E4
Seaview Terrace H5
Shore Road C7
Simpson Court (4) G5
Smeaton Court (6) G5
Solway Place F4
South Beach Esplanade D7
South Beach Lane E8
South Beach D7
South Drive G6
Southward Way G2
Southwood Road G9
Spallander Road G3
Spey Road G5
Stable Wynd J5
Staffin Road G4
Steeples View F2
Struthers Place G1
Symington Court E4
Tay Road G4
Telford Court E4
Templehill C6
Teviot Place F5
Titchfield Road B7
Troon Road H6
Union Street C6
Victoria Drive E7
Walker Avenue E4
Wallace Avenue E3
Wallacefield Road E6
Wardlaw Crescent H4
Warrix Gardens F9
Warrix House F9
Welbeck Court C7
Welbeck Crescent C7
Welbeck Mews C7
Wemyss Crescent F8
West Crescent G5
West Grove G5
West Portland Street C7
Westward Way F2
Whins Road F2
Willockston Road F7
Willow Lane E5
Wilson Avenue G7
Wood Court B7
Wood Place B7
Wood Road B7
Yorke Road E7
Young Avenue E3

Index to Turnberry

Drumbeg Road B3
Drumdow Road B3
Girvan Road B3
Kirkoswald Road C3
Lodge Road B2
Maidens Road B2
Milton Wynd C3
Station Road C2
Turnberry Cottages C1
Turnberry Lodge Road B2

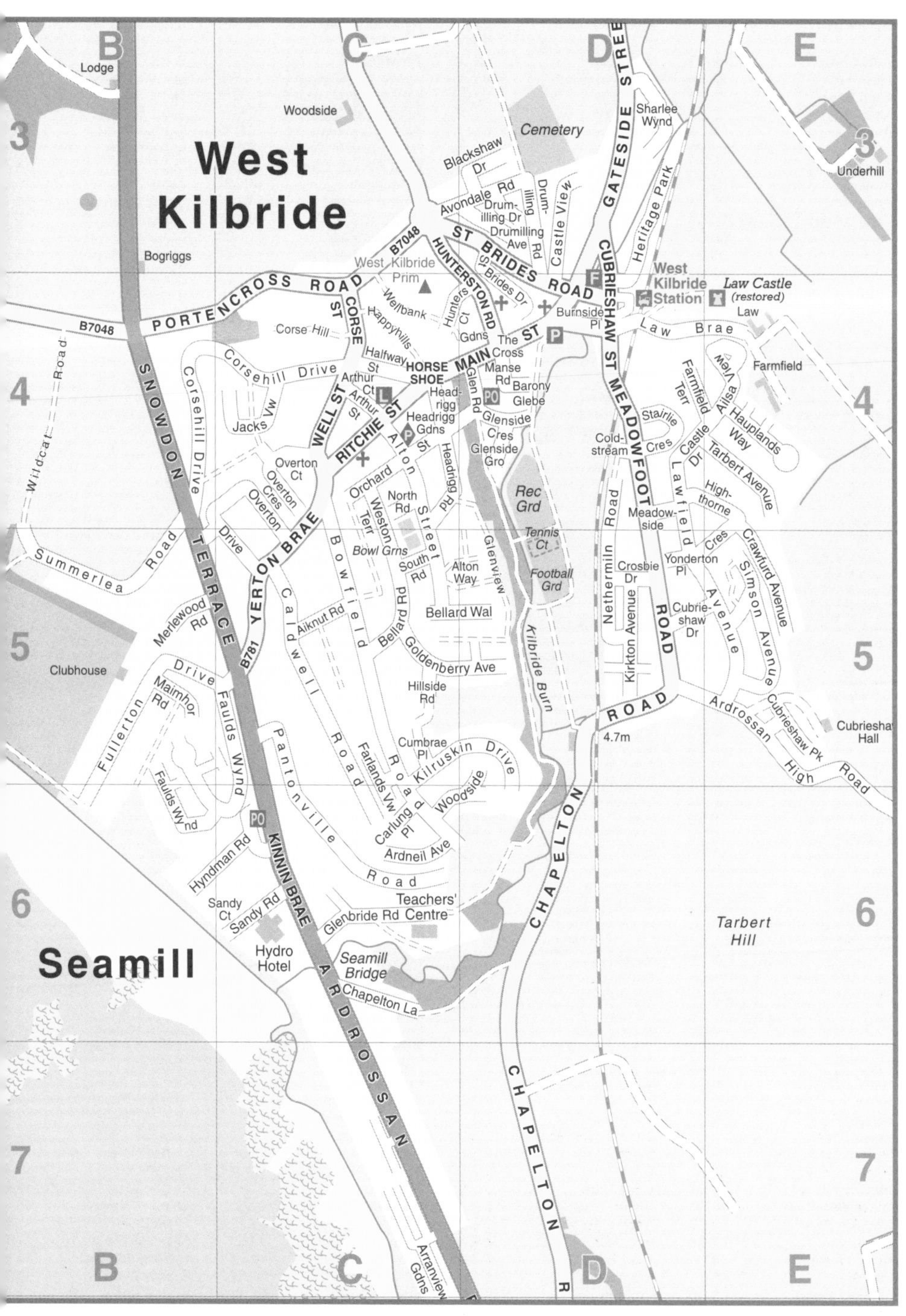

Index to street names can be found overleaf

INDEX TO WEST KILBRIDE & AYR

Index is shown by street name, page number then grid reference

Index to West Kilbride

Aiknut Road 93 C5
Ailsa View 93 E4
Alton Street 93 C4
Alton Way 93 D5
Ardneil Avenue 93 C6
Ardrossan High Road 93 E5
Ardrossan Road 93 C6
Arranview Gardens 93 C7
Arthur Court 93 C4
Arthur Street 93 C4
Avenue, The 93 D2
Avenue, The 93 E1
Avondale Road 93 D3
Barony Glebe 93 D4
Bellard Road 93 C5
Bellard Walk 93 D5
Blackshaw Drive 93 D3
Bowfield Road 93 C5
Burnside Place 93 D4
Caldwell Road 93 C5
Carlung Place 93 C6
Castle Drive 93 D4
Castle View 93 D3
Chapelton Lane 93 C6
Chapelton Road 93 D6
Chapelton Road 93 D7
Coldstream 93 D4
Corse Hill 93 C4
Corse Street 93 C4
Corsehill Drive 93 B4
Corsehill Drive 93 C4
Craufurd Avenue 93 E5
Crosbie Drive 93 D5
Cross, The 93 D4
Cubrieshaw Drive 93 D5
Cubrieshaw Park 93 E5
Cubrieshaw Street 93 D4
Cumbrae Place 93 C5
Drummilling Avenue 93 D3
Drummilling Drive 93 D3
Drummilling Road 93 D3
Farlands View 93 C5
Farmfield Terrace 93 D4
Faulds Wynd 93 B5
Fullerton Drive 93 B5
Gateside Street 93 D3
Glen Road 93 D4
Glenbride Road 93 C6
Glenside Crescent 93 D4
Glenside Grove 93 D4
Glenview 93 D5
Goldenberry Avenue 93 C5
Halfway Street 93 C4
Happyhills 93 C4
Hauplands Way 93 E4
Headrigg Gardens 93 C4
Headrigg Road 93 C4
Headrigg 93 C4
Heritage Park 93 D3
Highthorne Crescent 93 E4
Hillside Road 93 C5
Horse Shoe 93 C4
Hunters Court 93 C4
Hunterston Road 93 C3
Hyndman Road 93 B6
Jacks View 93 C4
Kilruskin Drive 93 C5
Kinnin Brae 93 C6
Kirkton Avenue 93 D5
Law Brae 93 D4
Lawfield Avenue 93 D5
Maimhor Road 93 B5
Main Street 93 D4
Manse Road 93 D4
Meadowfoot Road 93 D4
Meadowside 93 D4
Merlewood Road 93 B5
Morton Way 93 C3
Nethermiln Road 93 D5
North Road 93 C4
Orchard Street 93 C4
Overton Court 93 C4
Overton Crescent 93 C4
Overton Drive 93 C4
Pantonville Road 93 C6
Portencross Road 93 B4
Ritchie Street 93 C4
St Brides Drive 93 D4
St Brides Road 93 D3
Sandy Court 93 C6
Sandy Road 93 C6
Sharlee Wynd 93 D3
Simson Avenue 93 E5
Snowdon Terrace 93 B4
South Road 93 C5
Stairlie Crescent 93 D4
Summerlea Road 93 B5
Tarbert Avenue 93 E4
Well Street 93 C4
Wellbank Gardens 93 C4
Weston Terrace 93 C4
Wildcat Road 93 B4
Woodside 93 C6
Yerton Brae 93 C5
Yonderton Place 93 D5

Index to Ayr

Abbots Crescent 17 A21
Abbots Way 16 B20
Abercromby Drive 16 C19
Academy Street 14 E14
Afton Court 15 G17
Ailsa Place 14 D14
Ailsa View 17 A21
Ailsa View Gardens 17 A21
Ailsa View Place 16 B21
Ailsa View Wynd 16 B21
Airlie Court 14 D17
Albert Terrace 14 F15
Alder Bank 15 J17
Alderston Avenue 12 F12
Alderston Park 12 F12
Alderston Place 12 F12
Alexandra Terrace 12 F12
Allan Place 13 H12
Allenfield Road 15 J17
Allison Street 12 F13
Alloway 16 D22
Alloway Park 14 D16
Alloway Place Lane 14 D15
Alloway Place 14 D15
Alloway Street 14 E16
Altry Place 17 A22
Anderson Crescent 17 G19
Annfield Glen Road 17 G19
Annpit Road 12 G11
Ardlui Road 12 F11
Argyle Park 12 F13
Armour Drive 15 H17
Arnprior Place 17 E21
Arran Mall 14 E15
Arran Terrace 14 D14
Arranview Court 12 G11
Arrol Drive 14 C18
Arrol Park 14 D18
Arthur Street 14 E15
Ashgrove Street 14 F16
Aspen Court 15 J18
Aspen Road 15 J18
Auchenbeg Crescent 17 F20
Auchendoon Crescent 16 C19
Auchentrae Crescent 16 C19
Auld Nick's View 16 D22
Back Hawkhill Avenue 12 G13
Back Peebles Street 14 E14
Baird Road 16 D21
Ballantine Drive 14 E17
Balminnoch Park 16 B22
Bankfield Park 17 H20
Barnford Crescent 17 F21
Barns Court 14 E15
Barns Crescent 14 E16
Barns Park 14 E15
Barns Street 14 E15
Barns Street Lane 14 E15
Barns Terrace 14 E16
Barns Terrace Lane 14 E15
Bath Place 14 D15
Bathurst Drive 17 F22
Beagle Crescent 16 B20
Beech Grove 15 H15
Bellesleyhill Avenue 12 G12
Bellesleyhill Court 12 F11
Bellesleyhill Road 12 F12
Bellevale Avenue 14 E18
Bellevale Qaudrant 14 E18
Bellevue Crescent 14 D16
Bellevue Lane 14 E16
Bellevue Road 14 D16
Bellevue Street 14 E16
Bellrock Road 12 F11
Belmont Avenue 14 F18
Belmont Crescent 14 F18
Belmont Drive 14 F18
Belmont Place East 14 F17
Belmont Place West 14 F17
Belmont Road 14 F18
Belvidere Terrace 12 F13
Bentfield Avenue 14 D17
Beresford Court 14 E16
Beresford Lane 14 E16
Beresford Terrace 14 E16
Birch Road 17 H19
Blackburn Drive 14 C17
Blackburn Place 14 D17
Blackburn Road 14 D17
Blackfriars Court 14 E15
Blackfriars Walk 14 E15
Blackhill Street 15 G18
Blackhouse Place 15 H15
Boat Vennal 14 E14
Boswell Park 14 E15
Boundary Road 13 J11
Bourtree Park 14 F16
Bowman Road 14 E17
Bracken Park 17 H20
Bradan Drive 17 G21
Braehead Avenue 13 H13
Braehead Crescent 13 H13
Braehead Road 13 J13
Braemar Square 13 J13
Braeside Road 13 J13
Briar Grove 17 H19
Britannia Place 12 G12
Broadwood Park 17 F22
Broomfield Gardens 14 E17
Broomfield Road 14 E17
Broun Drive 16 D22
Browncarrick Drive 17 A22
Bruce Crescent 14 D14
Buchan Court 14 D14
Burnbank Place 17 C
Burnbank Road 17 C
Burness Avenue 16
Burnett Terrace 15 C
Burns Statue Arcade 14
Burns Statue Square 14
Burn's Wicket 16 D
Buttermarket Close 14
Cage Walk 14
Cairn Crescent 16 C
Cairnsmore Drive 16
Caledonia Road 15 C
Callendar Place 12 C
Callendar Road 13
Cambusdoon Drive 16 D
Cambuslea Gardens 12 C
Cambuslea Road 12 C
Campbell Court 15 H
Campbell Street 12
Camphill Place 15 C
Campion Court 17 C
Carcluie Crescent 17 C
Carrick Avenue 14
Carrick Gardens 14
Carrick Park 14
Carrick Road Lane 14
Carrick Road 14
Carrick Street 14
Carseloch Road 17
Carwinshoch View 14 C
Cassillis Street 14 D
Castle Square 17 A
Castle View 17 A
Castle Walk 16
Castlehill Court 15 C
Castlehill Crescent 14
Castlehill Road 14
Cathcart Street 14
Cedar Road 15
Celandine Bank 17 H
Cessnock Place 15 H
Chalmers Avenue 14
Chalmers Road 14
Chapel Park Road 14
Charlotte Street 14 D
Charlotte Street Lane 14 D
Cherry Hill Road 17 C
Chestnut Road 15
Church Court 14
Churchill Crescent 15 H
Churchill Tower 12 D
Citadel Place 14 D
Clarendon Place 15 H
Clarke Avenue 14 D
Clochranhill Road 16
Cloverhill 15
Content Avenue 14
Content Street 14
Coranbae Place 17 A
Cornhill 17 C
Corsehill Park 14
Corsehill Place 14
Corsehill Road 14
Corserine Road 17 A
Corton Howe 17
Corton Lea 17
Corton Shaw 17 C
Cowan Crescent 13 H
Craig Drive 17 A
Craighall Place 17
Craigholm Road 15
Craigie Avenue 14
Craigie Lea 15 C
Craigie Road 14
Craigie Way 15 C

aigneil Place 16 C19
aigstewart Crescent 16 B22
aigston Avenue 15 H17
aigweil Place 14 D16
aigweil Road 14 D16
anesbill Court 17 G20
ocus Bank 17 H20
ofthead Road 15 H18
omwell Road 14 D14
oss Street 14 E14
ossburn 17 A22
own Square 12 E13
own Street 12 E13
zean Road 16 C20
nning Park Drive 16 C20
nningham Crescent 15 G17
nningham Drive 15 H17
nningham Place 15 H17
rtecan Place 14 E17
isy Cottages 12 F12
lblair Arcade 14 E15
lblair Court 14 E15
lblair Road 14 E15
lmellington Road 15 G18
lmilling Crescent 13 J13
lmilling Drive 13 J13
lmilling Road 13 K13
lton Park 17 A21
rnside 12 E13
vidson Place 14 F14
ngola Road 14 F17
nnini Court 14 D14
onbank Park 16 C23
onfoot Road 16 C20
onholm Park 17 E23
onholm Place 16 E22
onholm Road 16 E22
onvale Drive 17 F23
onvale Place 17 F23
onview Gardens 16 B21
onview Wynd 16 B21
rnoch Park 14 D17
uglas Lane 14 E15
uglas Street 14 E15
umellan Road 17 F21
ummond Crescent 13 K13
ke Terrace 12 F13
mfries Park 17 F22
nlop Crescent 15 K14
nlop Terrace 15 J14
nure Road 16 B21
tch Mill 16 D23
rls Way 16 B20
st Park Road 12 G12
st Road 13 H10
enhall Road 12 G11
inton Place 14 D14
inton Terrace 14 D14
a Court 14 F14
a Gardens 14 F14
a Street 14 F14
sland Place 15 G17
sland Square 15 G17
nbank Street 12 F12
glewood Avenue 12 G10
planade 14 D15
rick Place 12 G11
enfield Avenue 14 E18
enfield Gardens 17 F19
enfield Park 17 E19
enfield Place 17 F19
enfield Road 17 E19
rfield Park 14 D16
rfield Road 14 D16
lkland Park Road 12 F12

Falkland Place 12 F12
Falkland Road 12 F12
Falkland Yard 12 F11
Farrell Place 12 G13
Fellhill Street 15 G18
Fenwickland Avenue 17 F19
Fenwickland Place 17 F19
Ferguson Street 13 H13
Fern Brae 17 H20
Finlas Avenue 17 G20
Finnick Glen 17 F20
Fir Bank 15 H18
Flaxton Court 14 E17
Forbes Drive 13 H11
Forehill Road 15 H17
Forest Way 15 H18
Forge Road 12 G11
Fort Court 14 E14
Fort Street 14 E15
Fotheringham Road 14 F15
Foxglove Place 17 H20
Fullarton Street 14 E15
Fulshaw Crescent 13 L13
Fulshaw Place 13 K12
Galloway Avenue 13 H13
Garden Court 14 E14
Garden Street 14 E14
Gartferry Court 14 D17
Gavin Hamilton Court 15 H17
Gearholm Road 16 C20
Gemmell Court 15 H14
Gemmell Crescent 15 H14
George Place 17 A21
George Square 14 F14
George Street 14 F14
George's Avenue 12 G12
Glebe Road 12 E13
Glebe Crescent 12 E13
Glenalla Crescent 16 B22
Glencairn Road 15 G17
Glenconner Place 15 G17
Glenconner Road 15 G17
Glendale Crescent 17 G19
Glendale Place 17 G19
Glenmount Place 17 A22
Glenmuir Court 13 J13
Glenmuir Place 13 J12
Glenmuir Road 13 J13
Glenmuir Square 13 H13
Glenpark Place 17 G20
Glenriddel Road 15 G17
Gordon Street 12 F12
Gordon Terrace 14 F15
Gorse Park 17 H20
Goschen Terrace 12 G13
Goukscroft Court 16 C20
Goukscroft Park 16 C20
Gould Street 12 G13
Gowanbank Road 17 G21
Gower Place 17 G20
Grange Avenue 17 G21
Green Street Lane 12 E13
Green Street 14 E14
Greenan Grove 17 A20
Greenan Park 17 A20
Greenan Place 16 B20
Greenan Road 17 A20
Greenan Square 17 A20
Greenan Way 17 A20
Greenfield Avenue 16 C21
Greentree Park 17 H19
Griffin Dock Road 12 D13
Guiltreehill 17 F22
Halls Vennal 12 E13
Hamilton Crescent 14 F17

Harebell Place 17 G20
Hartfield Road 14 E18
Harthall 13 K13
Hawkhill Avenue Lane 14 F14
Hawkhill Avenue 12 F13
Hawthorn Drive 17 H19
Hay Hill 15 J15
Hazelwood Road 14 E17
Heather Park 17 H20
Heathfield Road 12 G10
Heathpark 13 H10
High Street 14 E14
High Maybole Road 16 D23
High Road 13 K12
High Thornyflat Wynd 13 K12
Highfield Drive 13 K12
Highfield Road 17 G19
Hilary Crescent 14 F17
Hillfoot Crescent 15 G18
Hillfoot Road 15 H18
Hilltop Place 15 J18
Hollow Park Court 17 G21
Hollow Park 17 G21
Holly Bank 15 J18
Holmston Crescent 15 H16
Holmston Drive 15 H17
Holmston Gardens 14 F16
Holmston Road 15 G16
Home Farm Road 17 F21
Honeysuckle Park 17 G21
Hope Street 14 E14
Hunter's Avenue 12 G12
Inkerman Court 14 D14
Inverkar Road 14 F17
Iris Court 17 H20
Ivy Place 15 J18
James Brown Avenue 13 J13
James Campbell Road 15 G15
James Street 14 F14
John Street 14 F14
Juniper Green 15 J17
Kersepark 17 G22
Kilbrandon Crescent 17 A21
Kilbrandon Way 17 A21
Killoch Place 14 E16
Kilnbank Crescent 15 J16
Kincaidston Drive 17 G20
King Street 14 F14
Kings Court 14 F14
Kirk Port 14 E15
Kirkholm Avenue 12 F11
Knoll Park 17 E20
Knowe, The 14 E18
Knoweholm 16 B21
Kyle Court 14 F16
Kyle Street 14 E15
Laburnum Road 15 H17
Laigh Mount 17 F22
Lamford Drive 16 B22
Lansdowne Road 12 F12
Larchwood Road 17 H19
Larghill Lane 15 G18
Laughlanglen Road 17 F21
Laurel Bank 17 H19
Lawson Street 12 G13
Leeward Park 17 F22
Leslie Crescent 14 F17
Liberator Drive 13 K11
Limekiln Road 12 E12
Limonds Court 14 F14
Limonds Wynd 14 F14
Lindsay Street 13 H13
Lindston Place 17 F21
Linfern Place 17 G20
Lisburn Road 12 F11

Loaning, The 17 F21
Loch Park 16 B20
Lochlea Drive 15 G17
Lochside Court 12 G13
Lochside Road 12 G13
Longbank Drive 17 F19
Longbank Road 17 E19
Longhill Avenue 16 B22
Longhill Place 16 B23
Longlands Park 17 E19
Lorien Court 13 H11
Lorne Arcade 14 E15
Lothian Road 14 F16
Low Road 13 K12
Luath Walk 14 E15
Lymburn Place 15 G15
McAdam Place 14 F14
McAdam Square 14 F14
McCall's Avenue 12 F12
McColgan Place 13 H12
McLean Street 13 H13
McNairston Road 15 K18
Mackie Street 13 H13
Main Holm Road 15 K14
Main Road 13 J13
Main Street 14 E14
Mainholm Court 15 K14
Mainholm Crescent 15 J14
Mainholm Road 15 J14
Maple Drive 15 J18
Marchmont Road Lane 14 E16
Marchmont Road 14 E17
Marguerite Place 17 H20
Marigold Square 17 G20
Marlborough Court 14 D14
Marlepark 17 F20
Maryfield Place 12 G11
Maryfield Road 12 G11
Masonhill Place 15 H18
Masonhill Road 15 J18
Maybole Road 17 F20
Meadow Park Drive 14 F18
Meadow Park 14 F18
Merkland Road 17 F21
Mews Lane 14 D15
Midton Road 14 E18
Mill Brae 14 F16
Mill Brae Court 14 F16
Mill Street 14 F15
Mill Wynd 14 E15
Miller Road 14 E16
Milton Park 17 G20
Monkwood Place 17 G21
Montgomerie Terrace 14 D14
Monument Road 16 E20
Moor Place 13 H11
Moor Road 13 H11
Morrison Gardens 15 G15
Morton Avenue 14 F18
Morton Road 14 F18
Mossgiel Place 14 F17
Mossgiel Road 14 F17
Mosside Road 13 H11
Mote, The 17 F23
Mount Charles Crescent 16 C21
Mount Oliphant Crescent 14 F17
Mount Oliphant Place 15 G17
Mount, The 17 G19
Murdoch's Lone 16 D22
Murray Place 13 H12
Murray Street 13 H13
Nelson Place 12 F13
New Bridge Street 14 E14

INDEX TO AYR & IRVINE

New Road 12 E13
Newark Crescent 17 A22
Newmarket Street 14 E15
Newton Park Court 12 G12
Nile Court 14 E15
Noltmire Road 13 H11
North Harbour Street 14 E14
Northdoon Place 16 C20
Northfield Avenue 12 F12
Northfield Place 12 F12
North Park Avenue 12 G12
Nursery Grove 15 G18
Nursery Road 15 G18
Nursery Wynd 15 G18
Nurseryhall 13 J13
Oakwood Avenue 13 K13
Old Bridge Road 13 K12
Old Bridge Street 14 E14
Old Farm Road 13 J12
Old Hillfoot Road 15 G18
Orchard Avenue 14 F17
Orchard Place 15 G17
Oswald Court 12 F12
Oswald Lane 12 D13
Oswald Place 12 F10
Oswald Road 12 F10
Overmills Crescent 15 J16
Overmills Road 15 J16
Park Circus Lane 14 D16
Park Circus 14 E16
Park Terrace 14 D15
Park View 16 E22
Parkhouse Street 14 E16
Paterson Street 12 G11
Pattle Place 16 E22
Pavilion Road 14 D15
Peebles Street 12 E13
Peggieshill Place 15 G18
Peggieshill Road 17 G19
Pemberton Valley 17 F21
Philip Square 14 F14
Pine Brae 15 H18
Piperhill 17 F21
Poplar Way 15 J18
Portmark Avenue 16 B22
Prestwick Road 12 F12
Primrose Park 17 H20
Princes Court 12 F13
Promenade 12 F11
Quail Road 12 F11
Queen Street 14 F14
Queens Qaudrant 14 F14
Queens Terrace Lane 14 D15
Queens Terrace 14 D15
Racecourse Road 14 D17
Racecourse View 14 D18
Raithhill 17 G22
Recawr Park 17 G20
Rigwoodie Place 16 D22
River Street 14 E14
River Terrace 14 E14
Riverside Place 14 F15
Robertson Crescent 15 J14
Robsland Avenue 14 E18
Rockrose Park 17 G20
Roman Road 17 H19
Ronaldshaw Park 14 D17
Rosebank Crescent 14 E18
Rosebay Park 17 G21
Ross Street 12 G13
Rosslyn Place 12 G12
Rowallan Court 14 D14
Rowan Crescent 15 H18
Rozelle Terrace 17 G22
Rush Hill 17 H21
Russell Drive 12 F13
Russell Street 14 F14
St Andrew's Street 14 F16
St Catherines Road 13 L13
St George's Road 12 G12
St John Street 14 E14
St Leonards Court 14 F18
St Leonard's Road 14 F18
St Leonards Wynd 14 E18
St Phillans Avenue 15 G17
St Vincent Crescent 17 F21
Saltfield Lane 12 E13
Saltpans Road 12 E12
Sandgate 14 E15
Sandyhill Road 15 K17
Sandyhill Terrace 15 K17
Sannox Place 13 J13
Sannox View 13 K13
Sanquhar Farm Road 13 J11
Savoy Court 14 D16
Savoy Park 14 D16
Scaur o'Doon Road 16 B20
Sea Tower Court 14 D17
Sea Tower Gardens 14 D17
Seabank Road 14 D14
Seafield Crescent 14 D18
Seafield Drive 14 C18
Seafield Road 14 D17
Seaforth Crescent 12 G11
Seaforth Road 12 G11
Shalloch Park 17 A21
Shanter Place 16 D22
Shanter Way 16 D22
Shanter Wynd 16 D22
Shavin Brae 15 J17
Shawfield Avenue 17 F19
Shiel Hill 17 G21
Shieling Park 14 D16
Shore Road 12 E12
Slaphouse 16 E19
Sloan Place 13 J13
Sloan Street 13 J13
Smith Street 14 E16
Snowdrop Square 17 G20
Somerset Road 12 G13
Sorrel Drive 17 H20
Souter Place 15 G18
South Beach Road 14 D14
South Harbour Street 14 D14
South Lodge Court 14 D17
Southfield Park 14 F18
Southpark Road 14 D17
Speedwell Square 17 G20
Springbank Road 12 G11
Springvale Park 14 E17
Springvale Road 14 E17
Spruce Park 15 J18
Spur Road 12 D13
Station Road 14 F16
Stewart Road 12 G11
Stewartlea 14 E17
Stobhill Crescent 15 G18
Stonecrop Place 17 H19
Stonefield Park 16 B21
Strathayr Place 14 E14
Strathdoon Place 16 C21
Summerfield Cottages 16 E20
Sunningdale Avenue 17 F20
Sycamore Crescent 15 J17
Syms Lane 14 F14
Taybank Drive 17 F20
Taylor Street 12 E13
Teviot Street 12 G12
Thistle Walk 17 H20
Thomson Street 13 H13
Thorneyflat Crescent 13 L13
Thorneyflat Place 13 L12
Thornwood Avenue 13 K13
Thornyflat Drive 13 K13
Thornyflat Road 13 K13
Thornyflat Street 13 K13
Tig Road 12 F12
Treebank Crescent 15 H18
Trefoil Place 17 H20
Trenchard Court 14 D14
Tryfield Place 12 F13
Tweed Street 12 G11
Union Avenue 12 F12
Upper Crofts 16 E22
Upper Loaning 17 E22
Victoria Park 14 D17
Victoria Street 14 F14
Viewfield Road 12 F13
Virginia Gardens 12 F13
Waggon Road 12 E13
Walker Road 12 G13
Ward Court 12 G11
Ward Road 12 G11
Wattfield Road 14 E17
Weaver Street 12 E13
Weir Road 12 E13
Wellington Lane 14 D15
Wellington Square 14 D15
Wellpark 16 E21
West Place 14 F18
West Sanquhar Avenue 12 G12
West Sanquhar Place 12 G13
West Sanquhar Road 12 G13
Westfield Road 14 D17
Westwood Avenue 15 J14
Westwood Crescent 13 K13
Wheatfield Road 14 D16
Wheatpark Place 13 K12
Wheatpark Road 13 K12
Whin Hill Road 17 G21
White Street 12 G11
Whiteford View 15 J16
Whitfield Drive 13 J12
Whitletts Road 15 G14
Whittle Road 13 H12
Whittletts Court 13 K13
Willow Park 17 H19
Wills Road 13 H13
Wilson Street 12 G13
Windward Park 17 F22
Wood Park 17 G19
Woodend Road 17 E22
Woodfield Avenue 12 F10
Woodfield Crescent 12 F11
Woodfield Road 12 F11
Woodlands Crescent 17 G19
Woodlea Place 17 G21
Wrightfield Place 16 D21
Wyburn Place 12 F12
York Place 12 E13
York Street Lane 12 E13
York Street 12 E13

Index to Irvine

Aberfeldy Terrace 43 J3
Aberlour Place 42 H3
Aberlour Road 42 H3
Academy Court 44 D6
Academy Gardens 41 D5
Academy Road 44 D6
Adam Walk 45 G7
Afton Court 44 D7
Ailsa Road 44
Alder Green 4
Alexander Place 41
Alford Place 42
Allan Square 45
Anderson Drive 42
Annandale Way 4
Annick Court 44
Annick Drive 46
Annick Road (Irvine) 45
Annick Road (Dreghorn) 46
Annick View 45
Archers Avenue 42
Archers Court 42
Ardbeg Court 42
Ardmore Court 4
Arkwright Way 45
Arran Place 41
Arranview Court 44
Ashgrove 42
Auchenharvie Place 42
Avon Court 4
Ayr Road 44
Ayr Road 49
Balgray Way 4
Ballot Road 45
Bank Court 42
Bank Place 42
Bank Street 42
Bank Street 45
Bankhead Avenue 47
Barbeth Place 4
Barclay Gardens 43
Barony Court 42
Barr Crescent 41
Barra Crescent 46
Barra Lane 46
Barra Place 46
Barra Wynd 46
Beach Drive 44
Beaton Terrace 41
Beech Avenue 45
Bell Crescent 42
Benbain Place 43
Bencleuch Place 46
Bensley Avenue 42
Bensley Rise 42
Benthill Terrace 44
Beresford Grove 42
Berry Drive 45
Berryhill Avenue 43
Bilby Terrace 41
Bimson Place 44
Bimson Row 44
Birks Hill 4
Birkscairn Place 46
Birkscairn Way 46
Blairdenon Way 46
Blaven Head 4
Bodesbeck Court 46
Bonnyton Place 4
Bonnyton Row 4
Bowhouse Head 43
Bowhouse Rise 43
Bowmore Court 4
Boyle Street 44
Braefoot 42
Braehead 42
Braeside 42
Brewster Place 49
Bridgegate 44
Broomlands Busway 45
Broomlands Court 46
Broomlands Drive 45
Broomlands Gate 46

omlands Place 45 F7
omlands Road 46 K8
ughton Green 43 K3
wn Walk 42 E4
ce Terrace 42 F4
ce Knox Court 43 J3
nbrae Crescent 43 L4
nbrae Drive 43 L4
ns Crescent 43 J4
ns Street 44 D6
nside Place 41 D5
sbiehead (2) 43 K4
e Court 46 L8
rngorm Court 43 K4
rnmount Road 42 H2
rnsgarroch Way 46 K7
rnsmore Way 46 K7
don Road 42 E5
mpbell Place 46 J9
mpsie Avenue 46 K6
mpsie Walk 46 K6
mpsie Way 46 J7
pel Place 46 K7
pringstone Foot 43 K4
don Place 46 K7
dow Crescent 43 J3
mel Drive 47 Q8
michael Place 41 D4
noustie Place 45 G10
rick Drive 41 D4
ron Place 42 E3
son Drive 45 E9
ters Place 45 E6
ters Rigg 44 D8
stle Keep Gardens 42 H5
stle Place 44 D6
stle Street 44 D6
stlepark Crescent 41 D3
stlepark Road 41 D3
dar Road 42 F5
ntenary Road 45 H10
ntury Court 45 H10
almers Place 49 H11
apel Lane 44 E7
apelgill Place 43 J5
erry Gardens 42 G4
eviot Court 46 J6
eviot Head 46 J6
eviot Way 46 J6
urch Street 44 D7
rk Drive 45 G6
yton Avenue 41 E5
ach Brae View 47 N7
chrane Street 44 D7
ckburn Place 49 H11
eburn Court 42 H3
Gardens 46 K9
se Avenue 47 Q8
sehill Mount Road 46 J8
sehill Park 47 M9
sehill Terrace 47 N7
serine Bank 45 H6
ton Row 45 E7
ig View 47 P7
igmark Place 42 H4
ignaw Place 46 K7
malt Court 46 J6
mond Place 46 H7
mond Way 46 H7
ven Grove 42 H4
cus Grove 41 E5
ft Terrace 47 P7
fthead Court 46 J6
fthead 46 J6
mpton Way 42 G5
Cuillin Place 43 J5
Cumbrae Court 46 L9
Cunninghame Road 44 D9
Cypress Gardens 42 G4
Dale Crescent 42 F5
Dalgain Court 43 J4
Dalmailing Avenue 46 J8
Dalmore Place 42 H3
Dalmore Way 42 H3
Dalrymple Court 45 G6
Dalrymple Drive 45 F6
Dalrymple Place 45 G6
Dalwhinnie Court 42 H3
Darnshaw Close 43 L4
Dick Crescent 42 F4
Dick Terrace 42 F4
Dickson Drive 41 D4
Donaldson Drive 42 F5
Doon Court 44 E7
Doura Drive 42 H4
Doura Place 41 E4
Dreghorn Road 47 M10
Drumelzier Court 43 J5
Drummond Crescent 48 G10
Drummuir Foot 43 K4
Duncan Drive 45 F7
Dundonald Road 46 L8
Dunlop Crescent 46 K8
Dunlop Drive 48 G13
Dunlop Place 49 H13
Duntonknoll 41 E5
Dunvegan Place 42 F3
Earlswood Avenue 42 G3
Earlswood View 42 G3
Earlswood Way 42 G3
Earlswood Wynd 42 G3
Earncraig Green 46 J6
East Bowhouse Head 43 K4
East Bowhouse Way 43 K4
East Broomlands 46 K7
East Road 44 E7
Eastwood Avenue 42 F5
Eglinton Gardens 44 E6
Eglinton Street 44 E6
Elmbank Terrace 42 F5
Eriskay Court 46 L9
Esplanade 44 B8
Etive Place 42 F4
Fairlie Drive 43 K3
Fairways, The 41 C2
Fencedyke Close 42 H5
Fencedyke Way 43 J5
Finnie Terrace 47 P7
Fintry Place 46 K7
Fintry Terrace 46 K6
Fintry Walk 46 K7
First Avenue 44 E9
Fleming Terrace 41 D4
Ford Avenue 47 M8
Fortacre Place 43 K4
Frew Terrace 41 E4
Friars Croft 44 D7
Fullarton Street 44 E8
Gailes Road 48 E12
Galloway Court 43 K3
Galt Avenue 45 F6
Gardens, The 43 L3
Garelet Place 46 K7
Garnock Court 44 E7
Garrier Court 47 P7
Garrier Road 47 P7
Gateside 42 H3
George Court 45 E6
George Terrace 41 E5
Gigha Crescent 46 K7
Gigha Lane 46 K7
Gigha Place 46 K7
Gigha Terrace 46 K7
Gigha Wynd 46 K7
Gilbertfield Place 45 F7
Girdle Gate 42 H4
Girdle Toll 43 J4
Glasgow Vennel 45 E7
Glebe Avenue 46 L9
Glebe, The (Irvine) 45 E7
Glebe, The (Dreghorn) 46 L8
Glenbervie Wynd 45 F9
Gleneagles Place 45 G10
Glenleith Place 46 L7
Glenlyon Grove 42 G4
Goldcraig Court 43 J4
Golf Place 41 D4
Golffields Road 45 F8
Gottries Place 44 C8
Gottries Road 44 C8
Grampian Court 43 K5
Grange, The 43 L3
Gray Crescent 45 E9
Green Avenue 41 E5
Greenbank Court 45 E8
Greenbank Road 45 E8
Greenfield Drive 45 F7
Greenhill Court 43 K3
Greenside Avenue 47 Q8
Greenside Terrace 47 Q7
Greenside Way 43 J5
Greenside 43 J5
Greenwood Road 46 L8
Gullane Court 45 F9
Gulliland Place 45 F8
Haddington Gardens 43 K3
Harbour Road 44 C8
Harbour Street 44 C8
Harris Court 46 L9
Harris Terrace 46 L9
Heatherhouse Road 44 D9
Heatherstane Bank 46 L7
Heatherstane Walk 46 K7
Heatherstane Way 46 L7
Heathfield House 44 D6
Hepburn Way 43 L2
Herbertson Crescent 42 F5
High Street 44 E7
Highet Gardens 41 D5
Highfield Place 42 H3
Hill Street 44 E7
Hillshaw Foot 46 L7
Hillshaw Green 46 L7
Holms Avenue 47 M8
Hopetoun Bank 46 L7
Howat Crescent 45 G6
Hunter Drive 41 D3
Inverleven Place 42 H2
Iona Court 46 L9
Iona Place 46 L9
Irvine Mains Crescent 41 E5
Irvine Road 41 C1
Islay Court 46 L9
James Crescent 41 D5
Jermond Drive 42 F4
Jura Court 46 L9
Kames Court 43 K3
Katrine Place 42 F3
Kennedy Park 46 K9
Kerr Drive 45 F7
Kerr Place 45 F7
Kersland Foot 42 H4
Kidsneuk Gardens 41 C3
Kidsneuk 41 C3
Killoch Place 42 H5
Killoch Way 42 H5
Kilmarnock Road 47 Q7
Kiln Court 45 E7
Kiln Walk 45 E7
Kilpatrick Court 46 J6
Kilpatrick Place 46 J7
Kilsyth Crescent 46 J6
Kilsyth Walk 46 J6
Kilwinning Road 41 C2
Kirk Vennel 45 E7
Kirkgate 44 E7
Kirkhill 43 L3
Kirkland Terrace 47 P7
Kirkstyle Court 43 K3
Knockentiber Road 47 Q7
Kyle Avenue 47 P7
Kyle Road 44 D10
Ladyburn Court 42 H3
Ladyha Court 43 K4
Lamberton Gardens 43 L4
Lammermuir Court 46 J6
Lamont Drive 44 E9
Lamont Place 44 E9
Lanfine Row 43 J3
Lanfine Terrace 42 H3
Lanfine Way 42 H3
Langmuir Avenue 43 L4
Langmuir Court 43 L4
Lawers Place 43 J5
Lawthorn Road 43 K3
Leven Place 42 E3
Lewis Court 46 J7
Lewis Crescent 46 H7
Lewis Rise 46 J7
Lewis Terrace 46 J7
Lewis Wynd 46 J7
Linkwood Court 43 J3
Linkwood Place 43 J3
Linthouse Vennel 44 C8
Lismore Drive 46 K9
Lismore Way 46 K9
Littlestane Court 43 J3
Littlestane Rise 43 J3
Littlestane Road 42 H3
Littlestane Row 43 J3
Livingstone Terrace 41 E4
Loach Avenue 45 F8
Lochcraig Court 46 J6
Lochlibo Court 43 J3
Lochlibo Road 42 H4
Lochlibo Road 43 J1
Lochwood Place 42 H3
Lomond Place 42 F3
Lomond Way 43 J5
Long Drive 42 F2
Long Drive 45 H7
Longrow Gardens 42 H2
Loudoun Rigg 44 E8
Low Green Road 44 D6
Lowther Bank 46 L6
Lugar Avenue 43 J3
Lugton Court 44 E8
Lyle Gardens 45 F8
MacAdam Place 45 H8
MacAllan Place 42 H2
MaCara Drive 45 G6
MacKinnon Terrace 42 G5
MacKintosh Place 45 H8
Macredie Place 43 M3
MacRobert Avenue 46 K8
McClure Gardens 44 E6
McDonald Drive 42 F5
McGibney Drive 45 F8
McKinlay Crescent 44 D8
McLean Drive 47 M9

McMillan Place 49 H11
Maid Morville Avenue 46 L9
Main Road 47 N7
Main Street 46 L8
Malcolm Gardens 45 F7
Mansfield Way 43 J4
Manson Road 42 G5
Manuel Court 46 L9
Manuel Terrace 46 L9
Maple Terrace 42 F5
Marble Avenue 47 M8
Maree Place 42 F2
Marine Drive 44 C9
Marress Road 44 D6
Martin Avenue 42 F4
Maxwell Green 43 J5
Maxwood Place 43 J4
Meadow Avenue 41 E5
Meadowhead Avenue 48 G13
Meadowhead Road 49 H14
Meikle Place 43 K3
Merrick Place 46 K7
Merryvale Road 44 E8
Metcalfe Place 49 H11
Mid Rig 43 J5
Middleton Park 43 J5
Middleton Road 42 H5
Milgarholm Avenue 45 F8
Mill Crescent 45 G7
Mill Road 45 F7
Millbank Row 47 M8
Millburn Terrace 43 J2
Milldown Place 46 L7
Millfore Court 46 J6
Milton Court 47 M8
Milton Crescent 46 L8
Milton Road 46 L8
Monach Gardens 46 K9
Montgomery Lane 44 D8
Montgomery Place 44 C8
Montgomery Street 44 C8
Montgomeryfield 46 K9
Moorfoot Place 46 J6
Moorfoot Way 46 J6
Morar Place 42 E2
Moss Drive 48 G12
Mossgiel Drive 42 F5
Mount View 46 L8
Muir Drive 45 F6
Muirfield Court 45 G10
Muirhall Place 46 L8
Mull Court 46 J7
Mull Crescent 46 J7
Mull Place 46 J7
Mull Terrace 46 J7
Murchland Way 44 D6
Murdoch Place 49 H11
Neil Avenue 42 F4
Nevis Way 43 J5
New Street 44 D7
Newfield Place 43 J4
Newhouse Way 43 J4
Newtonhead (1) 43 K4
Norman Crescent 41 D4
North Vennel 46 J6
Nursery Gardens 47 Q7
Oaklands Avenue 42 E5
Ochil Court 43 J4
Old Caley Road 41 E4
Ormiston Place 43 K2
Overton Place 43 K4
Overtoun Court 47 Q7
Overtoun Road 47 P6
Paddock, The 43 L4
Park Place 41 D4
Parkside 46 K6
Parterre 44 E7
Paterson Avenue 42 F4
Paterson Crescent 42 F4
Peden Place 44 E7
Penbreck Court 43 K3
Pennyvenie Way 43 J4
Pentland Place 46 J7
Perceton Row 43 L5
Peter Street 44 C8
Piersland Place 43 J4
Pladda Avenue 46 K7
Pladda Court 46 K7
Pladda Crescent 46 J7
Pladda Terrace 46 K7
Pladda Wynd 46 J7
Portland Avenue 44 D9
Portland Place 44 D9
Portland Road 44 D9
Puddle Ford 44 E7
Purdies Close 44 E7
Quarry Road 44 E6
Queen Road 41 E4
Queens Court 45 F7
Racecourse Place 41 D4
Ramstane Place 43 L4
Ranken Crescent 45 F6
Ranken Drive 45 F6
Rannoch Place 41 D2
Ravenscroft 41 D4
Redburn Gate 41 C2
Redburn Place 41 D4
Regalia View 42 G3
Renton Park 43 L2
Rigfoot 43 K4
Riverside Avenue 46 J10
Riverside Road 47 M8
Riverside Way 45 G9
Riverway 44 D8
Ronaldsay Court 46 K9
Rosebank Gardens 42 H2
Roseholm Avenue 45 G7
Rowan Terrace 42 F5
Rowantree Gardens 43 J4
Rubie Crescent 44 E9
St Andrews Way 45 F9
St Bride's Place 41 E4
St Inan Avenue 45 G6
St Kilda Bank 46 H7
St Kilda Court 46 G7
St Kilda Place 46 J7
Sanderson Avenue 44 D8
Sandy Road 41 C4
School Lane 44 E8
Scott Road 44 E8
Seagate 44 D6
Seaton Terrace 41 D4
Second Avenue 44 E9
Shalloch Place 46 K7
Sharpe Avenue 47 M9
Shawholm Gardens 45 E6
Shewalton Road 48 G11
Shiel Place 42 E3
Shielhope Court 43 J5
Sidlaw Foot 46 L7
Sillars Meadow 45 F7
Skye Court 46 K9
Slate Mill Gardens 45 G7
Sloan Avenue 45 F7
Sloan Place 45 F7
Smiddy Close 44 E6
Smith Avenue 42 F5
Smithstone Court 42 H4
Smithstone Way 42 H3
Somerville Park 43 K2
Somerville Way 43 K2
Sophia Crescent 41 D3
Sourlie Terrace 42 H4
South Newmoor Avenue 45 H8
South Vennel 46 J6
Southook Row 43 J4
Speyburn Place 42 H3
Springbank Gardens 43 J2
Springfield Gardens 43 J2
Springhill Terrace 47 P7
Springside Terrace 47 N7
Staffa Court 46 K9
Stanecastle Drive 42 G4
Stanecastle Gate 42 H4
Stanecastle Road 42 H5
Station Brae Gardens 46 L8
Station Brae 46 L8
Station Drive 47 P6
Station Road 47 P7
Steadman Place 46 J9
Steps Road 42 E4
Stewart Drive 42 F5
Strathmore Park 43 K3
Stroma Court 46 L9
Stronsay Court 46 J7
Stronsay Way 46 J7
Swinton Place 43 K2
Symington Place 49 H10
Tarryholme Drive 45 E7
Telford Place 45 H8
Third Avenue 44 D9
Thornhouse Avenue 45 F6
Thornwood Drive 45 E7
Tiree Court 46 K9
Titchfield Way 43 J5
Tollerton Drive 42 F5
Tollhouse Way 43 J4
Towerlands Farm Road 42 H5
Towerlands Farm Road 46 K6
Towerlands Gate 46 K7
Towerlands Road 46 L7
Townfoot 46 K9
Townhead 44 F7
Turnberry Wynd 45 F9
Victoria Crescent 44 D8
Vineburgh Avenue 41 E5
Vineburgh Court 41 D5
Vines, The 41 E5
Wallace Road 41 E5
Wardlaw Gardens 43 K2
Wardneuk Court 43 J3
Warrix Avenue 45 F7
Warwick Hill 43 K4
Watercut Road 41 B1
Waterside 44 D6
Watson Terrace 45 F7
West Bowhouse Gardens 43 J4
West Bowhouse Head 43 J4
West Bowhouse Way 43 J4
West Court 44 D7
West Road 44 D6
Whitehope Green 43 J5
Whitewisp Court 43 J5
Whittle Place 45 H7
Whyte Avenue 45 F8
William Burns Place 46 L8
Williamfield Grove 41 D5
Williamfield Park 41 D5
Willow Gardens 42 G4
Wilson Avenue 41 E5
Windelstraw Court 46 J6
Winton Place 41
Wood Grove 46
Woodhill Crescent 43
Woodlands Avenue 42
Wyvis Place 43

Index to Kilwinning

Abbeygate 63
Abbeygreen 63
Abbot's Avenue 63
Abbot's Place 63
Abbot's Walk 63
Ainsdale Court 62
Alexandra Terrace 62
Almswall Road 63
Annanhill Place 62
Ardmillan 62
Ashgrove Road 62
Ashgrove Workshops 62
Atholl Gardens 63
Baberton Way 62
Baird Avenue 63
Bankhead Road 63
Bannoch Gardens 63
Bannoch Place 63
Bannoch Road 63
Bannoch Road 63
Barqeny 62
Bartonholm Terrace 63
Beechwood 62
Belleisle Close 62
Bevan Gardens 63
Birkdale Close 62
Blacklands Avenue 63
Blacklands Crescent 62
Blair Road 63
Blairafton Wynd 62
Braeside 63
Braid Court 62
Braidwood Road 63
Bridgend Lane 63
Bridgend 63
Brodick Avenue 62
Brodick Close 62
Broomfield Street 63
Broomhill Court 62
Bruntsfield Avenue 62
Burns Place 63
Busby Place 63
Byrehill Avenue 62
Byrehill Avenue 63
Byrehill Place 62
Byrehill Road 62
Byres Loch 62
Byres Road 62
Calderwood 63
Cambusdoon Place 62
Carnoustie Court 62
Cartle Close 62
Castlehill Road 62
Cathkin Place 62
Chalybeate Court 62
Church Street 63
Churchhill Avenue 63
Claremont Crescent 62
Cloncaird 62
Coodham Place 62
Corsehill 63
Cranberry Court 62
Cranberry Head 62
Cranberry Moss Road 62
Cranberry Moss Road 62
Cranberry Place 62

ınberry Road 62 Q5
ınnog Way 62 R3
zean Place 62 R5
garven Wynd 62 R2
jarrock 62 Q5
mahoy Way 62 Q4
ry Road 62 S2
rmule Drive 62 R2
vid Gage Street 63 T2
vid's Crescent 62 S5
anfield Court 63 T4
rans Terrace 63 U5
rnoch Court 62 Q4
vecot Lane 63 U4
ıid Drive 63 T3
ddingston Avenue 62 Q3
ıure Courts 62 S4
en Court 62 Q4
son Place 63 T6
zell Row 62 Q4
inton Place 63 T4
erkine 62 Q5
elyn Terrace 62 S5
rhaven Square 62 Q3
gushill Road 63 U4
e Roads 63 V4
ge Vennel 62 R3
ındry Court 62 R3
ındry Wynd 62 R3
ırs Lawn 62 S4
garin Terrace 63 T5
nton Court 62 Q4
rden Lane 63 T4
rden Square 63 T4
rnock View 63 T3
rallan 62 R5
be Street 63 T3
napp Court 62 R5
napp Place 62 R5
nbervie Drive 62 Q4
nburn Close 62 R1
neagles Avenue 62 R3
ystones 63 T2
enfoot 63 T4
lane Place 62 Q4
nilton Street 63 T3
Hawthorn Court 63 T5
Hawthorn Place 63 T5
Hazel Grove 63 V3
Hazeldene Park 63 U3
Helen's Terrace 63 T5
Heronswood 63 T2
Highfield Street 63 U3
Hillcrest Place 63 U4
Hillpark Rise 62 Q4
Howden Avenue 63 T3
Howgate 62 S4
Hoylake Square 62 R3
Hunter Place 63 V4
Innerwood Road 63 T2
Irvine Road 63 U5
James Clements Close 62 R3
Keir Hardie Crescent 63 V4
Kelburne 62 R5
Kelvin Avenue 63 U6
Kilkerran 62 Q5
Killermont Place 62 Q4
Kilrig Avenue 63 T3
King Street 63 T3
Kinnis Vennel 62 R3
Kirkhill 62 R5
Kyleswell Street 63 T4
Ladyacre 63 T3
Ladyford Avenue 63 T4
Lainshaw 62 R5
Lauchlan Way 63 T4
Lissens Walk 62 R2
Lochwood Close 62 R2
Longford Avenue 63 T6
Loudoun Crescent 62 Q3
Love Street 63 V4
McGavin Avenue 63 V4
McGavin Way 62 S3
McLuckie Drive 62 R4
McLuckie Park 62 R3
Machrie Place 62 R4
Main Street 63 T4
Manse Court 63 T4
Matthew Place 63 T2
Meadow Park Road 62 R3
Meadow View 62 R2
Meadow Way 62 R2
Meadows, The 62 S3
Millside Gardens 63 U4
Moncur Court 62 R2
Moncur Road 63 V4
Monkreddan Crescent 62 R2
Montgomerie Terrace 63 V4
Montgreenan View 63 U4
Morville Crescent 63 T2
Mountcastle Wynd 62 S1
Muirfield Place 62 R3
Muirside Court 62 R5
Muirside Place 62 R5
Muirside Road 62 R5
Nairn Court 62 Q4
Nethermains Road 63 T5
Newark 62 R5
Ninian's Terrace 63 U5
Northacre Grove 63 T2
Northacre 63 T2
Nursery Drive 62 R2
Nursery Wynd 62 R2
Old Glasgow Road 63 V2
Old Woodwynd Road 62 S3
Orchard Grove 63 T3
Orchard Place 63 T3
Oxenward Road 63 T4
Papingo Close 62 R1
Park Avenue 63 T4
Park Lane 62 S2
Parkhead Avenue 63 U4
Pathfoot View 63 U4
Pathfoot 63 U4
Pennyburn Road 62 Q5
Pinmore 62 R5
Pollock Crescent 63 T5
Prestonfield Avenue 62 Q3
Priory Wynd 62 R1
Queen Place 63 V4
Queen Street 63 V4
Redstone Avenue 63 U3
River Walk 63 T2
Robert W Service Court 63 T5
Rosemount 62 R5
Rowallan 62 R5
St Joan's Crescent 63 T5
St Winning's Lane 63 T4
St Winning's Road 62 S4
St Winning's Road 63 T4
St Winning's Well 62 S4
Segton Avenue 62 R4
Seymour Avenue 63 U5
Shavian Terrace 63 T5
Simpson Place 63 U6
Skelmorlie Place 62 S4
Smiddy Court 63 T4
Smith Crescent 63 U5
Station Plaza 62 S4
Stevenston Road 62 Q4
Stobbs Crescent 63 T5
Stobbs Terrace 63 T5
Sundrum Place 62 S5
Sunningdale Square 62 R3
Sutton Court 62 Q4
Tammy Dale's Road 63 U4
Thornhill Court 62 Q4
Townhead 62 S4
Treesbank 62 R5
Turnberry Court 62 Q4
Underwood 62 S3
Vaults Lane 63 T4
Viaduct Circle 63 T2
Wallwood 62 R5
Waterside Road 63 U3
Weirston Road 63 V4
Wentworth Square 62 R3
West Doura Court 62 Q4
West Doura Way 62 R4
Whitehirst Farm Courtyard 62 Q2
Whitehirst Park Road 62 Q4
Winstanley Wynd 62 R2
Winton Avenue 62 R4
Wood Crescent 63 T3
Wood Street 63 T3
Woodburn Avenue 63 T3
Woodfarm Close 62 S1
Woodgreen Wynd 62 R2
Woodmill 63 U6
Woodside Road 62 R3
Woodside Road 62 R1
Woodwynd 63 T3